NICK CAVE

Sinner Saint: The True Confessions

NICK CAVE

Sinner Saint: The True Confessions

Thirty Years of Essential Interviews edited by Mat Snow

Plexus, London

British Library Cataloguing in Publication Data
A catalogue record for this book is available
from the British Library.

ISBN-13: 978 0 85965 448 7

Cover Photograph by Kevin Westenberg
Interior Photgraphs by Bleddyn Butcher
Cover and book design by Coco Wake-Porter
Printed in Great Britain by the MPG Books Group

Acknowledgements
I would like to extend my thanks for their help
in making this anthology happen to Sandra
Wake, Tom Branton and Oliver Holden-Rea of
Plexus Publishing; Sarah Lowe of Fifth Avenue
PR; Zoe Miller of Mute Records; Bleddyn
Butcher for both his wonderful photographs
and lively conversations over three decades
concerning the subject of this book; needless
to say every writer represented here, for many
of whom I entertain the warmest feelings of
personal affection; plus *The Guardian*, *The
Daily Telegraph* and *Word* magazine with
whose kind permission three pieces here are
republished. And, of course, I would like to
thank every musician in the Nick Cave orbit
who has talked to me over the years, and finally
the man himself; I hope he might find this
selection of pieces offers a fair if not always
adulatory chronicle of how his life and work has
been reflected by others.

Acknowledgement is hereby made to the
following for permission:
    'A Boy Next Door' by Michel Faber, *Rock's
Backpages*, August 2002. © 2002 by Michel
Faber. 'Sometimes Pleasure Heads Must Burn
– A Manhattan Melodrama' by Barney Hoskyns,
New Musical Express, 17 October 1981 (*Rock's
Backpages*). © 1981 by Barney Hoskyns. 'A Man
Called Horse' by Antonella Gambotto, *ZigZag*,
January 1985 (*Rock's Backpages*). Copyright
© 1985 by Antonella Gambotto. 'Prick Me
Do I Not Bleed?' by Mat Snow, *New Musical
Express*, August 23 1986 (*Rock's Backpages*).
Copyright © 1986 by Mat Snow. 'Of Misogyny,
Murder and Melancholy: Meeting Nick Cave'
by Simon Reynolds, *National Student*, 1987
(*Rock's Backpages*). Copyright © 1987 by
Simon Reynolds. 'The Needle and the Damage
Done' by Jack Barron, *New Musical Express*, 13
August 1988 (*Rock's Backpages*). Copyright ©
1988 by Jack Barron. 'Edge of Darkness' by Nick
Kent, *The Face*, December 1988. Copyright ©
1988 by Nick Kent. 'Nick Cave on 57th Street:
A Late '80s Memoir' by Kris Needs, *Graffiti*,
1988, Remixed with additional material 2009.
Copyright © 1988, 2009 by Kris Needs. 'Titter
Ye Not' by Andy Gill, *Q*, May 1992 (*Rock's
Backpages*). Copyright © 1992 by Andy Gill.
'The Return of the Saint' by James McNair, *Mojo*,
March 1997. Copyright © 1997 by James McNair.
'From Her to Maturity' by Jennifer Nine, *Melody
Maker*, May 1997. Copyright © 1997 by Jennifer
Nine. 'The New Romantic' by Ginny Dougary,
The Times, 27 March 1999. Copyright © 1999 by
Ginny Dougary. 'Let There Be Light' by Jessamy
Calkin, *The Daily Telegraph*, 17 March 2001.
Copyright © 2001 by Jessamy Calkin. Used with
the kind permission of *The Daily Telegraph*.
'Nick Cave: Renaissance Man' by Robert Sandall,
The Word, March 2003. Copyright © 2003 by
Robert Sandall. Used with the kind permission
of *The Word*. 'Nick Cave: The Songwriter Speaks'
by Debbie Kruger, Expanded chapter from
Songwriters Speak, 2005. Copyright © 2005
by Debbie Kruger. 'Old Saint Nick' by Barney
Hoskyns, Expanded from *Dazed & Confused*,
October 2004. Copyright © 2004 by Barney
Hoskyns. 'Nick Cave: Raw and Uncut 1' by Phil
Sutcliffe, Interview transcript for a *Mojo* feature,
21 October, 2004. Copyright © 2004 by Phil
Sutcliffe. 'Acropolis Now!' by Michael Odell,
Q, March 2005. Copyright © 2005 by Michael
Odell. 'Old Nick' by Simon Hattenstone, *The
Guardian*, 23 February 2008. Copyright ©
2008 by Simon Hattenstone. Used with the
kind permission of *The Guardian*. 'Nick Cave:
Raw and Uncut 2' by Phil Sutcliffe, Interview
transcript for a *Mojo* feature, 25 November 2008.
Copyright © 2008 by Phil Sutcliffe.

Contents

Foreword

Mat Snow

Nick Cave: Man or Myth?

On New Year's Eve, 1983/4, Nick Cave played the Seaview Ballroom in St Kilda, Melbourne, under the heading of that rhetorical question. The Birthday Party, of which he had been the singer and lyricist, had ceased trading six months before, and from its remnants his new, more fluid backing group the Bad Seeds would be christened five months later.

It's a teasing self-advertisement from a man who has always had an instinct for the telling phrase.

More than that, though, it's a family in-joke – and a message to the other side.

Seven years before, Nick Cave's father, Colin, was killed in a car crash, the news reaching the nineteen-year-old while he was being bailed out of police custody – and not for the first time – by his mother. Father and son were at loggerheads, forever now unresolved and unreconciled. Father was a teacher, an academic, a man of high cultural seriousness, as so many Australians are, often to the amazement and mild awe of urbane Brits for whom all Aussies are Bondi Beach backpackers pulling pints in Earls Court's Kangaroo Alley. Loggerheads for the usual reasons – the generation gap and the mismatch of paternal expectations with a son defining himself as different. The youngest of Dawn and Colin Cave's three sons, Nick had been usurped as the baby of the family by his younger sister Julie; his new role in the sibling order would be problem child and rebel. What was he rebelling against? What have you got? How about the paradox that father chastised his third son as a rebel while devoting himself to a far greater rebel (and irritant to the police) in his paper titled 'Ned Kelly: Man or Myth?'.

Well, dad, if only you could see me now.

Biographers are always looking for a key – actually, *the* key: the character, incident or relationship behind the scenes that willy-nilly shapes and directs what the star presents on the public stage, even the need to be on that stage at all.

Nick Cave at Beehive Studios in Chalk Farm, London, 5 December 1988.

Nick Cave seems acutely aware of the springs of his artistic self, and over the years has hardly concealed the keys that turn his clockwork. Many artists will deny such keys, even to themselves. Not Nick Cave. His life and art have long meshed. At first it was as comically self-disgusted punk star braggadocio (take the Birthday Party's 'Nick the Stripper', a song presumably inspired, even sired by the Stooges' 'I Wanna Be Your Dog'). But over the next few years a complex mechanism of personal self-exploration and revelation have, I think, found expression in a growing repertoire of musical voices and song styles. These can be summarised – deep breath – as a Baudelairean angel/whore bipolar sexual obsessiveness rendered serio-comically in the idiom of the Deep South as it might have been stylised in the music theatre of Brecht and Weill.

An extensive aside here on Nick Cave's rock'n'roll ancestry. He has owned up to many influences, ranging from Tom Jones to Jethro Tull, Alex Harvey to Van Morrison, Johnny Cash to the Stooges. Artists never mentioned include those so audibly influential that their omission in Nick's roll call of inspiration must be down either to amazing coincidence or else their presence hidden in the plain sight of music that everyone heard and knew – the background noise of '70s teenhood.

First, the tense and doomy soundscape of 'Dazed and Confused' by Led Zeppelin, from the group's 1969 debut album. Every teenage boy in the '70s knew Led Zep, even if only to repudiate them. I would find it hard to believe that this supercharged chestnut of dungeon bass and teenage bedroom air-guitar in particular failed to percolate into the budding Birthday Party's earshot.

Then, narrowing the focus of influence, the Doors. If bipolar Baudelairean sexual obsessiveness rendered in the idiom of the Deep South as it might have been stylised in the music theatre of Brecht and Weill is your bag, you could hardly avoid it in the six studio albums by the group before singer-lyricist Jim Morrison's death in 1971. If you were a rock fan at any time from 1967 onwards, you could hardly miss The Doors. Just two of their greatest hits, 'The End' and 'Riders on the Storm', bear a striking ancestral likeness in their lyrical themes, imagery, personae, and mode of delivery, especially vocal, to such Cave classics as 'From Her to Eternity', 'Tupelo' and 'The Good Son'.

From the same soured end of the late-'60s psychedelic spectrum, and sprung from the same high-art inclination to weave *Mittel* European psychodrama and rock-star narcissism into the Deep South's landscape of the blues and the Bible, two songs performed by the Rolling Stones in 1968 stand out as building blocks: the worldwide hit single 'Jumping Jack Flash', whose kinship to Nick Cave's 'Up Jumped the Devil' twenty years later is hard to deny, and their account of 'The Prodigal Son', the pre-war country blues song by the Reverend Robert Wilkins.

Which is where we came in. The parable from the Gospel according to Saint Luke is a text which, I believe, has profoundly shaped Nick Cave's narrative of his own life; it is a mirror in which he recognises himself and finds meaning in his own story. His 1990 song 'The Good Son' is the murderous fantasy of the overlooked brother of the prodigal son; he is the son who has abided by his father's commandments but goes without special reward or favour. Nick Cave tells that story in the third person. He is not the good son – but feels some sympathy. Nick Cave, I strongly suspect, prefers to cast himself as the prodigal son whose transgressions, acted out in life, are far milder than the unrealised fantasies of his right-living brother – of, indeed, all those straight arrows who nurture their dark urges in righteous repression rather than purging them when sewing their wild oats – and who returns to the fold and the fatted calf in an instance of divinely-sanctioned unfairness justified by the prodigal son's return from the near-dead.

For some sixteen years up to, and especially including, the album *Murder Ballads* (1996), Nick Cave entertained the most black-hearted bad-hat fantasies in his songs, provoking a debate that pitted feminists – who deplored the seeming approval visited upon the singer of 'I stuck a six-inch gold blade inside the head of a girl' and many more lyrics in that vein – against the libertarians of artistic license for whom publicly obsessing in dramatic monologue was to be clearly distinguished from actually preaching it as gospel. After all, did his poem 'To My Last Duchess' make Robert Browning a killer, and did any Victorian critic ever attempt to mount such a puritanical and preposterous argument?

Near-the-knuckle creative types in the public eye of the '80s and '90s, such as Nick Cave, Martin Amis and Bret Easton Ellis, were beadily scrutinised for any offences against the safety and status of women. By extension, it was implied by our guardians of public morality in the arts, such fabrications as Amis's Keith Talent and John Self, Easton Ellis's Patrick Bateman and any number of Cave's first-person monsters and murderers were in themselves validations or endorsements, glorifications even, of the most pernicious behaviour. Worse still, what with the personal also being the political, they could not but gleefully endow with artistic credibility the law of the jungle extolled by the free marketeers of the Reagan-Thatcherite complex.

That satire, gallows humour and grotesquery might have had something to do with it was often overlooked by the new breed of guardians of public decency for whom the '80s was a crisis which called for politically engaged and righteous artistic endeavour rather than nihilism and nasty games of perps-and-victims.

Add to the mix that othe r combustible of the '80s (and since), the unembarrassed addiction to dangerous drugs, and you had a rock musician testing the limits of what even a great many rock fans thought a rock musician should be allowed to get away with.

In the great scheme of things, however, it was a debate which commanded far fewer column inches and less pub and dinner-party conversation than whatever it was that Madonna was up to at the time. While Nick Cave, year by year, added to his record sales and fan base, he remained a cult, and one which was commonly lumped into the Goth movement (much to Nick's annoyance); according to his more blasé detractors, he was an arty poseur who couldn't or wouldn't disembark from the drunken riverboat drifting into the heart of theatrically contrived darkness because the spectacle had created for him such a viable career among impressionable kohl-eyed, black-clad teenagers. The worst thing you could possibly do was encourage Nick Cave by taking him seriously.

Suddenly, Nick himself seemed to agree. His album *Murder Ballads*, including the hit duet with Kylie Minogue, 'Where the Wild Roses Grow', is self-parody by overkill. It was as if all along Nick's body-count of damsels done to death was nothing personal, merely a student-adept's art-project grimoire of old-time folk and blues death songs, as executed with the flamboyant twirl of a panto villain's moustachio in a puff of theatrical brimstone.

An exercise in style, people, a joke! Get it?

What else would you expect from a man whose name really was not only *Nick* but *Cave*, and whose snub nose, rats'-nest hair and skeletal limbs conjured to mind one of Count Dracula's bat-daemons? (Perhaps nomenclature and physique really are destiny.)

The linguistic relish of the tale and the eye-rolling, blood-curdling conviction of its telling were always more the point than the storylines themselves. Revisiting his recorded repertoire from that perspective, such a song as 'Mutiny in Heaven' now jumps out as a Fabergé egg of erudite and intricately worked design whose elements – hellfire preacher, Catholic peon, ghetto junkie, sea shanty buccaneer – cartoonishly collage the cultural treasure trove of a roving mind with a flair for the exotic and the exuberance of a comedian on a roll riding his comic riffs to the brink.

Barely had Nick Cave thus repackaged himself as a parodist con brio, a sparks-flying intellectual showman with a taste for mockery and working up a naughty head of steam in the Ocker-with-attitude tradition of Barry Humphries, then sudden personal circumstance both wiped the satanic grin off his face and triggered his moment of personal redemption, whereby he fulfilled the mythic role into which he had cast himself.

The Boatman's Call, released just a year after *Murder Ballads*, was Nick Cave's first and only album of consistent high seriousness, and hit the chattering classes of Great Britain with the kind of posh-gossip back story (two failed love affairs, one with a fellow rock star, PJ Harvey, plus new fatherhood twice over by different mothers) that overnight lead to his discovery by the commissioning editors of the BBC and broadsheet newspapers as an Orpheus of broken-hearted spiritual redemption.

At last, the prodigal son had not so much found as had thrust upon him the fatted calf of fatherly approval as manifest by *The Times*, Radio 3 and, smack-dab in the old man's footsteps, academic lectureship. As Nick Cave concurred with several journalists who mentioned it in those years, his dad would have been very proud. That it was his own fatherhood of two boys, with two more to follow, that triggered his return in such pomp to the fold of his upbringing's cultural respectability, is unsurprising and human. New parenthood, especially in mature years, has a wonderful way of shedding the long half-life of adolescent rebellion and reconciling one to both one's parental values and continuity with one's forefathers at precisely the moment you add your own link to the great chain of being. Nick Cave had come in from the cold of his own semi-comic monstrosity, and for a while basked in the warmth of his embrace as the least likely cultural institution of the turn of the millennium.

These days, elevation to rock's peerage of belle-lettered and *bien-pensant* regard is seldom revoked, and so stretches out a safety net for those who dare to undertake further artistic high-wire acts.

In the most recent years he has a different itch to scratch, one foreshadowed by a song released on the B-side of *The Boatman's Call*'s spin-off single 'Into My Arms'. Titled 'Little Empty Boat', this quite brilliant song speaks sadly (yet very wittily too) of impotence, both of the body and the will: even were the spirit so inclined, the flesh couldn't manage the necessary inclination. Nick Cave was turning forty; and even if no such dispiriting event blighted the onset of the man's middle years (and the birth of twin boys to his wife Susie Bick happily suggests otherwise), the growth of some extravagant face furniture to draw the eye south from the dwindling roof garden tells the old, old story of how we menfolk start swinging shiny medallions once the bloom of youth wears off. And artistically, he has responded just as one might have predicted: half obsessively, half comically.

'There is something to be said for disappointing people,' Nick Cave told Phil Sutcliffe in 2004 in a long interview included in this anthology. 'To displease and disappoint keeps you on your toes, keeps you alive.'

Nick Cave's recent projects seem intended to displease and disappoint or, at the very least, test the tolerance of precisely those who so recently clutched him to their bosom as the new Leonard Cohen: he is reinventing himself as a thoroughly dirty old man.

So we have his 'hobby' band Grinderman's two Stooges-alike albums including the tune 'No Pussy Blues', and his second novel, *The Death of Bunny Munro*, the tale of an ageing, compulsively priapic South Coast cosmetic salesman's descent into humiliation, hell and Hove, whose acknowledgment page finds room to render an apology to the singer Avril Lavigne, presumably for Bunny's brief but graphic imaginative description of her vagina. Bunny, of course, is an utter loser whom you need to probe deeply for his sole redeeming feature – a genuine, albeit entirely self-centred and neglectful, love for his son.

Is Bunny a Cave alter-ego? All creative writers toy with such fantasies – do they not? – and students of Cave minutiae may note that Bunny was the name of a now deceased German secretary with whom he dallied during his Berlin sojourn. Also, Bunny's adolescent first love, Penny Charade, takes her name from Cave's first love. The Cave-core is teasingly invited to make as much or as little of that as we like. To quote Nick's hero Van Morrison, it's all in the game. The myth-maker's wheels grind on.

And so to the man.

I first saw him as the feral farm boy singing with the Birthday Party at the Moonlight Club in Kilburn in late 1980. My old school friend Barney Hoskyns, who had just started writing for the music papers, had taken me as a matter of urgency. They were the real thing, he advised, and had to be seen to be believed. Barney was right, and any regrets I felt for having missed seeing the Stooges and the Sex Pistols were offset by the conviction that this was third time lucky.

The group's first champion in the national music press, Barney had become a friend, one of the Birthday Party's London circle, and, as his mate and fellow fan, I joined him as a backstage irregular and fellow traveller during Nick Cave and guitarist Rowland Howard's pilgrimages of wee small hours after-show rest and relaxation; on one occasion, I recall, Nick set his hairdo alight when he nodded out into a candle.

In June 1983, in the interregnum between the Birthday Party's dissolution and the Bad Seeds' formation, Nick, his girlfriend Anita Lane and then his new best mate Blixa Bargeld became my sub-tenants for a few weeks in Tintern Street, Brixton, South London. It was a strange but perfectly amiable interlude. Nick was a hard-working, slightly aloof presence about the place, Anita a delightful kook who never seemed to get up before the six o'clock news, and Blixa an utter gentleman and ideal flatmate, though his ripped leather trousers and gumboots hardly raised the tone of the area. Chief of my memories of that time is the contents of the fridge: Nick's jar of Haywards Piccalilli and Anita's Dairylea cheese triangles, for which Nick was wont to chide her: 'Your diet is so processed, Anita.' Never mind his jar of bright yellow pickle, I chuckled inwardly to myself, what about the heroin? On that score Nick was so discreet I couldn't swear he used during the three or so weeks he occupied the top room in my flat. Nick observed a certain old-fashioned standard of decorum in his behaviour.

Which, I suppose, is a code of etiquette I breached some two years later when, having raved to the skies about the first Bad Seeds album on the reviews pages of the *New Musical Express*, I mentioned in print that I found its follow-up a disappointment. What happened next is told in the fourth of the twenty features in this anthology. A few months after that feature appeared, at a Bad Seeds show at Camden's Electric Ballroom, I bought for £1 the green flexidisc bearing the song 'Scum', which he'd written about me and the authoress of the third feature in this anthology, Antonella Black (née Gambotto). Hearing the record for the first time remains the most thrillingly double-edged experience of my life, and to this day never fails to horripilate the nape hairs, flush all four cheeks and send a shudder of both shame and pride yo-yoing up and down my spine. Come the time the stonemason needs the words of my epitaph to carve, 'Scum' is good to go.

Beyond that, the stories in this book speak for themselves. A few observations, though. In 1988, 'Edge of Darkness' by Jack Barron marked the lowest point in Nick Cave's relationship with the music press. Today, Jack says that he would not take such a tack again when interviewing a using drug addict. We were all very much younger then. Barney Hoskyns was twenty-two when he wrote his first feature on the Birthday Party, Simon Reynolds just turning twenty-four when he penned his penetrating analysis of the hidden persuaders in the Cave canon, and Antonella Gambotto (under the *nom de plume* of Antonella Black) a mere nineteen when her brilliantly entertaining discovery that her idol had feet of clay was published. What we might sometimes have lacked in such middle-aged virtues as moderation or proportion we more than made up for in our absolute intellectual, emotional and moral engagement with the music we loved.

Second, one might note how well, from 1997, the year of *The Boatman's Call*, Nick Cave responds to female journalists. It was a two-way street: female journalists now wanted to talk to him, whereas before many were put off by the consistent misogyny of his lyrics – as distinguishable from equal-opportunity misanthropy – and that, moreover, he appeared to occupy a heavy scene of self-medicating blokes where heroines counted for less than heroin.

Third, though one doesn't have to be female to get a good interview out of Nick Cave, being a diligent journalist whose curiosity manifestly springs from the work rather than the myth grants the man as well as the artist a respect to which he tends to respond positively. For fans who share the deepest interest in Nick Cave's work and how it arises from his life, particularly valuable in this collection are the interviews he gave Debbie Kruger and Phil Sutcliffe. I hope that readers will share my fascination with the back and forth of Nick's many hours under the Sutcliffe grill; some of this is the kind of stuff commonly edited out of magazines and newspapers for space reasons and to spare the patience of less committed readers. I have removed only one passage, which Nick clearly felt uncomfortable revealing because it might expose him to a slight legal risk. Otherwise, I have done no more than tidy up loose ends and dead ends, meanderings and repetitions; what you read is Nick Cave in the conversational raw.

Nor have I removed assertions of the Nick Cave myth which I know to have little foundation in reality. That Nick Cave didn't care to be reminded by Ginny Dougary of the time he wrote lyrics with a bloody syringe while travelling on the London Underground may have something to do with the fact, as I am reliably assured, that it never happened.

I have otherwise sought to edit this anthology with a light touch. Those who take the trouble to compare these republications with the originals in yellowing press cuttings may note that some lyrics by other songwriters have been removed where they are quoted for dramatic colour rather than as grist to the critical mill; this is simply a legal precaution lest music publishers, who happily turned a blind eye to such irregular practices at the time of a text's original publication, now start playing it exorbitantly by the book.

Finally, when I was commissioned to edit this anthology in 2009, I had hoped to express in this foreword a remark or two about what a pleasant surprise it is to find that every journalist who had interviewed Nick Cave in this anthology is still around to read their work reprinted as much as thirty years later; after all, such has been nature of the man and his milieu that some of us, especially in the '80s, have been moths flitting perilously close to the flame. Sadly, though, as the first draft of this anthology went to the publisher, Robert Sandall, who wrote the typically elegant and incisive cover story for the debut issue of *Word* magazine in 2003, succumbed to the cancer from which he had been suffering for several years. I dedicate this foreword to his memory.

Mat Snow

A Boy Next Door

Michel Faber

In February 2001, I was launching the Slovak translation of one of my books in a bookstore in Bratislava. I noticed that on an adjacent table there lay a Czech edition of Nick Cave's novel, *And the Ass Saw the Angel*, suspiciously thinner than the original text, but packaged in a sublime expressionist cover that put the British version to shame. As I stood there, turning the book over in my hands, I was struck by the oddness of Nick Cave and me both having become novelists, our books translated into languages neither of us understand, meeting here on a trestle table in Eastern Europe.

But we'd met once before, face-to-face, when I was nineteen and he was twenty-one. He wasn't a novelist then. He was the singer in a New Wave combo called the Boys Next Door, and I wrote reviews for *Farrago*, Melbourne University's student magazine. Nick was by this time already finished with tertiary education, or it had finished with him. His deliberately sleazy paintings, crowded with penises and grotesque voyeurs, had fulfilled their function of antagonising a female tutor at Caulfield Technical College, but failed to impress the examiners, and he'd been shown the door. His obsessions with religion, redemption and the power of the word had yet to find their outlet; he was, to the outside observer, yet another would-be pop star hungry for exposure.

By 1979, Nick and his fellow Boys Next Door were still cherishing some hope of a commercial breakthrough. A succession of amateur managers and record company shysters had assured them that they would be massive. British punk bands like the Jam and the Stranglers had stormed the charts overseas. Could it happen down under? If so, the Boys Next Door didn't want it to happen to one of the rival Melbourne bands that they despised.

Unfortunately, the music scene in Australia was even sleepier than Britain's. Punk had made little impact on the mainstream, and such groups as the Boys Next Door were considered, by the public and the music press alike,

Nick Cave onstage with the Birthday Party at the Ace Theatre in Brixton, London, 25 November 1982.

ephemeral distractions from more essential questions, like 'Is Eric Clapton still God?', 'Can Rod Stewart ever recapture former glories?' and 'Will The Beatles get back together?'

As far as Australia's reputation in the worldwide musical arena was concerned, all hope was pinned on MOR soul singers like Renée Geyer, Marcia Hines and Billy Thorpe. Fleetwood Mac reigned supreme, and an astonishing one in four homes owned a copy of Neil Diamond's *Hot August Night*.

These were not the only reasons why the Boys Next Door's exodus to England was inevitable. Melbourne, in 1979, was a city whose centre was roughly a mile square. Surrounding this modest metropolis were endless acres of suburbia characterised by eucalyptus trees, milk bars, carpet emporiums, scout halls and local chapters of the Returned Servicemen's League. Music venues where anything more radical than Doobie Brothers covers, heavy rock or blues could feasibly be attempted were few. When Nick Cave, in the interview that follows, refers to an audience of 'Homesglen skinheads', he doesn't mean skinheads in the British sense. He means denizens of a suburban wasteland of shopping centres and barbecues, the natural fans not of ska but of Suzi Quatro.

I grew up in just such a suburb, twenty miles out of Melbourne. My ignorance of city nightlife was total; I was too poor, too studious and too antisocial to go and see bands play live. Occasionally, walking from the railway station to the university, I would catch sight of crudely printed flyers sellotaped to lamp-posts, but I ignored these invitations to join a counterculture that was incompatible with writing essays on Dickens. Apart from the groups who performed free on campus at lunchtimes, David Bowie and Jethro Tull were the only rock acts I had seen play by the time I interviewed the Boys Next Door.

To help me prepare for my assignment, I was given a copy of the group's debut LP, *Door, Door*. Their record company, Mushroom, was the largest independent in Australia, with success stories including Skyhooks and Split Enz. Virtually anybody who was anybody in the blues, folk, glam or progressive rock scene ended up on Mushroom, which was run by an old-school rock promoter called Michael Gudinski. Punk meant little in his hirsute, reefer-fogged world.

Nevertheless, a junior Mushroom employee called Michelle recommended the Boys Next Door album with great enthusiasm, and gave me the phone number of Nick Cave's mum, in case I needed to contact him at home. The dire poverty Nick would experience in a London squat, hand-to-mouth with other scabrous expatriates, was still in the unimaginable future; right now, he was living in a large house owned by his mother, a librarian. In this, he was no different from many Australian punks. The spiky-haired chap who presented the punk show on Radio 2 PBS-FM lived in a mansion in Toorak, Melbourne's answer to Sloane Square.

At home in my brick bungalow in Bayswater, I played *Door, Door* dutifully, many times. Then, as now, I had eclectic tastes, favouring any unusual band who made their own rules –Kraftwerk, Pere Ubu, King Crimson, Neu, Yes, Throbbing Gristle. The only thing I disliked was mediocrity – which the sanitised punk-pop of the Boys Next Door struck me as being. Side one of the album, recorded in

June 1978 and produced by Les Karsky, was a string of short, humdrum rock'n' roll songs written by Nick; side two, recorded in January 1979 and produced by the band in collaboration with Tony Cohen, was mainly written by new recruit Rowland Howard. Nick's sole contribution to the recent material was 'Dive Position', an exercise in glam archness reminiscent of Steve Harley & Cockney Rebel. Rowland's pieces were all stolid, multi-layered affairs that resembled Magazine or Television at their most pretentious. 'Shivers', a paean to romantic insincerity, had been a staple of his previous outfit the Young Charlatans.

I wondered if it would break Michelle's heart if I told her that I wasn't overly impressed with her favourite band.

At the *Farrago* office, opinion of the Boys Next Door was low. The editor, who looked like a stunted fifth member of Status Quo, informed me that Nick Cave had been educated at the posh Caulfield Grammar School, that the group were talentless poseurs and bandwagon-jumpers. This drawled tirade was interrupted by the arrival of the first Boy Next Door – Phill Calvert, a smiling, affable lad who did indeed look like someone who might run errands for grateful elderly neighbours.

'The others are always late,' he explained, and immediately seized upon an acoustic guitar that was lying around the office. After some tuneless doodling, he picked out a hackneyed riff worthy of Chuck Berry.

'Brilliant,' I commented sarcastically.

'It's a new song we've written,' he smirked.

Phill was keen to chat. The most industry-savvy member of the group, he was already demonstrating the impatience for commercial success that he would eventually find (albeit fleetingly) as drummer for the Psychedelic Furs. Before the tape recorder was even switched on, he'd told me excitedly that the group was going to England later in the year.

Nick Cave and Rowland Howard arrived together, apologising for being late. The other members, Tracey Pew and Mick Harvey, couldn't make it. This was just as well: there was only room on the *Farrago* couch for three boys sitting hip to hip.

Although biographies like Ian Johnston's *Bad Seed* emphasise that Cave had been a compulsive boozer since the age of twelve, and that by the age of twenty he was using hard drugs, the Nick Cave I met was a fresh-faced, fairly healthy-looking young man. His hair was washed and fluffy, he wore a schoolboy-ish shirt and a stylish jacket; indeed, neither he nor Phill Calvert would have looked out of place in an early line-up of Duran Duran. Within a couple of years, Nick's appearance would undergo an alarming metamorphosis and his visage would loom out of the British music papers like a public health warning – a puffy, pock-cheeked, swollen-lidded Halloween pumpkin with a shock of greasy black hair. On the day we met, adolescent resilience and the comforts of home were still holding him back from the leap into Hell. Seated side by side on the couch, Nicholas Edward Cave and his fellow Boys Next Door were on their best behaviour.

I began by asking:

Why are the band called the Boys Next Door? Is it ironic or is genuinely

how you see yourselves in relation to your audience?
NICK: No, we're intending to change it very soon.

Was it forced upon you?
NICK: No, we just thought of it years ago and we've regretted it ever since.

What was the thought behind it when you made it up?
ROWLAND: Oh, you know, we were just the clean-cut, normal looking boy-next-door people.
NICK: It was a reaction against the names that were going around at the time. The more vulgar names. *[Nick probably had British bands in mind here, such as Slaughter and the Dogs, the Buzzcocks and of course the Sex Pistols. The only Australian contender for a vulgarly-named punk band I can think of pre-1978 is Johnny Dole & the Scabs. Splendid examples like Thrush & the Cunts and the Slugfuckers were yet to, erm, come.]*

So it was ironic?
NICK: Yes, at the time, but it's lost all meaning now.

Someone told me that you started off as the archetypal spitting, jumping-around punk band. Would you agree with that?
NICK: No. For a start we always admitted that we were, um . . . in the days when it was a problem whether you had 'credibility' and whether you were poor or not, we were always . . .
PHILL: . . . delighted by the fact that you were middle-class.
NICK: . . . the first to say that we weren't, and that we were educated properly, et cetera.

Someone said to me earlier, 'Ask them about their public school background.'
NICK: Yeah . . . People still whisper behind their hands: 'They've come from public school, you know,' as if we care. But . . . we were a lot wilder in the early days. But so was our music.
PHILL: But we weren't covered in chains . . . I don't think Nick ever gobbed on the audience.
NICK: I did, at the first gig we ever played. All these skinheads – Homesglen skinheads – were screaming at us, 'Punks!' and stuff like that. And it suddenly occurred to me that we were punks, because everyone said we were. So I just sort of thought, 'What things do punks do? Will I fart, shit, gob, spit or whatever?' So I spat, and consequently got beaten to a pulp.
PHILL: Ah, that's right, yeah: that was wonderful. It just dissolved into one huge fight.

Do you see yourselves as moving away from basic rock'n'roll?
NICK: I think we've already moved away from it.

The thing that bothered me most about the LP was the gulf between the two halves. There's such a vast difference between the material on the first side and the material on the second.

NICK: There's about a year's difference.

Well, it's six months in the recording, but I suppose the songs were written longer apart.

PHILL: Yeah.

ROWLAND: It's more than six months, isn't it?

PHILL: No, not between recording, no.

It's seven months between recording. How far apart were the songs written?

PHILL: Well, a lot of the songs on the first side had been in our repertoire for quite a time before we recorded them. Same with the second side, actually.

ROWLAND: Oh, not really.

PHILL: Not as drastic a difference.

ROWLAND: When we recorded the songs on the second side we were quite enthused; they were fairly new still.

NICK: The first side is basically a rock'n'roll sort of record, and the second side is far more adventurous. But the new material that we've since written is a step away again.

So the implication of putting it on the first side is to say, 'Right, that's left behind.'

NICK, ROWLAND, PHILL: Yeah, yeah.

ROWLAND: It would have been ludicrous to mix the tracks up.

Would you have liked to re-do them, though?

PHILL: Oh yeah.

ROWLAND: Well, if we'd had the chance we wouldn't have re-done the tracks; we'd probably have done more new ones.

I suppose that's beyond your control.

PHILL: Well, it was at the time. See, that whole first side was part of an entire album. And we picked those tracks from that album and then recorded the second side in January. 'Cause Gudinski was going to release the album in its old format, which was done with four members prior to Rowland joining. When Gudinski said he wanted to release it, we said, 'No, no, we've gotta do more recording 'cause it's not a fair representation of us as we are now.'

So Door, Door was a compromise.

PHILL: Yeah.

NICK: It still isn't –

PHILL: – it still isn't a fair representation now, 'cause since it's come out, the band's different again.

NICK: But I'm sure that happens with everybody.

Nick, are you still writing basic rock'n'roll songs or is it just –
NICK, ROWLAND, PHILL: No! No!

Because the way the album's put together, it comes across that Nick Cave's the rock'n'roller on the first side, you know. *[Mocking laughter from Phill and Rowland]*
NICK: Well, that's unfortunate, but it's only because Nick Cave wrote those songs over a year ago, or a year ago, and I didn't really get much of a chance to show the newer songs that I'd written because we wanted Rowland to have songs on the album that *he'd* written.

ROWLAND: But also you only had two new songs.

NICK: *[sheepishly]* Yeah, that's true. *[Phill laughs]* I went through a dry spell. You're not supposed to say this, they'll think we're bastards. *[Rowland and Phill both laughing]*

I found the first side very disappointing. Except for 'Friends of My World', which I thought had a bit more going for it.
PHILL: There's some really crass synthesiser on that.

Those session musicians, were they your idea?
PHILL: They were all our friends!

ROWLAND: Who did they *[i.e. Mushroom Records]* want to have playing on the first album?

NICK: Mal Logan *[veteran of the Australian R&B scene, who by 1979 was playing keyboards for the execrable Little River Band].*

PHILL: Mal Logan . . . And they wanted Wilbur Wilde and Joe Camilleri on sax.

Oh God . . . *[Wilbur Wilde, latterly a producer of commercials, was the mainstay of nostalgia act Ol' 55, as well as a session player for the likes of Roy Orbison. Joe Camilleri was the leader of Jo Jo Zep & the Falcons, whose name speaks for itself.]*
PHILL: I mean, Wilbur's a great sax player, but not for us.

NICK: We spent about half of our studio time arguing with the producer that we refused to have this person . . .

PHILL: *[contemptuous]* – Mal Logan –

NICK: . . . Mal Logan on our record.

PHILL: And also Karsky kept rushing into the studio with guitars going, 'I've got a great bit for here!' and we're going, 'No you haven't.'

NICK: He was incidentally responsible for the really pompous backing vocals, the harmony. That's all him, you know.

PHILL: It's his singing, too.

The second side is pretty well produced.
PHILL: Yeah! It's not bad, is it?

Let's talk about the individual songs a bit. On 'Shivers', there are lots of Frippish things. You know, like two notes going on and on like a police siren and similar sorts of textures to what Fripp uses.
NICK: Yeah, I think there were vague influences there . . .
ROWLAND: *[dubiously]* Yeah . . .

You don't consider yourself very influenced by Fripp?
ROWLAND: Um, yeah, I would admit that that does sound rather like Fripp. That's not typical of my guitar playing.

What sort of music did each of you grow up on?
PHILL: Nursery rhymes.

None of the currently hip things like the New York Dolls and the MC5?
ROWLAND: The New York Dolls are wonderful. In their place. I really enjoyed them when their first album came out, but there's no way it had any influence on me.

What did influence you?
ROWLAND: Oh well, there's really obvious people like Bowie, Roxy Music and Eno and things like that, and more recently people like Pere Ubu and the Pop Group.

That doesn't really come over on the album, Pere Ubu and the Pop Group.
ROWLAND: Oh no. In a way, that's one thing we really hate about the second side of the album, is that it's so contrived and organised.
NICK: And consequently the music that we're writing now isn't. That's why the demos will be so much different. We'll be treating them in a different way.

That sort of roughness that Pere Ubu get.
NICK: Yes, just the sort of real spontaneous sound that they get. And things like they start themes off at the beginning and never bother to end them. And just a real wit about their music.

What sort of things are you progressing into for the next album?
PHILL: Well, the next album's a long way off. So I'd say . . . What'll happen is, before we go away to England we're doing some demos, which'll probably – which might be this weekend, fellas!
NICK: Might they?

PHILL: Might be, yeah. I'll find out from Keith *[Glass, their then-manager]* this afternoon. We're doing some demos of recent material to take to England with us. And what we're going to do is, we'll give the stereo master to Gudinski and try to convince him to release an EP prior to us going away, you know. Of say three or four tracks, so that people can have a more recent piece of music from the Boys Next Door. *[In fact, the mutual disaffection between Gudinski and his protégés led to a split from Mushroom shortly after this interview, and the EP surfaced much later on Keith Glass's own Missing Link label.]*

NICK: Those songs will be far less clinical. The way that the second side of *Door, Door* was recorded is a very clean sound, very contrived. The way we'll do these ones is just a real spontaneous sort of thing. With each song I've been writing, the lyrics are becoming more and more meaningless. The main reason for that is that I don't think anyone ever really draws anything from lyrics anyway. Only that they like them. I don't think lyrics ever affect people in any way or affect their lives.

Do you take much interest in experimental music, like [Cornelius] Cardew's Scratch Orchestra or Throbbing Gristle?
NICK: Um . . . I like Throbbing Gristle's stuff. You don't, do you, Rowland? *[Rowland looks unconvinced]*
PHILL: I really like people who use natural sounds like breaking things and banging things against other things.

There's nothing like that on the album.
NICK: I don't think anything we've been talking about that we'd like to do is –
PHILL: – related to the record at all!

At this juncture, Bernard, *Farrago*'s photographer, suggested we go out and take some photos. The Boys were undecided, partly because 'There's only three of us here', and partly because 'We really like doing interviews'. It was agreed that we would take the snaps, then come back to the office and carry on with the interview. Phill Calvert made it clear that he could talk about the group all day. So few publications were interested in the Boys Next Door that this feature in *Farrago*, read by scores or maybe even hundreds of potential fans, was a golden opportunity.

Photographer Bernard, looking mightily impressive with his SLR camera (although the eventual pictures would be feeble) shepherded the boys into the Rowden White Library, a large recreation room. Here, thirty-five airline-type seats, each equipped with a pair of headphones, piped a choice of music into the ears of shaggy-haired students. The library had a surreal atmosphere, created by a herd of post-adolescents singing tunelessly along with different records that were playing into their headphones, or drumming on their knees. Nick, for all his reputed exhibitionism, was reluctant when asked to pose in their midst. The prospect of being stared at by thirty-five teenagers groaning along with the

Eagles, Bob Dylan and Elvis Costello didn't appeal. Instead, the Boys Next Door ended up posing behind a magazine rack, awkwardly pretending to peruse old copies of *Rolling Stone*.

Back in the *Farrago* office, the boys were relieved to get back to serious business. Mindful of their unease at the photo session, I asked:

How does your record company try to market you now?
NICK: I don't think they've tried at all really. At least, the Mushroom people haven't done any promotion whatsoever, as far as I can see. Except for things like that . . . *[points to the promo picture conspicuously pinned to the Farrago office door]* But they haven't gone out of their way to promote us. They still think that we're a novelty act, that not many people are going to like us.

So Mushroom doesn't have any consciousness of the potential for New Wave bands?
NICK: No, no, not at all. If we were Plastic Bertrand *[cartoon French punk who had a minor hit with the Ramones-like 'Ca Plane Pour Moi']* they might like us, but he doesn't like us the way we are – that's Gudinski.
PHILL: There's just one person in the whole of the Mushroom building who thinks we're good. And that's, um . . .

Michelle.
PHILL: Michelle, yeah. She likes us. *[laughs]*
MF: Would you appear on *Countdown* if you were asked? *[Countdown was Australia's equivalent of* Top of the Pops, *with a comparable air of artificial unreality.]*
PHILL: *[laughs]* We're going to, soon.
NICK: I don't see why not.
ROWLAND: I mean, it's communication. We've got to try to communicate with as many people as possible and *Countdown* is the obvious medium. As much of a compromise as it may be.
PHILL: I don't consider it a sell-out.

Is it possible to play live on Countdown?
PHILL: No.
NICK: No.
PHILL: No one does it.
BERNARD: It takes an hour to do soundchecks and such.
PHILL: An hour? It'd take them all day! The way they run that show, there's so many dress rehearsals and Christ knows what . . . And all the miking up: they'd have to set aside a whole separate area.
BERNARD: And they've got a few bands to get through.
PHILL: Yeah. People used to sing vocals live, but the only people who did that were . . . Well, Marc Hunter *[lead singer of pop band Dragon]* did it and I can't

think of anyone else.

ROWLAND: People that generally don't care.

PHILL: Yeah.

ROWLAND: Chris Bailey . . .

BERNARD: And apparently they play the backing track at such a low level that it's hard to hear.

PHILL: Oh, it's ridiculous, it really is. We've done it once before.

NICK: We have been on *Countdown* once, a long time ago. It was disastrous.

PHILL: Probably will be this time, too.

How long ago was that?

NICK: Oh, at the same time as the single, 'Boots'. We did that. I mean, the volume they played it at . . .

PHILL: Like, you've got a drum set going onstage; that drowns most of it out anyway. You've got to hit it to look vaguely convincing.

So, what's the single you'll be promoting?

PHILL: 'Shivers'.

That's doomed.

PHILL: I don't think so. There's lots of long songs on the radio at the moment.

No, not so much because it's long, but because of what it is.

PHILL: I think it's really catchy as buggery.

It depends. John Cale's catchy as buggery too, but no one's ever going to play him.

NICK: I know what Phill's saying but I don't think anyone thinks it's going to be a hit. I think we're doing *Countdown* next week, are we?

PHILL: It should be this Saturday.

NICK: But we can't submit a film clip. They don't have film clips of Australian bands unless you appear once live and it takes off, and then you're allowed to submit a film clip. So we'll have to stand there with those mindless idiot cameramen . . .

ROWLAND: . . . zooming in on the fingers on the guitar neck.

NICK: There's no way you can get any emotion across and do a convincing show on *Countdown* with their cameramen.

PHILL: We did a really good film clip for 'Boots Are Made for Walking' which if they had've put that on, the record would've sold a lot more copies. We spent a lot of money on it, but they just didn't want it. It's sitting around someone's studio somewhere.

When you play a song like 'Shivers' onstage, do you change the dynamics? Like, 'We can't afford to let the audience get bored, so we'll

put a guitar solo at the end . . .'
NICK, PHILL, ROWLAND: Oh, no no. God no.
NICK: I think they'd be more bored if we did. *[laughter]*
ROWLAND: *[mockingly]* Hey, we could have a big build-up at the end and make it go faster and play a really fast soaring guitar solo, like Jab did with 'The Hospital'.
PHILL: Oh, yeah . . .

Doesn't everybody do that?
PHILL: We don't.
NICK: Anyway, 'Shivers' generally is never boring. It always goes over really well when we play it. People always shout out for it.

Everywhere you play?
ROWLAND: It goes over best in the outer suburbs. Much better than most of our other songs, usually.
NICK: It's only because it has all this mock emotion, you know; clenching the heart and stuff like that . . .
PHILL: Hand motions, you know.
NICK: . . . which for some reason people seem to like.
ROWLAND: And also we're not making a tremendous amount of noise which they object to most of the time because they can't talk, so when we allow them to talk to their friends *[laughter]* they clap us for it.
PHILL: A lot of our audience, the new material, the stuff that we're enjoying playing more, they don't react to as well. They like the real headbanging stuff. A lot of people like to go out and get drunk and watch the Boys Next Door jump around, and stuff like that.
ROWLAND: And shout out for 'Boy Hero'.

What's 'Boy Hero'?
PHILL: It's on *Lethal Weapons*. It's the B-side of the ['Boots'] single.
ROWLAND: It's just a sort of medium-paced rock'n'roll song, and it's fairly catchy.
NICK: We've played it at practically every performance we've ever done.
ROWLAND: That's an example of where people just tolerate our newer songs, sort of thinking, 'Okay, I'll let them fuck around with this,' but they think that the real highpoint of the gig is the songs we did years ago . . .

Like people sitting through King Crimson concerts and hating the whole experience but just holding out for –
PHILL, ROWLAND, MICHEL: '21st Century Schizoid Man'.
PHILL: *[laughing]* Yeah, true.
NICK: But we don't compromise the organisation of our sets for that either. You know, we don't end the set with a whole lot of oldies – which I think Keith, our manager, is wanting us to do more. To have a lot of fast, headbanging songs at the end so that they . . .

It's the rock'n'roll thing to do, isn't it?
NICK: Actually we organised it a bit like that the last time we played, and the audience went really crazy at the end of the night, only because we had four oldies.
ROWLAND: Except that it was totally unsatisfactory because you knew they only did it because of the four songs at the end. You could see the little lights appear in their eyes as you launched into 'Boy Hero'. *[laughter]* It was truly disgusting and I would rather have gone down really awfully, because I didn't want to go down well for the four old songs, I wanted to go down well for the new songs.

What sorts of things do you do usually, when you play live?
NICK: *[mock offence]* You're interviewing us and you've never even seen us?
FARRAGO EDITOR: I saw you once, a long time ago. At Swinburne [College].
PHILL: *[ruefully]* That long ago? Remember that night, Nick?
NICK: No.
PHILL: Swinburne, with the Negatives – oh no, what were they called then? – the Reals. And the Babeez.
NICK: Oh, the first night! Oh yeah, that was great, that. Fantastic. *[Phill giggling hysterically]* We did twenty-minute 'Louie Louie''s and –
PHILL: 'Gloria'.
NICK: Yeah, a really grotty perversion of that. *[remembering the original question]* Um . . . I don't know how to describe what we do onstage.
ROWLAND: What we're wearing in this photo *[indicates promo picture]* is what we look like onstage generally.

Hmm. Vague overtones of Split Enz there which I'm not sure I like.
PHILL: That's vague overtones of a very wide angle lens.
ROWLAND: People call me 'Split Enz' when I walk down the street dressed like this. I'm sorry, I can't help my funny nose, or whatever it is.
PHILL: Ha, Noel! *[he's suggesting that Rowland looks like Noel Crombie, the geeky, pointy-nosed percussionist of Split Enz]* That's just a wide angle lens that makes us look like we've got funny heads.

We're descending into trivia now, so we might as well call it a day, okay?

And that was that. the Boys Next Door said cheerio, and I hurried to a tutorial on medieval poetry. Later, in my suburban bedroom, with the Mahavishnu Orchestra or Tangerine Dream no doubt playing in the background, I transcribed the interview.

Although I didn't say so, I was pretty sure that the Boys Next Door would betray their brave declarations of experimentalism, and sell out to the record industry. Still fresh in my mind was the disappointment I'd felt with David Bowie the year before. The Thin White Bullshit-Artist had told awestruck Australian journalists that he was considering touring Oz with a repertoire of half-written songs, to be improvised to completion live onstage. Such risk-taking would take the boredom out of the rock'n'roll charade, he said. Of course, when I trotted along to the Bowie concert, it was a predictable trawl through the hits, with not a note out of place.

Talk, I realised, was cheap. Each week, *New Musical Express* was full of pretentious New Wave bands who namechecked the gods of the avant-garde but failed to deliver anything remotely challenging. The Boys Next Door, I suspected, would do whatever they felt was necessary to succeed in the marketplace, and would either hit commercial paydirt or quit in disgruntlement to become furniture removalists.

By the following year, I realised I was wrong. The *Hee Haw* EP was released while the Boys Next Door were away in London, already mutating into the Birthday Party. The music was everything they'd promised it would be, and more. *Countdown* was a distant memory, 'Blast Off' was just around the corner.

By 1983, when I attended one of The Birthday Party's final performances, they had amassed an extraordinary body of work, frenzied, unsettling and exhilarating. At that gig, the forward surge of the crowd pushed me up onto the stage, and I spent most of the set squatting in front of Tracey Pew's leather-clad legs. Phill Calvert was long gone, Mick Harvey had jumped the sinking ship and been replaced by a worried-looking Des Hefner. Every time Nick Cave fell down – which was frequently – a shudder would pass through the wooden boards. Rowland Howard, seething with disdain, kicked Cave in the ribs and yelled 'Get up, ya cunt!' The boyish solidarity the group had shown four years before had fizzled out like a firework.

Throughout that gruelling and humiliating gig, Cave looked like a corpse reanimated with thousand-volt shocks. If someone had predicted that he would one day publish a fine literary novel, and croon piano ballads like 'Into My Arms' to a hushed audience at the Barbican, I would have laughed. Once a man has landed in Hell, I would have said, there's no returning.

But of course, there is.

Michel Faber, *Rock's Backpages*, August 2002

Sometimes Pleasure Heads Must Burn — A Manhattan Melodrama

Barney Hoskyns

It's a chill, exposed night in New York City. The East Coast has only just recovered from a week of torrential rains, and winds sweeping up the island's avenue from Battery Park to Harlem threaten more.

But the show must go on, and at a swanky rock disco in Union Square it's only just beginning. Strutting their stuff to English imports like Duran Duran's 'Planet Earth' and Way of the West's 'Don't Say That's Just for White Boys' are second division preppies and neatly-pressed executives from New Jersey. They are trying to get their dates drunk.

The night is flowing by pretty amorphously when suddenly, at one o'clock, the lights on the Underground's floor scatter back to their source and the sound dies. Everyone looks round, seeking the cause of this unwelcome interruption. Instantly their faces drop in disbelief, for onto the stage are climbing five . . . five . . . but words just give way to alarmed grimaces. Let's just say five very undesirable aliens.

One, festooned in split-crotch gold lamé drainpipes, his bruised, labial features twitching through black flames of hair, appears to be the singer. Another, busy strapping on a bass guitar like a giant dildo, sports a fishnet vest, a Stetson, and the sort of moustache you might cultivate if you were shaping up to hustle some meat on gay Christopher Street. Perhaps most disturbing of all, a kind of gangling, psychotic hillbilly, squeezed into a ridiculous suit out of some garment district garbage can, is fastening on a guitar like he was about to run through a rehearsal for *The Texas Chainsaw Massacre*.

Hyperboles aside, it's not quite what the management was expecting. Hell, they haven't even played a note and already half the crowd is filing out. A single drumbeat portends ill, and next moment all the worst premonitions are justified. Cranking out of the guitar amps comes this murderous death-rattle, like the gaze of Medusa freezing in their steps the few foolhardy adventurers who dare to look.

Nick Cave onstage with the Birthday Party at the Ace Theatre in Brixton, London, 25 November 1982.

The bass, lurching obscenely into the foray, scrapes and shunts in subterranean seizures. St Vitus's Dance here we come!

Finally, his body doubling up in unholy convulsions, the macilent wreck of a singer starts to spit and fume: *'AMERICAN HEADS WILL ROLL IN TEXAS!! AMERICAN HEADS WILL ROLL!!!'* Hmmmm . . . like, what *is* this? Some of the observers turn away in nervous laughter, others comb their scattered brains to remember where Pigbag – polite, groovy little Pigbag – are playing. The rest suck on straws and pray it's over soon. *'I mean, shit, the Sex Pistols were one thing . . .'*

When the song ends, however, an ugly pause ensues. Something's wrong with the guitar. Suddenly, there's this ashen-faced nut behind the keyboard shouting into his mic, very slowly, again and again and again: *'WHAT'S THE MATTER WITH YOU BASTARDS? WHAT'S THE MATTER WITH YOU?'* It's a party-trick which fails to amuse the management. After the second song, 'Zoo-Music Girl', someone's climbing on the stage and telling the band their time is up. Scarcely acknowledging him, they thunder into one last, most outrageous exhibition of carnal mayhem and then disappear.

This little scenario is roughly what the Australian group the Birthday Party call 'a really great gig'. I mean, how degenerate can you get?

*

'There is no empty space in nature which we do not believe that, at one time or another, the human mind can fill.'
(Antonin Artaud, 'On the Alfred Jarry Theatre')

In this Apollonian climate of cold design and concealed despair, the Birthday Party take the concept of stage performance about as far as you are likely to see it go. Live, the songs of singer Nick Cave and guitarist Rowland Howard are driven to an emotional edge where pain and pleasure fuse – in cathartic madness for the performer and dithyrambic joy for the audience. Their concerts are feasts of energy, chaotic spectacles which break the surface of art and carry sound and lyric to ultimate violence. If Captain Beefheart or Pere Ubu seem too quirkily surreal, the Birthday Party in performance burst through the constrictions of intellect to a 'raw power', that original sin which Iggy Stooge so rightly perceived as 'laughing at you and me . . . '

'A man who believes is peculiar. BUT SINCE SOME ARE BORN PLAY ACTORS . . .'

The Birthday Party do not suffer from delusions of grandeur.

'I mean, fuck it,' says Nick Cave, 'what we're trying to do is the biggest musical cliché in the world. It's just that some people forget the cliché. Can you imagine Echo and the Bunnymen trying to let themselves go?'

He sprawls across the bar, trying to find his drink.

'I think it's really important to rely on clichés – like Suicide did. Not that it sounds like a cliché. As a matter of fact I think "King Ink" is one of the best songs ever written. That song can become so intense it puts me on another planet, though I don't think the recorded version is at all good.'

'*Prayers on Fire* stinks, quite honestly,' announces Tracy Pew, the group's super-macho bassist. 'The engineer slept through the entire session for a start. But then even "Release the Bats" isn't as good as it could be.'

'It's just too conventional at the moment,' resumes Cave. 'The record, as a cultural event, is a very limited concept. With the cover and everything, it can be much more than just the music.'

The Birthday Party come to shake us out of our inhibitions. They militate against the sedative boundaries of pop.

Cave: 'There's a real need for an intelligent but aggressive group in London. All the treasured groups are just so softcore. At one time there was a real upsurge of new young groups and incredible records like "She Is Beyond Good and Evil" . . . you know, the Pop Group before they sacrificed the music for that soapbox, toilet-roll politics. The groups that came out of the Pop Group have got back to primitive funk, which is good . . . I saw Rip Rig and Panic at Action Space and there was a real directness and irreverence, as opposed to Pigbag, who are just happy to be convincingly funky.'

What about their own bacchanalian night at Action Space?

Pew: 'The last two gigs in London have been the best yet. Before that the audiences were like a little bunch of eggs with faces. They lost control when they were told to, like Pavlovian dogs taking a leak.'

Cave: 'Compared to the gigs in Australia, especially in Sydney, they're nothing. You remember when that girl was slicing me up with a key, Tracy? In Australia, you really feel you're turning decent people into monsters. But look, we're not setting ourselves up as some kind of demonic force, it's just that things are generally more successful when they become blind and unconscious, when you feel anything could happen.'

Pew: 'In England that doesn't happen very often, because you media people have turned kids into robots, little UB40s . . .'

So what's kept you from the threshold of madness?

Cave: '*Funhouse*, the two Suicide albums (also the new live cassette) . . . *Slates* by the Fall. The Fall are a great group. *Slates* is one of the best things I've ever heard. It has a violence and humour which is off-putting to sheep.'

Is a popular music culture an important thing?

Cave: 'When the history of rock music is written – which, since it's practically dead, will be soon – it'll just be remembered as a sordid interruption of normality.'

Pew: 'Rock will be remembered as the anus of culture. Not Del Shannon but Iggy Pop.'

Cave: 'The last two years in London will be swept under the rug. This I can tell you: *THE LONG FRINGES WILL NOT BE REMEMBERED*. The point is that the creative process is not some fucking craft. *WE'RE A LIVING MUSICAL CLICHÉ*.'

*

'Who would care to contribute to a culture that cannot be satisfied no matter how much it devours, and at whose contact the most vigorous and wholesome nourishment is changed into "history and criticism"?'
(Nietzsche)

New York suffers terribly from its reputation and consequent sense of duty. It has convinced its spoilt children in their chic little headbands and PX offcuts that the entire point of their lives lies in snorting excessive amounts of cocaine, staying up till eight in the morning imbibing nauseous, overpriced cocktails, and taking non-stop taxis from one club to the next. All, of course, in the name of Fun and Style. But it doesn't feel like fun, it feels like a routine.

That the Birthday Party have been the most exciting live act in London for some six months cannot seriously be doubted by anyone who's seen them. In New York this excitement was seen simply as transgression – in the case of the band's Ritz show, incitement of the audience to a 'PiL-style riot'.

According to Cave, however, the Ritz was 'a really boring, conservative gig'. True, at several junctures he climbed into the pit of zombies below him, but it was quite obvious that to provoke a riot he'd have had to set fire to them. Three quarters of the way through the set, the lights came up, the disco came on, and the Birthday Party were quietly and efficiently shoved off the stage.

This sort of treatment, which might have left anyone else permanently embittered, only seemed to strengthen the group's immediate taste for America.

'If our natural path is disaster,' groaned Mick Harvey stoically, 'then so be it.'

Drunk on culture schlock, roaming the streets and sleeping with TV eyes on, the 'boys from down under' (as they were so tastefully described in the city's music listings) swallowed the pill and survived the comedown.

'What would you rather be in,' demands Rowland Howard, 'Dolly Parton's backing band or – an English New Wave group?'

The others hear the answer within the question: it doesn't brook reply. 'Yep!' bawls Tracy Pew, carefully adjusting the angle of a new Stetson and ignoring the question, 'The gig at the Underground was one of my all-time favourite gigs.'

*

At the root of Australia's open rock revolt, its avowed overthrow of Western chic and transatlantic pussyfooting lies a) the experience of pure boredom down under, and b) one all-important testament: *Funhouse* by the Stooges. Long deleted in this country, practically unheard of by Britain's post-punk youth – kids who will swear by crap like *Lust for Life* and *New Values* – this apocalypse of Middle America, with its unrepeatable anthems 'Down in the Street', 'Loose' (of which the Birthday Party do a version), 'TV Eye', and '1970' (from which Radio Birdman took their name), is very simply one of the greatest rock'n'roll records ever made. The Saints knew this when they recorded two of the other 'greatest rock'n'roll records ever made', *(I'm) Stranded* and *Eternally Yours*. And lead

Birdman Deniz Tek, who was born in Detroit and brought the word of Ig to his predestined true believers, the forgotten street rebels of Australia, knew it before anyone.

Despite the extraordinary contempt and derision Birdman have since suffered, it was the group's first tour of Australia which set off the few real triggers of discontent that awaited such a call to arms. The Birthday Party, whatever they may say to the contrary, bear the memory of seeing Birdman for the first time as powerfully as anyone. As a rather average five-piece combo called the Boys Next Door, all of whom, excepting Rowland Howard, had been playing together since third form in high school, their conception of music was radically changed by the experience.

Within a year they had effectively established themselves at the centre of Melbourne's 'alternative' music scene.

'It took us about three years,' says Cave, 'to get a group of about fifty people together and for them to convince another 300 or so that it was all worthwhile.'

'Yeah,' snarls Pew, 'all those fuckwits who used to throw glasses at us . . .'

'Actually,' whispers Rowland Howard in another time and place, 'we were regarded as a bit of a bloody joke.'

Nineteen-seventy-nine: one strangely pop-punk LP as the Boys Next Door, called *Door, Door*. Great cover, great lyrics, but songs and sounds like any Anglo-American powerpop band. A spite marriage of the Ramones and XTC.

Cave: 'We went through a year in Australia of playing the most disgusting kind of shit. Like *Door, Door*.'

Pew: 'We became a bunch of snivelling little poofs.'

Cave: 'I used to wear frilly shirts and pigtails before any of this English shit. We committed the unpardonable error of playing to the thinkers rather than the drinkers.'

Between *Door, Door* on Mushroom Records and *The Birthday Party* on Missing Link there is a gulf as wide as that between, say, the Knack's 'My Sharona' and Beefheart's 'When Big Joan Sets Up'. So what happened?

Howard stares into his drink for an answer. 'I guess this is hard to believe, but it was really just a case of natural progression.'

Like there's a 'natural progression' from the state of a person's mind before he drops acid to the trip itself. Tell us another.

'It's the honest truth,' he protests. 'Things just got a little . . . wilder, that's all.'

That's obvious. *The Birthday Party*, recorded back home and released at the beginning of 1980, is unobtainable in this country at present but features the singles 'Mr. Clarinet'/'Happy Birthday' (just re-released on 4AD) and 'The Friend Catcher', two of last year's most invigorating and disturbing single releases, plus the extraordinary 'Hair Shirt' and a manic version of Gene Vincent's 'Cat Man'. If you see it, you know what to do.

It's on this album that perennial influences such as the Stooges and Beefheart and more recent ones like Pere Ubu and the Pop Group begin to coalesce in Cave's and Howard's songwriting. The result is unique and unmissable.

By this time, the group had been so inspired by the weird sounds imported from possible goldmines abroad they decided it was time to leave. Their sights naturally settled on England.

Both find this idea hilarious. I venture to ask how they feel about England after having lived in London for nearly two years. Cave clears his throat with an evil grin.

'Coming to London has been one of the most disillusioning experiences of my life, partly for a lot of obvious reasons, like everything closing down at eleven o'clock, but more important, because when we came here we thought here at least people were doing more than standing around twanging their guitars. I was really shocked. When we arrived, we saw this package show at the Lyceum, with Echo and the Bunnymen, A Certain Ratio, Teardrop Explodes and so forth and ... well, I've never been able to take English music seriously since. It was horrible.'

*

The Birthday Party arrived in England just as the last, perhaps most intense vestiges of punk energy were burning themselves out. When the Pop Group split, the whole thing – the anger, the revolt, the sensuality – went into a coma. Perhaps most unfortunate, the influence of brilliant groups like Joy Division and brilliant individuals like Daniel Miller was partly responsible. They inadvertently changed countless bands and musicians who were incapable of absorbing and using that influence to any effect. The Birthday Party, in dismay, had to watch this almost inevitable breakdown unfold.

By 1979, a new but fatally unclear concept of 'Pop' had taken hold of the nation's alternative music scene. Today this meta-pop has become the actual state of pop, an ideal for some, a living death for others.

Certainly there's no reason why inoffensive music as produced by electronic groups like Depeche Mode and Soft Cell shouldn't co-exist with an aggressive alternative to chart music. But what the Spandau hype has done is to brainwash people into formulating a nouveau-glam capitalist ethic which, to put it bluntly, stinks. The music, cushioned in a kind of feebly opulent production, is the pure expression of this ethic, an ethic of adaptation to an environment that ensconces one in Plasticine beauty and soft, smooth luxury – the environment of nightclubs, fashion shows, and videos.

Of course there will, and must always be, fluctuations in the state of musical angst. It's not something that can be topped up when depleted. But why does England have this hang-up about real musical violence – that is, a music that is neither Saxon nor the UK Subs, that has soul and dirt and physical desire?

In the end, one can only conclude that it has something to do with the stranglehold the music press has on youth's cool minority. After all, look what happens to a band when it refuses to co-operate. Look what happened to the Saints when, like a circus animal refusing to play dead, they wouldn't play 'punk'.

Fortunately for the Birthday Party, they've taken the heritage of the Saints into another dimension, and won the kind of critical approval whose terms simply don't apply to the likes of Spandau Ballet. 'Release The Bats', a 'voodoo rockabilly' anthem which knocks the Cramps into the shadows of complete insignificance, saw three weeks at the top of the alternative singles chart. *Prayers on Fire* has been in the indie LP charts ever since its release. And attendance at London gigs has been growing all the time.

After the year of 'Pop', 1980 – a miserable year spent trying to fit in with the new nonchalance – the Birthday Party realised the only solution was . . . TO ATTACK.

*

A concert by the Birthday Party – Nicholas Cave (vocals), Rowland Howard (guitar), Mick Harvey (guitar, keyboards), Tracy Pew (bass) and Phill Calvert (drums) – can break and dissolve the semantic frame which supports this language. In it you can forget for maybe an hour all the other names and categories that flood forward in the name of pop to imprison your emotions.

Have we not all secretly yearned, since the deaths of those beings whose bodies, while they could not contain their own desires, diffracted and melted ours in the passing heat of their majesty – the bodies and voices of Hendrix, Joplin, Curtis – for that pure incandescence of being wherein we might at last yield up the barricades of knowledge?

What we must lose now is this insidious, corrosive knowingness, this need to collect and contain. We must use our brains that have been stopped and plugged with random information, and once again must our limbs carve in air the patterns of their desire – not the calibrated measures and slick syncopation of jazz-funk but a carnal music of total release. *WE MUST MAKE OF JOY ONCE MORE A CRIME AGAINST THE STATE!*

Is it possible for the tirelessly rational system which is 'popular' music ever to *GO BACK ON ITS WORDS?* Or has this music become so cognisant and inter-referential that all desire for escape and release has been extinguished? Will we never be 'lost in music'?

These questions *must be asked.* For if music is no more than cultural reference-point, *THEN IT IS NOTHING.*

From the spirit of this tragedy must come the birth of a new music – a music whose warning signals have already been received: 'Transmission ', Radio Birdman's '194', the Saints' 'Night in Venice', and the Birthday Party's 'King Ink'.

Of course we may continue to display ironical love for such advanced cultural artefacts as Prince, the B-52's, Michael Jackson, Disco, the Rolling Stones (the playing on 'Start Me Up' is among the year's great performances), or even such kitsch diamonds of MOR dance production as Dollar's 'Hand Held in Black and White'.

Naturally we shall not forget the Drifters, *Astral Weeks*, Etta James, Phil Spector, 'Liar Liar' by the Castaways, 'Jeepster', and all real SOUL music . . . nor shall we allow history to bury the names of Alex Chilton and Arthur Lee . . .

In fact, we shall try to remember as much great music as it is possible to do.

But what we will banish from memory is the whole heap of trash that is held in power by fools and phonies: REO Speedwagon, Bruce Springsteen, Lionel Ritchie, Fleetwood Mac, Paul McCartney, Debbie Harry and, worse still for the sycophantic love bestowed on them, Spandau Ballet, A Certain Ratio, Linx, August Darnell, the Teardrop Explodes . . .

'Oh wretched ephemeral race, children of chance and misery, why do you compel me to tell you what it would be most expedient for you not to hear? What is best of all is utterly beyond your reach: not to be born, not to be, to be nothing. But the second best for you is . . .'

I cannot finish the quotation. You must excuse this torrid rhetoric – angry, confused and above all, perhaps, misplaced – as the only possible substitute for the bitter silence of my tears. As this last sentence commences, a voice breaks in all the pain of its suppressed longing . . .

Sung in the words of 'A Dead Song':

'HIT IT! WITH WORDS LIKE/ THOU SHALL NOT/ THE END.'

Barney Hoskyns, *NME*, 17 October 1981

A Man Called Horse

Antonella Gambotto

I am crushed between a maniac with a Mohican and a screaming string-singleted Scot in the audience – sweating, drunken, belching, retching, hopeless, drugged – at London's Electric Ballroom.

Bad Seed guitarist Blixa Bargeld snaps two strings but few notice because it is too difficult to hear anything other than the wall of feedback. Cult anti-hero and underground diva Nick Cave staggers about the stage wailing and writhing, bumping into speakers, moaning and burping about redheads and rockets, bats and veils and wells of misery, rats (lots of rats) and 'sticken' needles in his arm. Few question the real impact of his lyrics and behaviour on the young – Cave's dark romance with heroin has never been a constructive force. He is a scary-looking thing, something like six-feet-four with great tentacle-limbs, a glutinous mass of hair, and a big sullen boo-boo pout. He sings a little, trips over a wire, and the audience goes bananas. The disaster makes the most dysfunctional of his followers feel far, far less inferior.

Backstage after the performance, Bargeld – more shadow than man – blends into a corner whilst speaking German to an equally emaciated blonde. A jumbled American heiress overflowing from a tube of black vinyl repeatedly bleats 'Nick'. Band members pour each other drinks and seem to take turns in collapsing, looking sick, haggard, and starved: they look, in short, as if they are about to die. Suddenly, Cave lurches in and crashes into a stool. The wraiths descend. Cooing, the heiress strokes his head. Cave blinks and nods and wobbles on one leg and then indifferently begins to divest himself of his trousers.

It is one o'clock in the morning. I leave the room.

'I'm not really interested in the audience's enjoyment,' Cave mumbles once he has changed into nice clean pants. 'It doesn't bother me one way or another. I just don't give a shit. People feel more and more disappointed with each concert because less and less happens. It's really easy to suck an audience in. Like, I can wiggle my bum and backflip on my head and they love it. I could make an audience love me until the end of my days. There's just no point in it anymore. I wish they'd just . . . die.'

Cave has been the darling of the international alternative music scene for years. Writers are infatuated with his hostility, the melodramatic posturing, that spluttering and frequently near-incoherent rage. Such negative reinforcement is a kind of curse. Like the pugnacious and vaudevillian Norman Mailer, he is the stuff of which bad myths are made. The London-based editor and writer Mat Snow, who housed Cave and his girlfriend of the time for a number of weeks, remembers him as a 'lovely, sweet boy who walked around the house in red pyjamas'. And then there are the sex stories, the drug stories, the overdose stories, the assault stories, the waiting-to-score-outside-public-baths stories: sad stories told by those who know Cave very well. To others, he is the prince of darkness, king of the bats, a god and genius, the true voice of all suicidal impulses. That which no one ever mentions is that Nick Cave can also be a puling bore.

Born in Warracknabeal, Victoria, in 1957, Cave was agonisingly middle-class (father, Victoria's adult education director; mother, librarian). A friend recalls his parents as 'incredibly straight people', and believes that Cave 'really lost it when his father died'. Cave's father was 'very literate and intelligent' and his mother, to whom Cave is profoundly attached, apparently dotes on her unsavoury son. He once told a journalist that she 'doesn't complain about the 4:00am phone calls [and] doesn't bother [him] if [he] wants to watch television for two weeks'.

One can only marvel at Mrs Cave's exemplary maternal instincts.

Cave was a student at Caulfield Grammar, the school at which he formed the Boys Next Door, his first band. The fine arts course at the Caulfield Institute of Technology followed. 'He always looked geeky,' a fellow student comments. 'He wore tight jeans and these 1950s Hawaiian shirts, the ones made from nylon with those big floppy sleeves which his skinny arms dangled from. At that point, there was a new punky scene starting up in Melbourne, and I remember going to see him perform. I was totally shocked. There was shy Nick onstage, extremely pissed, wearing one of those thin suits with a thin tie and thin trousers, singing "These Boots Were Made for Walking" while this rather unattractive woman who called herself "Vulva" threw minced meat at the audience.'

In 1977, the band recorded *Door, Door*, their first album. Cave sneers at the memory. 'I'll give you a bit of buttock-clenching information. When I was young I was very shy, and music was my way of getting girls.' It was also a means of temporarily expelling an acute degree of emotional tension. 'The object is to create as much chaos and drunken revelry as possible,' Cave remarked at the time.

The Boys Next Door recorded the *Hee Haw* EP in 1979; in 1980 and possibly inspired by the work of Harold Pinter, they changed the band's name to the Birthday Party. Eager for success, the newly punked-up boys left for England, where they starved, retched, toured with American performance artist Lydia Lunch (with whom Cave reportedly shared more than a stage), and recorded *Prayers of Fire*, *Drunk on the Pope's Blood*, *Junkyard*, and *Mutiny*. They were muscular recordings, and ugly. After the band's inevitable implosion, Cave recorded *From Her to Eternity*, a small masterpiece of nihilistic despair.

'We created a monster,' Cave told one writer. 'I realised that when we were billed in Germany as "The Most Violent Band in the World". They were confiscating things like twelve-inch pipes from the audiences who had come to "enjoy an evening of music". It was ridiculous. It became like a bloodbath.' The creation of this monster attracted the attention of Anita Lane, the woman who became his muse. An associate recalls her as 'waifish-looking, a vacant kind of pretty girl who was attracted to interesting guys. She was totally nouvelle vague. The kind of girl who gave up her personality for whichever man she chose to be with.'

Cave became progressively stranger over the years, imitating Elvis Presley, immersing himself in Confederate lore, slapping swastikas on the covers of his European releases, and reportedly locking himself in a suitcase for a day or so when Lane left him for an Australian journalist. Instead of questioning his mental health, friends and fans all thought he was just too, too cute – a response which in retrospect, could only have encouraged his emotional instability.

It is 3:00am and I am standing in the kitchen of the dilapidated, rocking Chelsea houseboat owned by one of Cave's dear friends. I am exhausted by the concert and waiting for an obsequious hack to conclude his interview with Mister Music. Cave stops the interview to stumble in and carve himself a great slab of chocolate walnut cake. Scattering crumbs and icing over his crumpled white shirt, he wolfs the cake down. He then returns to the sofa to drone – as indefatigably as an air conditioner – while the obsequious hack smiles and nods. Outside on the Thames, several thousand ducks are having a war.

The obsequious hack finally leaves.

Balefully, Cave stares at me. 'You wanna do the interview now?'

When I nod, he disappears into the bathroom and emerges some fifteen minutes later. His unrolled shirt sleeve is speckled with blood. Cave manages the obstacle course the room has become and collapses on the sofa. He slowly waves a monstrous hand at the tape recorder, indicating that the interview has begun. He then nods off. Uneasily, I stare at him. I cough. He blinks a bit. I clear my throat and, in an effort not to overtax him, ask him an easy question: what does he consider important?

Without opening his eyes, he slurs: 'Uh . . . things . . . that affect me personally.'

I gently ask him to elaborate.

'Uh . . . personal things . . .'

Most anything can be interpreted as personal, I say.

'You think so?' he asks, momentarily surveying me through bloated slats. And then: 'I guess you're right.'

Change approach. Keep it simple. What does he find inspiring?

He shifts a little on the sofa to pull the Superman quilt over his knees. 'Ummmm . . . I find writing to be the one solitary consistent . . . faithful . . . ummmm . . . activity that . . . that I am able to indulge in . . .'

Sighing, I ask if he feels wounded by his experience of love.

His head droops. Slowly, he begins to drool. That thread of saliva is long. 'Uh . . . is this leading on from the other question?'

I reply yes.

He lifts his head. 'That was a lucky . . . coincidence, wasn't it?'

I explain that as he had described writing as the one consistently faithful thing in his life, I assumed that his experience of women was poor.

He pauses. I look over. He is immobile. Worried that he may, in fact, be dead, I try to rouse him with another question. Does he feel more betrayed by others or himself?

Shifting the ball of his shoulder, he hoists himself into a sitting position. 'Betrayed by . . . myself,' he mumbles. 'Actually, I would say that I am consistently betrayed by the . . . uh . . . total lack of rapport between my mind and my body . . . I . . . uh . . . think it was God's idea of a joke, I guess.'

I remind him of the quote that a 'drugless existence' terrified him.

'I think that . . . ummmm . . . the guy who wrote that . . .' His voice is rising. 'I'll start again.' He clasps his hands. 'If I had the inclination . . . and the . . . uh . . . energy . . . and the money, I would have sued that guy to hell and back for the bullshit he wrote about me . . .'

Watching him very carefully, I ask why he considers the piece to be 'bullshit'.

'Because . . . it was . . . untrue.'

Is he saying that he does not use drugs?

'No. No. I'm not saying that at all . . .' His eyes are open. There is a pause. He then topples from the sofa, crawls along the floor, and attempts to light his cigarette with one of the artificial fire's decorative logs. Still on the floor, he whines: 'Whadda pathetic question! I mean, if you wanna ask me a stupid question ask me a stupid question, and don't . . . uh . . . try to shovel the blame on that guy's shoulders for his stupid questions! I mean, the things that guy wrote about me in certain articles were just the . . . just the lowest form of sensationalist tripe that I've . . . ever . . . ummmm . . .' He is staring at the unlit tip of his cigarette. His expression is confused.

I offer him my lighter. As he drags on his cigarette, I question his own use of 'sensationalist tripe' – the swastika, say, or the glamorisation of heroin abuse in his lyrics.

'Oh, no,' he drawls, slowly shaking that big black matted head as he gropes his way back onto the sofa. 'Oh, no. That's something that's said about me . . . ummmm . . . the point I'm trying to make is that . . . ummmm . . . it's a point brought up by other people – it's not something I make a point of talking about . . .'

I suggest that his Southern Preacher shtick could be interpreted as sensationalistic.

'I don't do that!' He is outraged. 'Name . . . name one song where I make one statement . . . name one song where I'm didactic . . . one line . . .'

'Saint Huck', I reply.

He riles. 'Those lines are totally descriptive . . . they make no judgement whatsoever . . .'

Exasperated, I ask whether he would prefer his work to be described as inane.

'No, thank you very much! My work isn't inane. My use of language is . . . poetical . . . and descriptive . . . ummmm . . . the language certainly hasn't sufficient inference to warrant it being described as preaching . . . y'know, I mean, to me, the city in "Saint Huck" that this . . . particular character is going into is a great, grey, greasy city . . . and . . . uh . . . hence I've chosen those words to describe it. I'm not saying that, y'know, it's a great, grey, greasy city and don't go into it . . .' He begins to play with the quilt. 'I'm not making . . . a statement.'

Would he describe himself as happy?

He snorts. 'Have you abandoned the previous question?'

I repeat my question.

'I'm not happy at the moment, no,' he declares. A pause. 'I'm not generally happy . . . I don't see what this relates to . . . I'm not happy because . . . ummmm . . . why don't I think I'm happy? Ummmm . . . oh . . . because I don't feel happy.'

Does he feel the world is playing a cruel trick at his expense or does he believe he is the perpetrator of his misery?

'I think that it . . . is a combination of . . . the former and the latter. I think that anything has the capacity to make me feel sad . . . falling in love can make me feel sad . . . it can make me feel happy . . .'

I ask how he was affected by the disintegration of his relationship with Lane.

He starts. Pops up like a piece of toast. 'What are you talking about?'

I repeat my question.

He angrily drags on a cigarette. 'Where do you get your information?'

I shrug. It is a simple question.

'Yeah, and I'm asking you a fucken question – I'm asking where you get that piece of information from!' Lurching forward, he fixes me with a terrible stare.

Does he want to answer the question or not?

'No, I don't wanna answer it!' His voice climbs to a near-shout. 'Except to say that it seems to me that you're turning this interview into some sort of gross little conversation two people from Melbourne would have . . . an interview should be more than that . . . more than dwelling on that kind of . . . there should be an attempt to pull something intelligent out of a person . . . I think that there are a lotta things one could talk about that aren't just . . . uh . . . I mean, for Chrissake!' His ire is that of a Sunday school scold on PCP. 'I mean, you've really got a fucken gall . . . it upsets me because I wasn't aware that I was to sit down and talk about my personal life . . . I don't wanna have every disgusting face in Melbourne reading about how I felt when I broke up with my girlfriend . . .'

I interject: given that *From Her to Eternity* pivots on heartbreak, the question is relevant.

Cave is silent. Ducks are killing each other on the water. I wait a few minutes before trying again. I ask if he considers himself attractive.

For once, he doesn't hesitate. 'Yes, because . . . ummmm . . . I've become an attractive human being. Because I'm confident and I've been able to develop my ideas about things.'

I suggest some may consider him pathetic.

'Pathetic?' This surprises him. He furrows his big brow and thinks a bit. 'No,' he concludes, 'I'm not pathetic like other people . . . ummmm . . . why are they pathetic and I aren't? Because I say they're pathetic and they don't say that I'm pathetic . . . no . . . ummmm . . . not that I hear, anyway. But that's not a good answer . . . I might have to rewind the tape to find out the question . . . I think that they're pathetic because I know things that they don't know, and that they aren't able to know because they don't exist outside the norm . . . I'm badgered by such people day and night . . . it's only because I have the capacity to see beyond what they can see that I . . . ummmm . . .'

I wait and when the sentence remains unfinished, I ask how he knows his vision is so extensive.

'Because it's a . . . fact. It's something I know. It's something that I just know.'

He begins to play with a pair of plastic bug-eyed sunglasses. I watch as he pushes them up the bridge of his nose and then down the bridge of his nose. He pulls them off to examine them and then pushes them back up the bridge of his nose. With the Superman quilt tugged over his knees, his bony feet in a heap on the floor, his cigarette forgotten and burning in an ashtray, Cave begins to fall asleep.

'I think,' he murmurs, slumped against the sofa, 'half the world wants to be kicked in the head.'

Antonella Gambotto, *ZigZag*, January 1985

Prick Me Do I Not Bleed?

Mat Snow

Among Nick Cave's most prized possessions is a hardcover green book stuffed with press cuttings and private observations written in his painstakingly spidery hand.

'There was an academic painter at the turn of the century, whose name escapes me at the moment, who did portraits of rich people and aristocrats, like a poet laureate.

'When he died they found a trunk full of other paintings he did. And they all were obsessed with one theme: the reflection of a woman breaching the pinking surface of a puddle with her stride.

'They were not particularly obscene, but it was obvious he was using his artistic prowess for other reasons than to portray the rich who gave him money to do it. And this is my book; I'm allowed to write as much about whatever I like as I want.

'Rather than living out the extremes of our particular fantasies, most of us rid ourselves of these desires in other ways – beating the wife, the normal day-to-day things. In this particular book I indulge myself to the limits. I don't have to show this to anyone; I don't have to worry about whether my mother's going to read it . . .'

I believe it includes a song about the British music press entitled 'Scum'.

'I didn't write it about the press; I wrote it about *you*. See, here's a whole lot of scums. There's one; this is about you . . .'

He flicks through the pages, his pink-rimmed eyes not looking up once to meet mine . . .

'. . . You . . . you. This is just a kind of pastime. I write hate lyrics really well. It's not every day you can use them, really . . .'

This interview is not turning out at all as I'd hoped . . .

I had hoped for an interview which would amplify how Nick Cave's preoccupations have been revealingly side-lit by his new album consisting entirely of cover versions. Called *Kicking Against the Pricks*, its very title alludes not only to the verse from the Acts of the Apostles but perhaps also to Samuel Beckett's borrowing of the phrase; certainly, a pun of Cave's own devising is intended. And I suspect I might be one of the pricks.

As he explains in his measured, dictation-speed sigh of a voice, 'There's not a great deal of academic intellectualisation of the reasons why we did these particular songs. We're musicians and feel music more from the heart than the head. I'm not sure whether you can understand that.'

Ouch.

'There was no round-table debate as to what each particular song means. When I listen to a song, it strikes my heart whether it's worthwhile or not. There's something so basic and so simple it shouldn't even need to be said.'

What, however, constitutes that supposedly instinctive recognition of a song's worth is not so simple.

On his new album there are self-confessed tributes, like his version of 'The Hammer Song', originally by his schoolboy hero Alex Harvey, the piratical Glaswegian rocker whose Jacques Brel-derived theatricalism anticipated punk.

Missing from *Pricks*, however, are songs Cave loves which have already been fully realised elsewhere, offering no avenues for further exploration. Van Morrison's *Astral Weeks* LP is a case in point, though Cave reviles all his other records. Likewise damned is Jimi Hendrix, whose rendition of 'Hey Joe' Cave regards as an easily surpassable high point in an unappealing career. Not unlike Tim Rose's 1967 performance which he heard only after recording his own, Nick Cave's 'Hey Joe' invokes a brooding cosmic wrath surrounding Joe's *crime passionel* which echoes the heavenly portents which attended the birth of the Presley twins in 'Tupelo' (a song where he now faults his own gruff singing).

These are details, however. *Kicking Against the Pricks* is a richly exciting, dramatic record, not only for the choice of songs and their singing, but also for the revitalising aplomb and, where needs be, restraint of their performance by the Bad Seeds, whose highly talented maestro Mick Harvey (also of Crime and the City Solution) is too little recognised.

Pricks is, in addition, a further instalment in the remoulding of Nick Cave into one of the rock world's most striking and multi-levelled leading players.

For a start, Nick Cave hates the 'rock world'. Like fellow itinerant Australian musicians the Go-Betweens' Grant McLennan and Robert Forster, the Triffids' David McComb, the Moodists' Dave Graney, and former Saint and Laughing Clown Ed Kuepper, he is highly literate about rock and its many sources, but inclines towards its most earthy poets of passion, the balladeers and storytellers. Johnny Cash and Roy Orbison – like him, men in black – figure large in his taste, as do Elvis Presley and Bob Dylan, whose late records Cave particularly enjoys not least because he discovered them for himself amongst rock criticism's bargain-bin of talents supposedly declined into mawkishness and stupor.

Nick Cave in Stepney, East London, 23 March 1985.

Cave has sought amongst this canon those themes which most closely resemble his preoccupation – that of a jilted lover whose thoughts in abandoned desolation turn from regret to grief to vengeance. That the end of his relationship with his girlfriend of seven years, Anita Lane, in 1983 has inspired so much of his subsequent work has never been denied.

From that point, Cave has turned his life's big wound into art, and he has also plunged into that art as a safety-valve. Not for a long time has a more poignantly tragic figure – one whose downfall springs from an unbalancing ruling passion – starred in rock's obsessively scrutinised zone where private life and public image overlap.

His gravity of demeanour and much-trailed affinity with serious literary endeavour (likewise a characteristic of those other aforementioned Australians) not only mark him out from the frivolities of the pop industry, but also bestows on him a substantial tradition in which his tormented desolation may find a home.

Now is the winter of our discontent . . .

Whether 'tis nobler in the mind to suffer the slings and arrows of our outrageous fortune . . .

Not for Nick Cave the battlements of Elsinore; he stalks instead America's Deep South, a larger-than-life corrupted Eden of hot blood, primitive religion, swamplands, scarlet women, quack sawbones, whisky preachers, riverboat gamblers, white trash, slaves and the lynch-mob. In fact, Cave is barely acquainted with the area. But then, John Fogerty wrote evocative bayou songs for California's Creedence Clearwater Revival without getting so much as within sniffing distance of an alligator's tail.

This mythical Deep South serves not only as the landscape for some of Cave's favourite music, but also as a backdrop sufficiently wild and impassioned to project his tragic image onto – an Oedipus wreck in winklepickers.

'I just think Mat Snow is an arsehole who said this, and it's not true. I find it I hard to sit down and talk to someone who gave us a bad review.'

Tragic figures are usually proud – it goes with the territory. Petty-mindedness, however, tends to be comic. So how come neither of us are laughing? What had I done to poison this whole encounter?

In March last year I wrote of an Einstürzende Neubauten single that it 'musters the psychodramatic edge disappointingly absent from Nick Cave's forthcoming LP . . .'

That's all, yet his grudge has stewed in bile ever since. Nor is my reassurance, for what it's worth, that *The Firstborn Is Dead* LP has subsequently grown in my estimation, of any use. At least I am not alone as the target of 'Scum': also included are *NME*'s temporarily retired Barney Hoskyns for no reason I know of, *The Australian*'s Nicholas Rothwell for whom Anita Lane deserted Nick ('personal reasons' as Cave wrily explains), and Antonella Black who, in an interview for *Zigzag*, portrayed him as a petulant, dribbling junkie. That all four of us have also heaped extravagant praise upon his work cuts no ice at all.

'If someone says something good about me, they're doing their job; I have no complaints. They get no medal, they get their wage. That's all. But if they say something bad, then that really gets on my tits.

'I'm inconsistent, I'm illogical, I'm irrational about it. So fuckin' what?'

Cave's voice barely rises. He's as laboriously patient as an iceberg.

'There are some people who will take it in good stead and laugh. But I take it as a personal insult and harbour it. And then that person comes up to me and attempts to shake my hand with a smile and say, "Hi, longtime no see, burble burble burble."

'*Everything* that's said against me offends me, whether it's true or not. I can't fathom these people who flunked their arts courses and became rock journalists and are too goddamned ignorant about music or academic about their thoughts or have so many hang-ups that they can't bring themselves to perform. Yet it is these people whose opinions are heralded and lauded as being *gospel*.

'Some arsehole will go along to our concert in a bad mood because he will have prematurely ejaculated with his new girlfriend and then been shoved around by a few skinheads, and consequently give the concert a bad review. And people read it and imbibe!

'It really boils my blood and makes me sick to think that this is still perpetuated and the same idiotic process continues of me speaking a lot of shit to some fool. It's not what I consider to be a day that I enjoy, a day that I consider profitable.'

If, with few exceptions, Cave has scant regard for we earnest, back-stabbing scribblers, he 'doesn't give a flying fuck' for the other four-fifths of his audience, most of whom by my reckoning are full-time Goths, part-time slummers, wallowers and weirdos who are there to be fucked up the dirt-track, metaphorically speaking.

'I've got less and less inclined towards being some sort of colourful food for a lot of other people to consume. Writing allows me to be myself and not have to perform this filthy function which, no matter what I do, is inherent in being lead singer for some freak group.

'I don't know what the people who come and see me are like. I don't know what their reasons for doing *anything* are. I don't know the reason for the boy down the front who comes to each of our shows and screams out. "You're a fucking arsehole!" *Pays* every night to scream that at the group, and, if he gets a chance, to punch me.

'He's not there to pick up a girl, that's for sure.'

Spotlights and the smell of greasepaint hold no charm for Nick Cave. Nor, he claims, does the money amount to much.

'When you've finished a British tour playing all these horrible places, like the worst prisons in America, and finding that type of person at every concert, after a while you consider. What's the benefit of doing this? That person becomes more important to you than the rest of the audience. I don't want to be over-dramatic about it, but the whole thing seems to be an obscene comic strip . . .'

Sometimes during this supremely painful interview Nick Cave forgets himself and speaks eloquently and animatedly about something outside his immediate concerns; the American prison system, for instance, which he's been researching for a film project in Australia. When I ask about God and the Afterlife, he becomes more guarded. All he'll vouchsafe is that he believes evil will not go ultimately unpunished, even if it's rewarded on earth.

But he soon reverts to being the sod with a grudge and thin veneer of forced politeness.

'I'm just a sensitive guy,' he smiles inwardly. Very inwardly.

Mat Snow, *NME*, 23 August 1986

Of Misogyny, Murder and Melancholy: Meeting Nick Cave

Simon Reynolds

Talking to Nick Cave is a bit of a trial. He's not really a *proper* person. Like many artists, what makes him a genius also makes him difficult to get on with, to get to. He's afflicted and empowered by a certain, crucial deficiency of humanity. Or perhaps more accurately, he's drastically, wilfully, estranged from the confining notion of the 'human' that's been installed by the post-Live Aid popular culture – extroversion, civic engagement, the benign totalitarianism of caring/sharing/ opening up, the cult of health and efficiency.

Morbidly inward, unforgiving, creating art that is perhaps best seen as a kind of metaphorical automutilation, Cave goes against the grain of the times by being sick but refusing to be healed. His obsessions are wounds he deliberately keeps open, returns to again and again. The reason is simple: as he remarked elsewhere – 'my periods of pessimism are far more individual than my feelings of joy, which are fairly commonplace, if few and far between'. Like the Band of Holy Joy, Mark E. Smith and other poets of the abject imagination, he sees the mark of the 'real', what makes a person unique, as vested in flaws and scars – any kind of disproportion (obsessions, grudges, neuroses, bigotries, deformity), anything that warps or blinkers a clear vision, and endows the person with a *visionary* perspective. Beauty or virtue – always tending towards the ideal, the anonymity of the absolute – aren't interesting at all, suggest the bland perfection of innocence rather than the damage of experience. Really, Cave and his ilk are 'agitating' for a *broader* definition of the human, one that incorporates lapses into the human, incompleteness, a certain dilapidation and impoverishment of the soul. They're harking back to an older, more religious notion, one where it's not a question of wholeness of being, but of holes.

Nick Cave surfaced at a time when post-punk's handle on the workings of desire was diagrammatic and programmatic. Punk had bequeathed the idea that demystification was the route to enlightenment. 'Personal politics' was the buzzword: the acknowledgement of the 'dark side' was always grounded in progressive humanism, the belief that what was twisted could be straightened out, that the shadows could be banished. The ideal was that through deconditioning, unblocking, a ventilation of the soul, some kind of frank and free-flowing *exchange* was possible. Against this contractarian view of love (negotiation, commutativity, support), Cave, in the Birthday Party, was almost alone in reinvoking love as malady, monologue, abject dependence, a compulsion to devour and be devoured.

For Cave, love was nothing if not the doomed fantasy of possession, and its supreme expression could only be violence. In a post-punk climate of positivism, he dwelt on the tragic and insoluble, was the first to Biblical imagery (sin, retribution, curses, blight, bad seed) and to express an interest in country and western's imagery of destitution and betrayal (both of which were subsequently imitated by groups as diverse as the Triffids, Lloyd Cole and the Weather Prophets).

Consciousness-raising post-punk became self-conscious New Pop; 'personal politics' developed into ABC and Scritti's seductive deconstructions of the lexicon of love. For some, the Birthday Party were solitary heroes of literate oblivion. As New Pop regressed into a dismal impasse based around a combination of wistful vintage retrospection and a therapeutic revision of soul, Cave looked back even further, over the course of four solo records, to C&W and blues, in search of a more troubled, troubling kind of 'authenticity'.

The fireball became an ember. *Kicking Against the Pricks,* an album of cover versions, marked the key shift from poet-visionary of Sex and Death to balladeer, from torched singer to a croon the colour of cinders, from Dionysiac excess to a ruined classicism. On the LP that followed sharply on the heels of *Kicking,* Nick Cave and his Bad Seeds were to be found staging their own dilapidated equivalents to the epic melodrama of 'Wichita Lineman' and 'Something's Gotten Hold of My Heart' – the gently obliterating slowly gathering morose grandeur of 'Sad Waters', 'Your Funeral, My Trial', 'Stranger Than Kindness'. . .

Despite having been consistently and almost exclusively serenaded by sycophantic epiphanies the length and breadth of his career, Cave *loathes* journalists. The slightest slight is nurtured as a festering grievance. Today, I make a grievous strategic error. When Cave enquires if I have a copy of *Melody Maker* on me, I say: 'Yes.' Cave spends about twenty minutes reading my colleague Chris Roberts's cover feature on him, his countenance growing steadily darker, more furrowed and nauseous. Quite why I'm still not sure. But we embark upon the interview with his loathing and distrust given an unusually fresh and pronounced edge.

He's not in the best of states anyway, having just emerged from four eighteen-hour days in the studio working on the new album. Deep gashes of black under the eyes, skin the colour of ashes, stooped by fatigue. Eloquent body language (what the French describe as *coincé).* Cave's exasperation is exasperating, his weariness wearisome. There's a sardonic tang behind his civil and fastidious replies, his small, grave, gnarled voice, while all the while his face bears a look as though each question was a plate of your excrement offered under his nose. Often, he starts his replies by repeating the question, like a poor O-level candidate, as if there's a slight relish in parroting your own crassness back at you. Then again, if you do think of an unprecedented question, he's likely to answer: 'I don't know how to answer that question' – closer to a boast than an apology, because Cave doesn't like the idea of being seen as an intellectual, would rather deny the complexity of his work. There seems to be a grim pleasure in finding the most terse answer, the one that closes off any elaboration most decisively. Still, one bastard genius is worth a thousand affable craftsmen any day. So they say.

Cave is poised for another key shift right now, the transition to other media for expression, acting and writing, that are surrounded by such minefields for the restless rock performer anxious to inflame a settled career. Music can arbitrarily endow with force words that on the naked page might seem forced or gauche or mannered; equally there's no *guarantee* that the star's aura and presence can survive on film, in music's absence.

Was writing *always* the prime motivation, and music only a vehicle, the most convenient one at the time?

'No, no . . . the idea to take up writing literature seriously is only a recent thing . . .'

There was a need to perform, to be an exhibitionist?

'The reason I got involved in music was that I was thrown out of art school . . . I happened to be in a band at the time *[the Boys Next Door, a reputedly execrable power pop combo that* mutated *into the Birthday Party]* . . . and the band happened to take off. And it hasn't stopped since. There was never any big decision to be a rock star.'

Presumably, though, you feel that music imparts a dimension to the written word . . .

'The writing of lyrics is quite a different thing to writing a novel. I have very strong ideas about how they can be put across in a live situation . . .'

Do you ever suffer from writer's block?

'It's the general condition. One has to push oneself out of it. It's a state where your mind is always tricking itself . . . I constantly think that I'm unable to do anymore, that I've given all I've got . . . this isn't a new thing . . . it's been like this for years . . . but I always find at the end of the day I'm able to put something out.'

Do you find the same imagery recurring over and over? Or is that a strength, your *signature?*

'The themes I deal with . . . are not easily summed up, and can be approached again and again.'

How long is it before something you've written disgusts you? Is it immediate, as though the page was smeared with your own excreta? Does it get easier to live with the more distant you get from it?

'After the period of disgust, it doesn't have much effect on me; I find it pretty impossible to discuss or have much feeling about it.' (This reminds me of his famous statement about the Birthday Party being a slug, nomadic, its slime being its art, 'and we are barely conscious of its issue'.)

Your first book, though (coming out around now) is a collection of all your writing – lyrics, prose, poetry – all over the seven years. How can you bear all that being aired again?

'That book, *King Ink,* is more a product of the publisher than myself . . . I suggested the publisher [Black Spring Press] do it as something to go on . . .

because the novel, which he suggested, has taken almost three years to write, and it was supposed to have been finished two years ago. But it is not so much the writing of the lyrics as the way they are put across that I don't like. It's the records I find embarrassing now, not the lyrics.'

Do you own the records?

'No, I don't actually. I'm not really in a situation where I'm able to hoard things. I'm too mobile.'

The novel, *And the Ass Saw the Angel,* is it febrile and disordered, or is there a narrative?

'There's a narrative. It's set in a small valley in a remote region somewhere in the world – a sugarcane-growing valley. It's the story about the people who live there, based on a series of ironies that bring about a fairly suspenseful conclusion.'

Why are you fascinated by closed communities, limited lives?

'They breed a certain ignorance, can be a breeding ground for very extreme emotional releases. *Very absurd* emotional releases.'

One of the things that interests me is your oft-professed indifference to your audience, your lack of interest in how they respond to what you do . . .

'Yeah.'

As simple as that?

'It used to be like that . . . the relationship I have with my audience is probably quite different now . . . as the audience begin to have a more honest relationship with my work, I actually do respond to the way they respond to me . . .'

Are you ever intrigued by what it is they get out of it?

'I don't know if it's necessarily interesting to me . . . I just try to put as much *into* it as I possibly can . . . and that's more for myself than for me . . . I would hope they would glean something from that . . .'

Do you worry that they might misrecognise what you're about, respond on a superficial level?

'I've given up worrying about that . . . it used to worry me a lot . . . I went through some kind of crisis about the way the audience was responding to my performances . . .'

Do you need to have an audience at all, or would you create even if no one saw it? Is it like a biological need?

'Yes, I think so.'

You seem to see yourself as an Artist on High . . . rather than a participant in a (sub)culture. For instance, you clearly see the interview as an appallingly irksome chore done only for reasons of marketing – rather than an exercise in accountability towards an audience who relate to you. Is it just a monologue?

'When I get any real feeling about my audience is in a live situation. Otherwise it's a fairly one-sided thing.'

One level of interest that must annoy you is that Goth voyeuristic thing of being into the dark and the uncanny . . .

Stepney, East London, 23 March 1985.

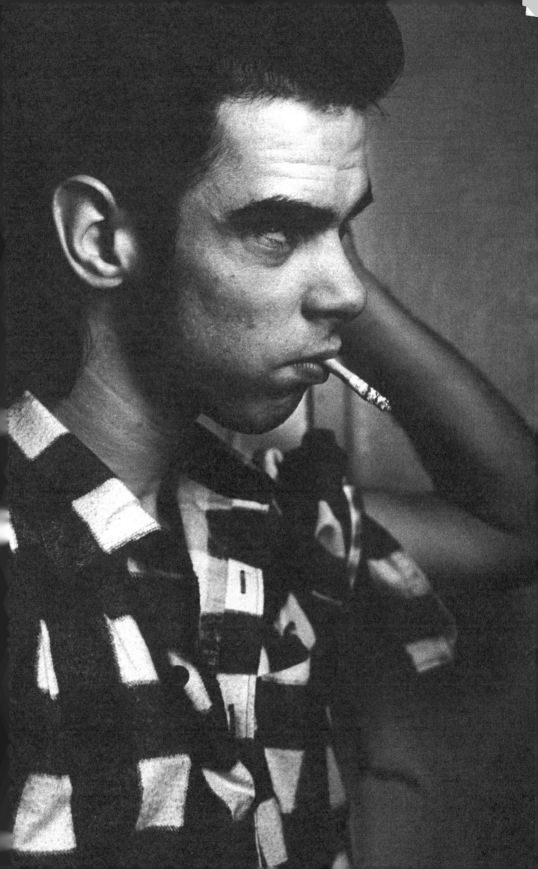

'Yes. But I don't think any mass of people are going to understand what I do properly anyway.'

Are you in touch with the culture in general . . . does pop impinge at all?

'To a degree . . . I follow my instincts . . . my instincts tell me that there's not much to be involved in.'

Was there a time?

'Some years ago the music scene was healthier; it was possible to find some inspiration in that.'

Your music's become steadily more structured, stately even . . . do you have sympathy anymore for the self-immolation school of rock Bacchanalia? If there was a band doing now what the Birthday Party did then, would you think it was redundant, played-out?

'Not necessarily . . . I would need to know what the music was like . . .'

Your songs are more like torch songs now than *torched* songs.

'I respond to that sort of thing now, rather than the other. I listen to the kind of things on *Kicking Against the Pricks.* Country and western. Blues music. I'm also interested in "entertainment" music, what some people see as corn. Tom Jones, Gene Pitney, and so forth.'

What do you see in them?

'I just find them exciting, I find Tom Jones's voice exciting. [*with immense, sepia weariness*] I haven't really thought of the reasons why.'

Do you prefer not to have a critical consciousness, this parallel layer of awareness?

'Yeah. Or rather . . . I just don't have it. I find it more *healthy* to be able to respond to things on a more immediate level.'

Healthy is a strange word from someone with such morbid preoccupations.

'I'm not trying to put across the idea that they're a favourable way of being. They just *interest* me.'

Do you ever feel angry about things that aren't concerned with yourself and your immediate environment?

'I don't feel *quite* so numb about social issues, these days.'

Cave makes two forays into celluloid this year. The first is a cameo in Wim Wenders's latest film. The Bad Seeds appear at the end, playing in a nightclub. 'Wenders approached me one day, and asked us if we wanted to be in his next movie . . . an SF movie . . . set in thirteen different countries. We were to represent Australia, musically. But it would have taken a long time, there were delays, and he embarked on another film in the meantime and gave us this small role.'

Cave has a slightly more substantial involvement in the other film, tentatively titled *Ghosts of the Civil Dead.* 'I have a not very big part, and was initially involved in writing the first two drafts. But by the sixth draft, there weren't many of my ideas left. The character I play is a kind of known provocateur. The character is brought into the prison, one of the new hi-tech ones, in order to disrupt the equilibrium of maximum security life . . . he's a psychotic with some kind of death wish . . . spends his entire time screaming abuse . . . he's a racist.'

You've been represented, and have represented yourself, as a misogynist.

'I think I've been stitched up in respect of that.'

Women do seem to get it in the neck in your songs, though . . .

'Yes, but I think men are subjected to the abuse of life as much as the women are. I just find there's something essentially more exciting about seeing women being abused. Possibly because it is usually men you see in films subjected to violence. There's a violence for women and a violence for men, and when you see a woman subjected to a man-size violence it's usually quite shocking.'

So women, being repositories for the sacred, are inviolate, and therefore it's a more powerful effect, artistically, when they're violated?

'Yeah, something like that.'

After punk's demystifying, secularising influence, you were the first to start using imagery of the sacred and desecration, the Biblical language of revenge and guilt. Is that because you think *that* language is truer, more primal, what all of us, in our hearts, still believe in?

'I'm not really sure I'm interested in whether people believe in it, or whether it's true to today's standards.'

Is it true to how you felt? Have you ever wanted to exact revenge?

'I think the worlds I create are kind of mythological . . . I don't know if they have much relevance to today.'

And is that *today's* loss? Is contemporaneity impoverished for losing touch with what you're about?

'I think there's a certain *numbness* in the world today . . . that accepts certain kinds of violence, but is against other kinds of violence.'

So you have a kind of ethics of violence?

'Yes, I do.'

Once again I think of *River's Edge,* the dialogue between Feck the reclusive fugitive from justice, the girl-killer who despises but above all *pities* the teenage killer because he had no reason to kill his girlfriend. Where Feck killed because of an excessive love (like a Nick Cave character), out of a deluded dream of possession, the teenager killed only to get a stronger grip on his diminished sense of his *own* being, depleted by media hyper-reality. A dialogue between two different ethics of murder.

Do you worry about your own mortality?

'I have periods where the thought of it is quite frightening. The only consolation is seeing that old people come to terms with it in some way. But I'm no way ready for my death myself.'

(A heavily loaded question:) Do you think you're doing the best you can to *avoid* dying?

There's the slightest of gasps, a tiny glimmer of semi-amusement, and for a moment we're almost communicating, 'Yes . . . I think I'm doing the best I can.'

Simon Reynolds, *National Student*, 1987

Nick Cave: The Needle and the Damage Done

Jack Barron

Nick Cave is a man of many voices. Right this second, outside the VIP Hotel in Hamburg's Holstenstrasse, his larynx has the timbre of The Reaper. 'You scum-sucking shit,' he screams at me, aiming a scuffed cowboy boot at my groin. Luckily he'll never play football for Australia, even the junior squad. The foot misses its target, resulting only in a bruised thigh.

I'm stunned. Reeling. 'You're nothing but a shit-eater,' he shrieks, taking a scythe with his fist at my head. He'll never get a gardening job chopping down weeds, let alone collecting my skull. It misses.

The hate in Cave's eyes burns more fiercely than a funeral pyre. We're too far into this ugly scene for him to quit or back down now. 'I'll fucking kill you, you bastard,' he bellows, trying to tear out my left eye with filthy spatula nails. He couldn't drive in a tack with a mallet. He misses.

Nick spies my travel bag nearby. He lunges after it. Picks it up and runs like an ostrich with its head still buried. Nowhere far. 'Where's that fucking interview tape,' he hisses, ripping the contents of the bag out into the street. 'If it means that much to you I'll give it to you,' I offer. It's no big deal. All I want is to get out of this damned city and never have to look at Cave and his dish-rag limbs again.

'What the hell do you think you're doing?' castigates Nick's press officer as Cave fumbles with my zips – the one's on the bag, you understand. 'Stop acting like a child. Do you think that Jack hasn't got a memory?'

Nick stops. Dead. Something is sinking in. But not far enough. While I kneel down in the street and gather up the gear Cave cocks his boot at my head. He'd have trouble pissing against a lamp post. It misses.

Eventually the press officer comes between Cave's gale-force windmill limbs and my passive resistance. I'm glad. Horrified. Angry. And scared. Nick has had his revenge. The 'fight' is over. The story has just begun. It's time to tear out the pages of his book and light a fire.

UP JUMPED THE DEVIL

Nick Cave is the voice of desperation onstage. A man trying to exorcise the ghosts inside his head through limited means. The cramped parameters of his singing are his strength. Vulnerability, sentimentality, bitterness, abrasiveness, humour and morbidness, all peel from his stretched larynx like a snake shedding skins. Above all he's hypnotic.

In a Dutch club whose corridors remind me of the entrance to the gas ovens in Auschwitz – not a flippant comment, since I've been there – this lanky piece of literate shit, in his waistcoat and bow tie, holds the audience around the neck by the hangman's noose of his sheer showmanship of inadequacy.

Inadequacy? Yes. The Cave constituency tonight in Utrecht, and virtually every night elsewhere, couldn't change its underwear without help. Barely moving, they're like hyenas attracted to carrion. The body they're feeding off is a mirror of their own emotional turmoil. The blood they're sucking is clotted.

Ironically, though the surface vibe may be different, the clothes cut from another loom, the uniform of personal as opposed to social alienation that Cave deals in is the oldest cliché in the book. Whether it be Biblical morality or unrequited love. Many of his recent songs have been a collapsing of both. With Cave's own unique slant.

The viewpoint of a wretch. Nick might feel sorry for himself beyond belief, but belief is often the problem, the search for or lack of it. That or cupid's eyes poked out blind. His talent is he can tell fantastic musical stories that encapsulate those emotions. From the Boys Next Door, through the Birthday Party, to the present day Bad Seeds, Cave has often strived for things that can't be resolved: salvation and unrequited love. Along the way he has left a narrative trail of picaresque characters. Nightmares. Delusions. Frenzy. Compassion. Romance. Idiocy. Fallibility.

And in the process became a junkie.

And so much for that. As the Bad Seeds sow the cyclical rumble of 'City Of Refuge', from the tentatively titled new album, *Tender Pray*, flagellated by the bullwhip guitars of Neubauten's Blixa Bargeld and Kid Congo (no Cramps solos here), I know Cave is a great. Up there with Dylan. Presley. Reed. Pop. Williams. Cash. Anybody you care to mention. Hey, but mention writers . . . because, as Nick is the first to admit, he's technically a lousy singer.

Backstage tonight it's like a grave. There's no party. Kid Congo, now with a moustache, diligently packs his guitars while Mick Harvey picks up the takings and the rest of the band flop out. A talented multi-instrumentalist, Harvey is the musical arranger for both the Bad Seeds and Crime and the City Solution. He's one of nature's organisers with a Filofax in his head rather than his pocket, as well as a wicked wit.

'Tour managers are parasites,' he later explains. 'They want ten or fifteen percent of your money and then drink all your booze. It's a joke, that's why I set up the tours. It's not hard. I have this new system. I get everything organised in advance. Then when members of the band come up to me and say, "Hey have you seen this or got that?" I just say "No". After all they're big boys now.'

Cave meanwhile is slumped in his chair. He looks ash-grey with exhaustion.

This is more than the result of tonight's exertions, it's a cumulative thing. Nick has been going through perhaps the most productive year of his life so far.

Aside from writing and recording the exercise in musical styles that form the forthcoming album, he's virtually finished editing his novel, *And the Ass Saw the Angel*, and had *King Ink* – a collection of lyrics, snippets of prose and short plays – published by Black Spring Press. On top of that the Bad Seeds perform in Wim Wenders's movie, *Wings of Desire*, while Cave has partly scripted and acted in another film, *Ghosts of the Civil Dead*.

The latter is the story of prison authorities deliberately making inmates lives hell in order to instigate an insurrection which they then violently squash, thereby gaining legitimacy for increased penal powers. In *Ghosts*, Cave plays a psychotic provocateur with a death wish. This simply involves a lot of swearing, rolling of eyeballs, gouging of flesh and spitting. Cave, on this appearance, doesn't seem to have the makings of a great thespian. The soundtrack parts provided by Bargeld, Harvey and Cave, are, however, fine.

Back in the dressing room Cave has been cornered by a piece of rotting flesh called Moan. We're all fatigued. Somebody doles out that vitamin known as speed. I don't refuse the offer. Two days and one country later, just before a glass comes whizzing by my head and smashes against a wall, Cave will insist that, 'People don't bring us drugs. All that happens backstage at our gigs is that people drink our alcohol.'

Right now though our hearts are pounding like jack-hammers. The world seems like a fine place, full of people to bore senseless with our speed-babble. As the sun comes up like a pat of rancid butter over the canals, it feels like we're engaged on a one-way trip to purgatory. Drugs can do strange things to people.

THE CARNIVAL IS OVER

Nick Cave's voice late afternoon in the bar of Amsterdam's Museum Hotel is laced with humour. He looks sharp, dressed in an immaculate black evening suit topped off by a belt with a massive gaudy buckle depicting Christ. He's just been doing television interviews.

'I couldn't believe it,' he laughs, 'they wanted me to go on one of those pedalos to do it. I told them, "No way," and took them off to interview me among the prostitutes. I mean, can you see me on one of those contraptions?'

Publicist, photographer, Seeds piano player, Roland, and I crack up at the thought. Together we head off to eat. Nick escorts us to a Surinamese cafe. As soon as we're seated he disappears off into the red light district.

With Cave gone and Roland captive it seems a good time to interview the classically trained German keyboardist. Our conversation goes like this:

We're dog tired. Do you know where to get any speed?

'No, I think it's a bad drug. It destroys your body, fucks up your mind,' says Roland.

So what do you recommend?

'Smack. Look how young-looking I am,' says Roland, who's twenty-three going on ninety-nine.

STRANGER THAN KINDNESS

The singer returns and takes us back to sample his go-faster vitamins at the hotel. Thirty minutes later he's onstage at the Paradiso Club. As the Bad Seeds' rhythm section of Harvey and drummer Thomas Wydler deliver the uppercut of another new song, 'Oh Deanna', Cave jack-knives around the stage. Nick's lyrical concerns might sometimes rattle like skeletons in shallow graves, but his current band set his prayers on fire like no other.

Riding on the wave of energy, with typical perversity Nick rasps. 'I remember the Paradiso. We played here when we were the Birthday Party. I remember smashing somebody's teeth in with my microphone stand.' Slowly, the band lower a coffin of scales and Cave, with a voice like freezing fog, groans, *'I am the crooked man, I walked a crooked mile.'* 'Your Funeral, My Trial' is in session.

IT'S THE SINGER NOT THE SONG

Three in the morning. Night hangs like a lead shroud. Nick Cave's voice speaks in quiet, measured tones in the hotel lounge. Any hesitation is due, not to inarticulacy, but to wanting to frame precise answers. I had hoped that Bleddyn would be here. Aside from being a fine photographer, Butcher is a long-time friend of Nick's who takes most of the shots for the Bad Seeds' record covers. Between us we hoped to map the definitive guide to Cave's creativity. The only problem is not even Jesus could raise Bleddyn from his bed. Lazarus? No problem. A tired Antipodean snapper? Well, miracles take a little longer.

Nick says he often comes over as retarded in interviews because he can't trust journalists, especially English ones, who nod in agreement to his halting answers and then ridicule him in print. He cites two interviewers who've recently grilled him for another British paper as a case in point. 'I only trust somebody when I feel that they are genuinely on my side,' he mentions pointedly.

Nick Cave is a journalist's nightmare. An artist, who through such emotional blackmail tactics, expects a writer to snip off the barbs of their questions and place their tamed tongues in his rectum. He wants respect but doesn't seem to respect a journalist's freedom to inquire. Cave has even written a song about two ex-*NME* writers called 'Scum'. It bookends his anthology *King Ink*. That's how obsessive he is about the press . . .

The songs on the upcoming album seem to have less narrative form than before. Why?

'Well, I think *Your Funeral, My Trial* was particularly narrative. The new record is coming back to a more conventional sort of lyric. There still are stories, but they're a lot more disguised. Like "Oh Deanna" is a retelling of a true relationship that I had with somebody through the story of somebody else, even if it doesn't begin with "Once upon a time". Deanna was a girl I knew when I was about eight. She lived in a trailer on the outskirts of the town with her old man who was basically this drunken wretch of a character. Our relationship was kept a secret from him because he frequently beat her. I was just one day older than her. It was a very equal relationship we had.

'Anyway, we used to play truant from school and go to this little hideaway that she had fashioned under this bridge over a dry river creek. It was impossible to get to because of the briar that surrounded it. But she made this tunnel through the briar. Inside this place she had a collection like a magpie's nest. We used to go on these day raids on the different houses around the town. We knew the people wouldn't be in the houses and we used to eat their food, lie on their beds, and steal all sorts of stuff like letters, cutlery, clothes and money. The story is important because I've tried to write a lot of songs about it.'

Do you mean you've actually written a lot of songs about her then?

'No, I've only tried. She was never any kind of threat. I never had any reason to feel anything against this girl because she was really my best friend at this time. The kind of things I've written after this time have a different kind of bent to them altogether, although they might be the same kind of melodramatic fantasies. So one day we robbed a house and found a handgun which we took back to our little grotto. We, I should add, robbed by ourselves, separately also. One day she was caught by this guy who was in this religious instruction teacher's house. The wife of this teacher thrashed her and the guy did something to her, but I really don't know what it was.

'The next day I was woken up by my mother and had to answer all these questions from the police. Deanna had gone back to the home and shot the strange man and woman in the religious teacher's house. How the stranger fitted into their lives was a bit of a scandal.

'That's the basis for the song. I've tried to write about it many times but I've never felt able to do it justice because it sounds like some sort of fantasy or some Disneyland type of thing. Nonetheless, after that happened she was taken off to some sort of child psychiatric place. And I was taken out of (the local) high school and sent to the big smoke to a strict all-boys boarding school to have a bit of sense knocked into me. I dunno.'

Neither do I. Cave is an epic storyteller of Grimm proportions. He'll make up what you want to hear.

We turn from the fantastic to the relatively mundane, the stylistic beggar's banquet to be heard on the upcoming album, *Tender Prey*. As the provisional title implies, the record marks a continued shift in Cave's attitude to, and use of, Biblical imagery, compared to say the Birthday Party's venomous *Prayers on Fire*, with songs like the almost redemptive tones of 'New Morning'.

'Each song has a very distinctive kind of style to it, as if it is the Bad Seeds playing '60s garage band music, as in the case of "Oh Deanna", or kind of Bacharach stuff like "Slowly Goes the Night". It's all fairly stylised and each song is very stylised within itself. As the record evolved we saw this happening and rather than rectify this disjointedness we decided we'd play on what would normally be a weak point within a record and make it its strength.'

Cave happily admits a lot of the musical tendons that lift his work are provided by the Bad Seeds, especially the arrangement and interpretation that Mick Harvey brings to bear on the embryos of Nick's ideas. Typically, in rehearsal, he describes in emotional terms – lechery, compassion, violence etc – the sort of atmosphere he wants the band to create. The fact that he can rope in some of the most gifted musicians of the era, be it Kid Congo or Bargeld, is testament to the esteem he is held in popular music's more fractious quarters. Either that or they all need a meal ticket.

Despite popular myth, Cave isn't always deadly serious. Anybody who rues on about his *'hump of sorrow and sack of woe'*, as he does on the new tune, 'Up Jumped the Devil', can't be as deadpan as rigor mortis.

Do you think you're lyrically funny at all?

'Well, I never said I was serious all the time. The way I'm portrayed I find particularly funny sometimes, this supposed pessimism I'm meant to harbour towards everything and anything. I think something like *Your Funeral, My Trial* has got its humorous side because I'm reasonably aware of the reputation that I've got. I find it curious to think certain people would find songs I write so continually harping on the same themes to be irritating, pathetic and so on. I kind of find some sort of enjoyment in that.

'I think my own view of things is quite irrational in a lot of ways; the way I see certain things, like the way an audience reacts, or the way people will interpret lyrics. Mick Harvey is continually telling me the way I've responded to a situation or what I've felt coming off an audience has not been really realistic . . . I think our group is capable of supreme disappointment, far more than other groups. I really care about what we do and I really care that the shows are good and try my hardest to make them that way and I'm always upset if they're not as good as they should be.'

A lot of this, obviously, hinges on Nick's voice itself. Is he happy with it?

'Only when I sing well. One has to use what resources one has and live with these things. I am quite aware that my voice is basically unlikeable. And I think what I've managed to achieve with it has been quite a feat in itself. It's like trying to play great guitar on some sort of Gibson copy or ten-dollar guitar. The edge and depth of my voice is not a natural thing that great singers have, like Chris Bailey or Tom Jones or even Simon Bonney. People whose voices automatically give you a nice feeling.'

Would you like to have a voice like Frank Sinatra's?

'No. That would be jumping out of the frying pan and into the fire. I think trading my voice for Frank Sinatra's would be a pretty poor deal all round. Neither of us would fulfil our potential.'

You're involved in a lot of different projects, films, records, a novel. To be honest I thought your acting was really over the top in *Ghosts* to the point of being funny. From what I've seen of you so far you seem quite the opposite of the character you portray in that you're quiet and considered offstage, despite the media image of you.

'Quite possibly. I'm quite nervous and not a racist, which is the opposite of this character. Is that what you mean? I dunno, but I suppose that's what acting is supposed to be about, playing a character opposite to your own. Anyhow, I really did enjoy doing the acting though I admit it was very kind of caricaturish. Basically in the script there were these big gaps which just had Nick Cave and no dialogue written down. I wasn't given any of the coaching the other actors were given, it was just assumed I could walk on and be this particular character. So basically I just had to be in front of the camera and scream abuse out.'

Cave part scripted *Ghosts* for producer Evan English. Ironically enough, Nick's first script for him, put together in LA several years back, was completely unfeasible and has now turned up as the basis of his novel, *And the Ass Saw the Angel*.

'Evan English and his partners were video-makers called the Rich Kids who wanted to make their first feature film. So they got me to write the script. The script I turned out was absolutely ridiculous. It would have cost millions to make. I had no idea of the expense involved in creating a film that would have an entire town in it and aerial zoom shots that started at one end of the town and zoomed in to a person's eyeball.'

Are you a voyeur as opposed to a participant?

'Well, I've always felt much more comfortable writing in the third person. I would find it impossible to write a book that was written from the author's point of view about myself. But I could write it quite easily by putting a character in to portray me and writing from an outside point of view. In *And the Ass Saw the Angel*, the photographer is in fact a chronic voyeur.

'His entire life is spent on the periphery of things. He acknowledges this fact and spends the entire time recording what goes on in the town that he lives in. It's only in the last two years of his life that he swings into action and creates situations with consequences. That's what the book is basically about, a voyeur, someone who's chastised by the townsfolk or the general mass.'

Are you aware that you've got this myth that you carry with you that could be held responsible for the launching of a thousand Goth bands? What a horrible thought!

'Heh-heh. Unfortunately all the worst sides of my output in my creative life seem to have been adopted by people as the most influential ones.

'What you become is that which is taken up and aped by other people. But when the things that people take from you are the most repulsive misconceptions about you – the way the Goths do, for instance – that's all pretty frightening. I'd hate to go down in history as the number one Goth, the man who spawned a thousand Goth bands with stacked hairstyles, no personality, pale sick people. I really don't want to be responsible for that sort of thing at all. I think there are a lost more interesting things about what I've done than what seems to have most affect on people.'

How much of an effort is it to keep recording?

'Every record I feel like I've really wrung the sponge out this time and there isn't anything left of me to give and I've felt that way ever since *Mutiny*. Only with the last couple of records I've realised that actually you do fill up again and can do it again. But I always really worry before I make a record that it's just not going to be there. And this is one of the prime reasons that I do continue to make records, to ward off this fear that grows in me after three or four months.'

Despite what he calls 'the monumental task' of editing his novel, Nick says he will still be unsatisfied with it when it is published. I wondered, therefore, whether he has been totally happy with any of his recorded work?

'There are a couple of moments that I'm really proud of but that's all. Like "Mutiny", that particular song, and "Sad Waters". Just a couple of moments here and there. But I find a lot of my work grotesque and tasteless in a lot of ways. Things like "Deep in the Woods" are diseased with grotesqueness.'

Do you feel that you are grotesque like some of your characters?

'Well, no I don't actually feel that. I feel like I tend to forget about really significant aspects of what I do that people will generally take notice of. On "Deep in the Woods" [*a song whose treatment of the female character was interpreted by many as misogynistic* – JB] I concentrated so much on sort of lyrical flow and nice use of words that the actual story behind the song is really ridiculous, a grotesque exaggeration that's ultimately really kind of comic book and shallow. I find I do that quite often.'

Sensing the interview winding down, I decide to put a final shot to Cave. It's a secret personal project that Nick is going to be involved in during the coming months, concerning his drugs problem. Nick is mortified when I broach the question, but leaves the tape recorder running while he talks extensively about the subject.

Because of an agreement settled upon the following day, that particular subject matter has been left out of this article.

Nick Cave, before we split for bed after our four-hour interview, summed up his feelings about his heroin addiction in the following way:

'I've always wanted to hone my music, writing and lyrics down so they are as pure as possible. It has always worried me that drugs retard the development of ideas. They also retard other things like your physical development.

'I don't want to encourage people to take drugs or be an example of somebody who takes a lot of drugs and hasn't burnt out just because I don't feel burnt out. But it does distress me that I have an influence over people in that way. I've seen myself have an influence over people, in regard to drugs. I really think drugs are quite an evil thing and I really wish I hadn't become involved with them myself because I'm in a situation now where it will take quite a concentrated effort to live without them and it will require quite a major life's fight to stop taking them.'

IF THIS IS HEAVEN AH'M BAILING OUT

The shitstorm begins. Packed and waiting to catch the next plane home, the sound of perhaps Cave's most possessed performance, an obscene song partly about kicking heroin, 'Mutiny in Heaven', replays itself in my mind.

Upstairs in the Museum Hotel, meanwhile, Cave is freaking out. He's already castigated his PR for talking to me about Simon Bonney and is now giving his friend Bleddyn Butcher the third degree. Nick is bitterly concerned that I haven't yet given an undertaking not to write about his secret project, despite the fact that he has offered to tell me the whole story after its completion.

Though I'm satisfied with what I've got on tape already, a compromise is eventually reached. I'm informed that Cave will quite happily talk about his use of heroin in detail so long as I draw a veil over his secret project. Given that Cave's drug abuse has only been snidely insinuated in the press, and this is a chance to get the story from the horse's mouth, so to speak, and in the process deglamorise the sick junkie chic that surrounds him, I agree. We fly on to Hamburg.

The PR is told by Cave that one of the singer's minions had been dispatched earlier to get us up. Our response to the invitation was supposedly to tell the minion to 'FUCK off!' A pretty neat trick since we were both asleep.

'You're the person, it's your type that are responsible for those people dying for insisting on writing about it.' Cave's voice is snarling now. Our second interview is closer to a war. Overnight it seems Nick has changed the game-plan. He doesn't want to talk about heroin anymore and we're well on the way to a head-to-head collision.

'I can't help it that I take this particular drug,' he continues. 'I mean, it is that evil and insidious and it does worm its way into your life and it's very difficult to get it out again. Never have I spoken about it in any other way.'

I haven't really seen it mentioned (openly).

'It isn't mentioned. I've talked about it a lot, in fact. Usually it's considered to be . . . There are reasons that I don't want you to write about it. Or one of the reasons. You know, I don't write endless songs about it, for example.'

This is, of course, true. Cave hardly has a mono-dimensional talent, as should be clear. The sensible thing to do would be to terminate the interview here and now. Instead we bicker on with the abuse level rising.

'I work from the time I get up to the time I have . . . I have to go to the sound-check and do the concert. I have to spend hours talking to fucking idiots like you who have no kind of notion about anything.'

Yeah, well, let's just forget it. Bollocks.

'Jesus Christ!' snaps Cave. 'You're insulting me so much and you don't even realise it.'

I haven't insulted you!

'You're so numb through your occupation that you can sit there and say that I'm responsible for the deaths of young children – or that your girlfriend told you that.'

About now I start collecting my belongings from Cave's room since the whole scene is getting beyond pathetic. Earlier on I'd telephoned my girlfriend who said a couple of friends of hers had become addicts in part because they dumbly wanted to ape the kind of lifestyle Cave exudes. His initial response to this was a) I didn't have a girlfriend and b) I'd made the story up. Now, apparently, he thinks I'm accusing him of killing young kids!

'Listen,' says Cave as I make for the exit. 'We started up a whole new interview while there are other people out there who've got to do interviews. We try to do it again and all you can ask me is questions related to heroin. Again . . . I talked to you the other night about heroin. I told you everything there was to know about it in relation to me. And I really regret ever having opened my mouth about it.'

'I'm sure you do,' I reply, opening the hotel bedroom door.

'Because I didn't realise what a fucking scumhill and what a filthy little prick you were,' snorts Cave, shoving me out into the corridor and slamming the door behind me. A couple of seconds later a glass comes hurtling past my skull and smashes against the wall. Nick, meanwhile, is getting a psychotic head of steam up.

Only this time he isn't play-acting.

Jack Barron, *NME*, 13 August 1988

Edge of Darkness

Nick Kent

By virtually anyone else's standards the events of the third week in October would have provided a perfect license for basking in a boundless high of self-achievement. Early in the week, Nick Cave's fifth album, *Tender Prey*, was finally released. By the Wednesday, the reviews of said record in all sections of the British music press were aglow with fervent critical hosannas of the kind that most other acts would kill for. Meanwhile, the streets of London were being seriously fly-postered with Cave's singular features staring plaintively out from within a frame of royal red.

Yet on a rainy Saturday afternoon, the mood of the flesh-and-blood Nick Cave that I'm interviewing is a million miles removed from one of blithe satisfaction. Ask him how it feels to be viewed by the *NME* as the 'Hank Williams and Bob Dylan of the '80s' and he refuses to be swayed. 'Whatever they say, I can't trust them. Next week it's just as likely to be the opposite.' I ask him how it feels to be lauded as the last rock star, the only authentically dangerous figure left, and he answers almost in a whisper. 'I certainly don't *feel* very dangerous.' The plethora of fly-posters similarly fails to excite him. 'I'd only look at them to see if they'd been spat on or otherwise defiled.'

This, it has to be said, isn't the diffident braggadocio of Nick Cave the badass junkie hellion of fabled myth and murk, but the sober self-questioning of a man whose public trials and tribulations have finally occasioned an inexorable breaking away from the swamp-like mire of a debilitatingly infamous past. The new album, he states, he hasn't actually listened to 'for ages. To be honest with you, I thought it was a piece of shit when we were making it. I'm still under the impression it's too scrappy. Half the songs have some point to them, but the other half are probably just filler. I'll have to listen to it again, but at the time of recording, it seemed to me like one long cry for help.'

The word 'caricature' comes into the conversation. 'Oh, that was happening anyway,' Cave states unblinkingly. 'For the past three years or more, I've been in

Nick Cave photographed in West Berlin, 3 August 1985.

a state of ever-increasing emotional and spiritual numbness. I mean, I've written a lot of songs where I've articulated my pain without actually being able to *feel* it. I don't think I've ever been able to be honest about the way I feel about things because I've been totally numb. At the same time, a lot of bad things have happened to me. Best friends of mine have died and all I've felt is guilty that I couldn't feel anything. That's maybe why I wrote in the third person. Maybe all along I've been articulating how I *should* feel without feeling it.

'I have no idea what my forthcoming music will be like, only that I'd imagine the themes will be different. *Before* now, if you'd asked me, I'd have been able to predict the exact themes that would turn up on my albums to date. Let's see: there would be the songs that dealt with "death", "loneliness", "alienation" . . .' He pauses. 'Oh, and of course, "low self-worth".' He laughs but he is not joking.

Up until now, the ongoing saga of Nick Cave and his attempts to terrorise the '80s with music has been creatively provocative, often (mostly in live performance) charismatically thrilling, but also worryingly dissolute and occasionally wantonly barbaric. It's not overstating things to refer to Cave as the most effectively 'driven' white rock performer since Iggy Pop. Yet the inevitable rub – the essence of Cave's charisma residing in his irretrievably 'doomed' demeanour and persona – has caused many to be repelled by his work, indicting him instead as a dangerously wayward influence on his audience.

By the same token, his private life has become a magnet for tall tales, sensational copy, high dudgeon, voyeuristic adoration and insatiable loathing. Six weeks before it ran its rave review of the new album, the *NME* published a long feature, 'The Trials of Nick Cave', probably the most controversial and feverishly debated piece it has printed in years. The writer, Jack Barron, basically set out to expose Cave's addiction to heroin, accusing the singer of being virtually a walking advert for the drug. An outraged Cave in turn tried to beat Barron up. A prominent news story chronicling the former's trial in London for possession of the drug and his subsequent entry into a rehabilitation clinic was grandstanded in the same issue. Since then, numerous outraged letters have flooded into the *NME*'s letters column, all of them fiercely damning of the article's sensationalist tone, whilst Barron himself has allegedly been a recipient of several death threats from incensed fans.

For someone so supposedly 'driven' and larger-than-life, Nick Cave's initiation as a singer was scarcely auspicious. 'I actually had no great desire to become a singer or be in a group. When I was a teenager, I wanted to be a painter. But I failed my art school entrance exam . . .'

He was born thirty-one years ago in Melbourne, 'the most tragic place on earth', he now stresses. 'It's hard to escape from there and because Melbourne and Sydney are centres for the Australian drug trades, young people living there often end up either drug addicts or alcoholics. My worst fear these days is having to accept a phone call from Australia because usually it means that one of my old friends have either overdosed or hung themselves.'

He was cajoled into singing with some school friends, a mongrel conglomerate influenced by punk and power pop named the Boys Next Door, joining 'not for musical reasons, more because it enabled us to get into clubs free and get drunk a lot'. How the seriously uneventful Boys Next Door ('We were another of those groups who ended up having to rhyme "my generation" with "masturbation"') metamorphosized into the seriously full-blown sensory cancer of the Birthday Party is a subject no one seems able to fully detail, but, clearly, something radical occurred.

'Nick sometimes likes to say in interviews that the Birthday Party got their early motivation from playing to extremely aggressive audiences in the outback. This isn't strictly true,' states Mick Harvey, the Birthday Party's drummer and Cave's continuing musical collaborator in the Bad Seeds. 'The real violence erupted later on.'

This 'violence' is not something Harvey recalls with fondness. 'There were gigs where guys would jump onstage wielding iron bars at us. You never knew what might happen next. We became a magnet for the audience's aggression and things became just very ugly.'

Harvey now guardedly refers to the band's daunting reputation since their breakup as 'overrated'. Cave, however, feels otherwise. 'I still have a lot of respect for the Birthday Party. I feel it was a very solid statement of intent that we put in a nutshell. Not that we had any control over it. Plus, we broke up when we were at our peak, which I'm particularly proud of.'

Certainly, if Nick Cave had retired from music after the group's breakup in 1983, his immortality as a performer would have been assured. Having moved to London in 1981, the group almost immediately attracted a following amongst the disengaged post-punk coterie, the group's most vociferous supporters often being young, impressionable writers for the music press. Cave's onstage demeanour – a seething coalition of reckless abandon and flaming arrogance – was eulogised fanatically, whilst his singular appearance – the lanky, raw-boned physique, a face that seemed to represent the very apex of poignant dissipation topped off by a wild corona of ink-black hair – became a perfect visual image for music journals being submerged by the early '80s antiseptic pop star prototype.

The fallout from the group's breakup is still something that deeply troubles Cave. (Not that he was necessarily the worst affected. The group's bass player, Tracy Pew, for example, died two years ago in a diabetic coma.) He admits, for example, that as early as 1981 when the album *Junkyard* was recorded, 'I thought I'd wrung the sponge, creatively speaking. I really thought I could never make another record. And since then, it's just gotten harder and harder.

'Recording sessions have dragged on longer and longer, I've had to fight more and more in order to assert some control over the music. Looking back, it sometimes seems like everything has been chaos, more chaos building up to yet more chaos.'

Cave's bleak vision of the past five years is considerably influenced by a further descent into drug addiction. His recollection of events during that time is somewhat impaired, whole album sessions are almost a complete blank memory now, whilst he readily admits he can't remember why he asked certain members of the Bad Seeds to join him in the first place.

The five albums he's recorded, however, culminating with *Tender Prey*, can boast a continuing ascent in song structure and quality. After an initial infatuation with the Delta blues form that seemed somewhat heavy-handed, Cave and the Bad Seeds recorded an excellent collection of cover songs, *Kicking Against the Pricks*, his most accomplished vocal performance to date. A year later, *Your Funeral, My Trial* began to capture that genuine sense of mystery and depth, replete with Brechtian keyboards and strident, almost militaristic drum patterns that Cave and his group had previously only glancingly hinted at. There was a sense of melancholia undercutting the previous clamour, a space and breadth to the sound that bolstered Cave's limited range ('I came to terms years ago with the fact that I couldn't sing like Barry White'). *Tender Prey* further tones up the dimensions to Cave and the Bad Seeds' august output, stretching all aspects of their abilities to great effect. Mostly though, it seems balanced in a weird, quasi-cathartic way between the often almost baroque style of the Bad Seeds' playing and the sound of Cave's vocals; the sound of a man literally on his last legs, being dragged to hell in a bucket.

The Nick Cave I'm interviewing has been out of drug rehabilitation for only three days ('I'd prefer it if you could downplay that aspect,' he states. 'If you could just say that I've been doing a lot of menial work for the past two months!'). On Monday he flies out to West Berlin to rehearse for a couple of days before embarking on a daunting European tour.

'There's been a lot of talk about how it might jeopardise his situation,' stated Mick Harvey the day before Cave came out. 'But if he was just doing nothing for a while it would be equally bad.' Everyone – from record company to group members – is being understandably cautious, choosing their words with the utmost care. Cave himself, however, appears relaxed and healthy.

'I thought I'd be emotionally and spiritually bankrupt after the experience, but I actually feel much the same about most things – surprisingly enough – only mentally, much clearer. My attitudes towards life haven't changed. I've just got a melancholic bent to my character. That won't change.'

He claims to be feeling 'nervous but exhilarated' by the upcoming tour. 'Actually, I'm not really worried. I feel quite confident about what I offer onstage. There's a lot of pressure on me, but I'm not going to dwell on that.'

The next immediate project is the final editing of his long-awaited novel *And the Ass Saw the Angel*. 'The end is in sight after two or three years of kidding myself. Now I have the chance to discipline my output. I know I can go back and finish it off in a couple of months. My publisher's a really happy man!'

His movie career too is progressing. Having completed an acting role in the Australian *Ghosts of the Civil Dead* as well as a cameo performing with the Bad

Seeds in Wim Wenders's *Wings of Desire*, both parties are talking about concrete projects with Cave.

'The Wenders film project . . . I don't know how much I should say, but he's been working on this vast shooting script for the past three years involving locations all over the world. It's set ten years in the future and involves various groups representing each country. We represent Australia, would you believe! He's asked us to write a song that will represent how we feel ten years from now . . . which is an interesting concept!'

Wenders is a big fan and sometime cohort of Cave's. 'He turns up at our gigs. I don't know what he sees in us because Wim isn't too much of a talker. Being in his company is rather like watching *Paris, Texas*. Kind of a random experience. But interesting.'

Then there is the music business. Cave is more guarded here.

'I'm currently reassessing what music can do for me. The press have upset me. I've been deeply, deeply embarrassed by a lot of what's been written. They were able to manipulate the way I felt good about myself. There's been too much personal upset. The places I was drawing my sense of self-worth from were so fickle and precarious. Like the way audiences felt about me. I was a very paranoid person. But I've had a lot of work done on my self-worth lately – I don't need to draw it from the same places anymore.

'I want to continue with music, but to do it in a way where I can simply make my contribution and then just step out. I mean, even though I don't know what's going to happen, what kind of themes or sounds I'll pursue.

'But basically, I don't see how I could make a worse record than before, now that I'm able to start tackling the way I *genuinely* feel about things.'

So there you have it. A happy ending. Nick Cave, come on down and step into the light. You have nothing to lose but your sack of woe.

Nick Kent, *The Face*, December 1988

Nick Cave on 57th Street:
A Late '80s Memoir

Kris Needs

Between 1986–88 I was New York correspondent for *Creem* magazine and a Canadian monthly called *Graffiti*, nursing both a fixation with the works of Nick Cave and a growing heroin habit. These three elements seemed to collide at regular intervals around this time as Cave, then also lolling in the arms of Morpheus to heroic levels, paradoxically enjoyed a period of creativity foreshadowing his current plateau of super-prolific multi-tasking.

In 1988 alone he released the *Tender Prey* album, lyrical anthology *King Ink* and completed his first novel, *And the Ass Saw the Angel*, as well as appearing in Wim Wenders's *Wings of Desire* with the Bad Seeds while making his acting debut in Evan English's harrowing *Ghosts of the Civil Dead*.

I'd been encountering Cave on a regular basis back in London before moving to New York in mid-1986, in the context of both massive fan and socially in situations usually involving drugs. In October 1986, he was busted scoring smack in Alphabet City, meaning that night's gig at the Ritz Ballroom on 11th Street was postponed. We somehow hooked up after he'd emerged from the two-day process which usually followed such an arrest and needed to refuel his tank, so to speak, spending the night sitting and nodding in the tiny 12th Street apartment I was staying in (a floor above Allen Ginsberg and next door to Richard Hell). A couple of days later he asked me to procure further supplies as he continued the tour, including a blazing rescheduled Ritz gig, and popped round one last time.

The next time we met was over two years later in December 1988, ostensibly as part of the conveyor belt to talk about *Tender Prey*, but also ended up covering the other projects. Nick had cleaned up three months earlier (albeit temporarily). Those around him said he was like a new person. This could only be a major contrast to our first interview encounter back in 1983, when the Birthday Party had just released *The Bad Seed* EP. Then Cave had seemed spectral, nihilistic and anaesthetised to the gills, that fearsome band's aura of cerebral drag-racing and simmering menace amplified by the larger-than-life, be-Stetsoned presence of their late bassist, Tracy Pew. In retrospect, though, there were signs then that Cave was realigning his literary sights from the Birthday

Party's shock and awe to the deeper literary strata we were talking about in New York, the germs of the novel maybe starting to jostle as he wrote a series of short stories with Lydia Lunch.

Ironically, by now I was in the final throes of my own stint with the drug and had come to the hotel from a current Avenue B heroin hot-spot with pockets stuffed, just in case. Well, junkies like nothing better than a sparring partner. It's like alcoholics doing their best to upend a former drinking buddy's wagon. But after just five minutes with Nick I decided to respect his new sobriety, repairing to his bathroom when the demon in my pocket called. Apparently that croaking ghost on the tape is me.

Sitting stirring his tea in his room at New York's Parker-Meridian Hotel on 57th Street, the be-suited figure before me certainly looked in better shape than the last time I'd seen him, often laughing or shrugging with dry humour and obviously happy with his recent work, even carrying an air of vulnerability and world-weariness as he talked about having to do interviews from the time he woke until around eleven at night. Having encountered Nick in a variety of conditions over the years it had to be said that this was the most open and friendly I'd seen him. He hadn't changed dramatically, and made no big deal of the rehab forced upon him by a court. Now he'd done it he carried an air of triumph too, and did seem more positive. Unclogged, if you like. 'It was simple,' he remarked, matter-of-factly. 'If I'd have gone on like that I would have died. I didn't have any sudden desire to clean up. It was forced on me, but I'm glad I did now. I haven't touched anything for four months!'

Facing the inevitable void which giving up heroin leaves, Nick had plunged himself into work. No change there, but this was the start of the vigorous work ethic he would famously turn into a fine art after finally kicking smack for good in the late '90s. First he had undertaken a European tour, then finally finished the biggest project of his life: his first novel *And the Ass Saw the Angel*, which became his grand passion as he bashed out its 500 pages cloistered in Berlin.

The book took Cave's fixation with the Gothic Deep South and Biblical imagery to black new depths even old Nick hadn't plumbed before, the story centring around a simple teen-mute called Euchrid Eucrow, bullied into his swamp sanctum by small-town thugs, the reader stuck in his poor mind, suffering redneck abuse from this stupid rank underbelly amidst growing dread and apocalypse.

'That's in its final stages now. We did the final edits on it and I just finished reading through it. I'm really pleased with it. I was quite worried about what I'd think about it but I'm really happy with it. I think it's really good. It holds together well.

'Primarily, writing that was a perfect kind of escape from a lot of personal problems I wasn't really dealing with,' he says, perched on a chair under low lighting. 'I'd just go and lock myself away for days. It was perfect in a way for this sort of book because it's about a boy's growing obsessions.'

Although I hadn't read it yet, Cave could be heard reciting extracts from the novel on a twelve-inch EP dished out with initial copies of *Tender Prey* which suggested strong plot-lines of persecution and human cruelty amped up with liberal smatterings of fire and brimstone.

'A lot of my past themes are dealt with,' he agrees. 'But it goes into it a lot more fetishistically. It starts at an all-time low and kind of sinks from there.

'The story was pretty much clear from the start. It was based on a film script that I'd written with Evan English, who was the producer of *The Ghosts of the Civil Dead*. But it never got made into a film so it turned into a book. I had no idea what it was like to write a film script and the practicalities of actually making a film, particularly someone's first film on a relatively low budget. To have made this into a film would've cost fucking millions; it's a really complicated story!

'I'd quite like to write some more film scripts. The prospect of writing another book at the moment is pretty daunting. I think if I wrote another one it would be quite different to this and much simpler. This one has just got everything in it. As a story I think it holds together really well. It's almost like a suspense story. It's almost like a Spielberg type of thing; not in a horror kind of a way. The book's very much to do with language and that sort of thing. I've got a lot of that sort of stuff out of my system now, really.'

Meanwhile, *King Ink* featured song lyrics both in finished form and some as sprawling epics later to be pruned and sculpted, dating back to when his old group first howled at the moon. Reviewing the collection at the time, I said, 'Cave has been a grossly-misinterpreted individual in the past, often dismissed as some kind of doomed Goth low-life laundering the blood off his shirt-sleeves in public. It's true that he has fixated on the rank lizard underbelly of the human condition, but this compilation stomps on the stone-throwing hands as, away from his flailing stage and studio sweatshop, Cave is simply a brilliant wordsmith. His subject matter might be from the dark side but I've rarely encountered such mesmerising image-building and sheer atmosphere in the written word.

'It's fascinating to watch the seeds of Cave's current style germinate, swell and sprout. By the time he gets to the arcane Deep South terror of Swampland we're at the grimy halt where he shut himself away in Berlin, started twitching at the Devil and the ass saw the angel.'

The tome, initially intended as a stop-gap when the novel over-ran its deadline, also includes unused song segments, pieces of prose, one-act plays (including five on the Salome legend), a 'fan letter' to Einstürzende Neubauten and the full novelette of *Blind Lemon Jefferson*, one of the character studies which made up the original novel idea but, instead, became a twisted blues on *The Firstborn Is Dead* album. There are also reproduced pages from his faithful notebook, doodles intertwining with first drafts.

'That book came about because I'd been contracted with Black Spring Press. I was supposed to finish by July 1984 or '85, I can't remember. It was only supposed to be 150 pages long or something like that. In fact, it took three years longer. In that time, the publisher quite graciously waited and didn't apply any pressure on me. He was just happy I was doing it, basically. So I just gave him the option of putting out a book of lyrics. I just gave him any material that I had and he sort of dug it up and put it together.

'There was much more than actually got put in the book. I gave him a lot of stuff and we basically made a decision. There were two types of book that could have been made. There was just one which was basically a reasonably concise book of my lyrical work up to this date with a few extra-curricular things thrown in, or else there was this idea that I had of a fat volume with just everything, with drawings. I don't know how many versions there were of "Your Funeral, My Trial". There must have been about twenty or so verses. To have all that sort of stuff in it almost documents the way a song's actually written and the way I actually write songs, where so much actually goes into one idea and then gets sort of pruned down into three verses.'

I never knew *Blind Lemon Jefferson* was a complete story.

'Yeah . . . *[laughs]* That was never a song. That was actually what the original contract was for with Black Spring Press: for me to write a book that had ten fact, fictional or mythological semi-factual biographies of different people that I was interested in. That was like an idea I never really took up. I just decided to actually write a novel instead. There was going to be Blind Lemon Jefferson and a variety of other people who I can't remember. I have written some other ones; a guy called Baliban, a rampaging Rumanian murderer in Australia.'

Where do you find the time for all this? You must be on the go all the time?

'I'm basically a workaholic. I'm only really happy when I'm working. On one hand it's the hardest stuff to do, but it's the nitty-gritty work I'm most happy being involved in; when I'm actually there writing a song, or writing prose or the novel or working in the studio on a record or whatever. It's the actual selling of the products, the concerts, whatever, are the things that I find most taxing. The work's already been done, now it's the performance of it. Then there's the interviews and photo sessions and other sort of stuff which is on another plane again.'

Cave's newfound clarity seemed to make him aware of his infamous relationship with the press at the time. 'I'd like to change my ideas about interviews; my basic hatred of them, in a sense, has become so embedded over the years. I would like to be able to look at interviews as where I'm keeping some kind of continuing communication with my audience, something like that in a more kind of creative way. Very often, at the end of the day, I just find there's so little to actually talk about. In a sense, there's so much I'm actually doing but to sit down and articulate in any other way . . . I always feel kind of cheated by it. I always feel like I've not explained myself properly or I've not done what I'm doing justice, just as much as I often feel the actual journalists aren't doing it justice.'

Listening to the tape now, the interview comes over as more of a rambling chat (with me doing most of the rambling), Nick more than happy to explain his books and the background to songs on the new album. He's not so comfortable talking about drugs but the given the circumstances, who would blame him? I tell him I only interview people who I'm interested in and want to find out more about, a selfish trait, in a way, which he finds quite unusual.

"I think that's quite rare, actually. It's quite strange to still think in those terms. A lot of journalists start off that way but then . . . It would be a very frightening prospect for me to be a journalist in this day and age! And to be a workaholic at the same time! To wake up in the morning and think, Who am I going to go out and interview today? The amount of bands worth talking to you can count on one hand, really. I feel really kind of divorced from modern music anyway. It's not deliberate. In a sense, I think I've been so self-obsessed with my own kind of tiny plight that I haven't really cared really about what else is going on.'

If *Your Funeral, My Trial* could be considered the album which saw the Bad Seeds come of age and set foot on their path to current glory, the tortuously-created *Tender Prey* was patchy, later even invoking disdain from its composer, but it's not without considerable magic, breadth and Cave's swelling religious fixation on tracks like the aching 'Mercy'. He explains, 'Basically, that's the story of John the Baptist. It's still a kind of demystifier basically. He's a kind of prophet who saw things and it talks about him seeing his own death that many times.' The album closes with the sun-through-the-clouds gospel optimism of 'New Morning', which Nick describes as, 'very much like "Amazing Grace" actually'.

But then 'Slowly Goes the Night', one of the album's somnambulant ballads, sports cooing MOR-style backing chorale. 'I like a lot of that sort of music, basically. "Slowly Goes the Night" was a bit of a problem in a way because it was a piano composition and the thing was so strong melodically it was a nightmare to put a vocal on. The refrain played by the piano was so strong it was almost an instrumental, in a sense. It was very much built up from an instrumental then putting vocal over the top of it . . . Barry White.'

Then there's 'The Mercy Seat': in my opinion, among the top three Cave compositions and Bad Seeds performances as it details to stunning effect the condemned man driven to distraction while waiting to fry in the electric chair, mind baking as he sees the face of Christ in his soup.

'That song was an idea we have been trying to do for a long time, which finally seemed to work and was to have some galloping, almost-thrash bass-line and then put a slow, chord progression over the top of it. So we wed these two things and it worked quite well.

'I don't really like to analyse but basically that song talks about judgement working on three different levels – divine judgement, social judgement and one's own personal concepts of what's good and what's evil. The bit that interests me most – which is the actual kind of spoken stuff – is this guy, who's by himself all the time, actually putting his own perceptions of what's good and evil on inanimate things until he's actually looking at his own hands and calling one good and one evil and actually passing judgement on himself and things around him.'

This leads neatly to Nick's latest movie role of a deranged-nasty prison in-mate called Maynard in *Ghosts of the Civil Dead*, based around 'super-maximum security establishments which don't work at all, basically'.

'I'm a psycho, yeah,' says Nick with some relish. 'The basic story is taken from a true account by this ex-prison guard called Dave Hale, who was forced out of the system after he saw this corruption going on there. It was about the administration deliberately provoking a disruption within the prison amongst the prisoners by changing their routines, just in little ways up to taking their belongings off them, just kind of provoking them in these insidious ways. Ultimately, the inevitable happened and two guards were killed and then this went to the media, who said, "Look at the situation here." Then they got a whole lot of money and got the prison on permanent lockdown, which is when they're kept in their cell. They're allowed out of their cell one hour each day, something like that.

'My role is that I'm actually put into the prison as a deliberate provocateur by the authorities to deliberately irritate everybody. I'm basically a nutcase who screams out shit all the time and irritates everybody. It's a solid political statement. This particular film is about new-age prisons, these kind of super-maxi security prisons. There's a lot of them being built over here [in the US], certain designs and so forth, supposedly built for more humane containment. The interiors are all painted in pastel purple colours, all done in psychiatrist's colours. They're all very sinister in that way. But they're really bad. They don't work at all, basically. But the thing is, in England the Home Office have had all sorts of plans for these sorts of prisons in order to build them in England as well. So England is by no means safe from them. The Home Office actually asked to see this particular film because it got so much interest when it was shown in England. You should see it. I don't really feel like going into it because it's such an incredible . . . It's quite difficult to explain unless you've seen it. It's a very solid political statement.'

How did you manage the six in the morning calls for filming?

'Well, they didn't do that with me. I think they conveniently placed my times which I was able to manage at that point. It was all filmed in Australia, which is a very unhealthy place for me to be . . .'

I ask Nick if he's seen *Dogs in Space*, the movie starring Michael Hutchence centred around Melbourne's drug-addled late '70s post-punk scene. 'Terrible,' comes the reply. 'It's a really stupid movie. It's supposed to be about a certain sector of the Australian punk movement. They're all kind of junkies and so on. In the end the heroine dies of an overdose and, to the strains of this terrible song, she's carted away in this Vaseline-lensed white limousine and this pale rider comes and sweeps her off to heaven. It's much worse than *Sid and Nancy*. I watch a lot of movies. I saw *Crocodile Dundee Two* on the plane coming over!'

Talk turns to when I'd last seen Nick after he'd been busted. Since then the same thing had happened to me; hauled into a wagon, taken to the precinct, finger-printed, thrown in a communal holding cell for hours with junkies, prostitutes and hardcore gang members before being consigned to overnight cells to await the eventual court appearance, which usually dismisses possession cases as misdemeanours with time served. 'It sounds like the same as me. I was in there for three days. Sitting in this dark van for hours waiting for it to start up. I went into this cell with this one other guy but before that they stick you in this big cage.'

That made it doubly amazing that he'd also created this body of work while finally cleaning up after being busted again in London.

'I'm quite amazed that I was able to cling on to so much of that, really,' he smiles. 'I really was really clinging on by the skin of my teeth, but there's a lot of stuff that was incomplete and had been hanging around for a long time, particularly the novel. The first thing was to get that out of the way.'

After this interview Cave would go on to clean up again, relocate to Brazil, settle down and make the lighter and more ordered *The Good Son*, which lived up to what he said when we started talking about the group again.

'I basically want to explore some different themes now. I kind of want my songwriting to be simpler anyway, get away from these incredibly sort of labyrinthine lyrical excursions like "The Mercy Seat" and things like this. I want the next record to be much simpler, much more a record of songs. It depends on what happens and how they come out, but I want to write some classic-type songs, more singer-orientated songs, possibly like some of the stuff on *Kicking Against the Pricks*, some of the more complicated singing type stuff. I find I can sing much better these days.

'I just used to sing flat all the time and that's certainly changed. That was certainly evident in the concerts we did this time round Europe. Everyone thought I'd taken a crash course in voice training or something like that!'

Not so, but he did visit a singing teacher who asked him to sing a song. He promptly serenaded the old lady with 'I'm Gonna Kill That Woman'.

Whereas the Birthday Party had been feverishly imitated, few dared venture near the Bad Seeds' cinematic sonic tapestries. (Some long-forgotten names tried but, by *The Boatman's Call*, Cave and the Bad Seeds were untouchable).

'I think we're a lot harder to copy these days,' he reasoned, uncannily predating comments he would make twenty years later when he said, 'The Bad Seeds is very much a kind of growing thing. This kind of journey of discovery; kind of self-discovery, whether it be lyrically or through different musical forms, even attitudes and so forth. The Birthday Party, which was very kind of youthful and impetuous, was there with a kind of nutshell statement, in a sense, right from the first thing we did. It was very much some dirty little thing that I think a lot of people took and scrubbed up and cleaned up and regurgitated in that way and made successes out of themselves by doing it.'

Do you ever sit back when your group are playing and think, 'Fucking 'ell!'?

'In the studio, yeah, sure. I'd actually like to push that more and kind of expand it; push the actual requirements of each musician so they do more, basically. I'm still kind of forming this in my mind, in relation to the next record and the way I'd like to structure what everybody does more, or have them structure it a bit more, particularly in terms of the guitars, which are very much the rogue elements in the music anyway. I'd like everybody to become more involved on the actual structure of the song; the actual basis would be put down, even the singing over the top, then have Blixa come in and fit himself in and around it: to actually employ them more.'

After laughing at a story then adorning tabloids that Elvis's dead twin brother was alive having escaped the confinement imposed after he was born mentally retarded, Nick reiterated his love of gospel music, before expressing deep admiration for Shane MacGowan and the Pogues. 'I think the Pogues are a great band, actually. Shane is a fucking great lyricist.' He's amused by *NME*'s idea to put MacGowan, the Fall's frontman Mark E. Smith and himself on their cover as 'a trio of three who survived. It's frightening . . . three geeks!'

I wondered if Cave's new sobriety had affected his obsessions or changed his perspectives?

'I'm still interested in the same things. I had to look at myself again but I still see the world pretty much as before.'

Including the UK, which he says still depresses him when I ask what it's like there now, seeing as I've been away for over two years. 'I'm not a very good judge of that because I've never found it any other way, even in its supposed heyday. I never really felt very much involved in any of the scenes or anything there. I'm not by any means bringing it down; I just felt quite alienated from them, in a way.'

Listening to the tape now, my wretched condition sounds painfully obvious. It takes one to know one and concern creeps into Nick's voice as he says softly, 'It sounds like a bit of trap here for you here at the moment . . .' At that point, the tape is turned off, maybe because I was about to confess all.

But I was about to leave that lifestyle for good. Nick's struggle would be a longer one and, when I encountered him in later years, he wouldn't remember much of this period. The main thing that stayed with me afterwards was, no matter what state he was in, Nick Cave was already pushing towards greatness with the results of his self-imposed, punishing work ethic. Imagine what he'll come up with if he sticks to sobriety, I mused as I walked into the cold New York night to pay a return visit to 13th Street and Avenue B . . .

Kris Needs, *Graffiti*, 1988, Remixed with additional material 2009

Titter Ye Not

Andy Gill

Nick Cave sighs. He sighs a lot, as if weary of the world and all that's in it. Specifically, you suspect, weary of the questions he's being asked, which he gives the impression of having answered a hundred times before. His answers, when they come, proceed via a stutter of aborted sentences, as he seeks a more accurate way of phrasing.

Cave, who lives in Brazil these days, is in London to promote his forthcoming album, *Henry's Dream*. His profile's as high as it's ever been, what with his appearances in the movies *Wings of Desire* and *Ghosts of the Civil Dead*, the runaway success of his first novel *And the Ass Saw the Angel* (an astonishing 16,000 hardback sales, followed by 35,000 more in the Penguin paperback edition) and the equivalent success of his previous album *The Good Son*, which has sold more than a quarter of a million worldwide, reaching number one in Greece and, of all places, Israel – pretty good going for an artist still considered very much a fringe interest. The success, however, doesn't make the work any easier.

'It was a complete and utter nightmare writing the songs for this record,' he shudders. 'It just gets harder and harder with each record. I'd like to think it was because I was becoming more and more selective, but the notion of writer's block is something that looms over me continually. I'll walk past the room with the piano and see it sitting there, waiting for me to do something on it . . . I'll sit down at it for five hours, and absolutely nothing comes out – it's incredibly depressing.'

One of the more panic-inducing aspects of writing this particular record, claims Cave, was the kind of material he came up with. 'I had a lot of songs that were like, just hitting one chord on the piano and singing these endless lyrics over the top of it,' he says. 'So there wasn't that immediate, "Wow, that's a catchy tune" aspect to it – it took a lot of effort on the part of the band members to do something with that one chord. I'd sing them the song and they would sit there

West Berlin, 3 August 1985.

looking at one another with their mouths open. The song would end and there'd be a kind of deathly silence after it, and I'd say, "Well, that's the first one!"'

His recording career is, however, but one of several strings now operative on the Cave bow. He's now also a published author, and a successful one at that. Cave's novel is surprisingly well written for a rock star, in a prose style which attempts to capture the inner voice of a mute psychotic in some Southern mountain valley in the early decades of this century. It amounts, he believes, to a purging of various themes that have recurred time and again in his work: the American South, death, religion, vengeance, sex . . . the usual stuff. Though it must be said that his new LP is only three lines old before yet another preacher man makes his appearance. What is it with old Nick and men of God?

'I've had my experiences with them in the past,' he says, darkly. 'I also like to put them in because [Bad Seeds guitarist] Mick Harvey's father's a preacher, and he's never been able to show him one of our records yet!'

While it shares themes with his lyrics, Cave admits he found writing the novel vastly easier, and liberating, in its own way.

'I seemed quite possessed when I wrote that book,' he recalls. 'It was just pouring out, unstoppable. It took five years to do, an enormous amount of time. I had a sort of freedom with the book because I didn't really feel I would ever see it published. Whereas when it comes to writing lyrics, there's a horrible pressure about it: you know that every line's going to be looked at, and that can be quite a constipating thing.'

Nick sighs again. I've asked him whether he finds his past a burden, whether the Nick Cave of legend – boozer, junkie, arty wastrel and all-round roaring-boy reprobate – still dogs his steps.

'No, not really,' he says. 'People expect certain things from me, and I guess they're disappointed when they don't get it. Some people stop me in the street and say, "What are you wearing a suit for? You've sold out!", like I'm a yuppie or something. I just tell them to fuck off.'

Cave admits he 'kicked up a little dust' back in the '80s, but feels he was unfairly singled out and boycotted by some of the music papers at the time. 'There were,' he asserts, 'some editorial meetings to discuss which groups made some effort to educate the world in political and social affairs and problems – and we certainly weren't one of them – and which ones were openly self-destructive, on whom there was, effectively, a ban. I may be wrong about this, but there was a period there when we didn't get much written about us.'

That's changed of late, but then so has Nick. 'Basically, what I've done is stop taking heroin and speed,' he explains matter-of-factly. 'I'm certainly not "in recovery", or whatever you're supposed to be. I tackle the alcohol problem on a daily basis, just try and drink one day at a time. But I don't feel like I've gone through something and risen into this blazing white light, or whatever. My life is still as chaotic and disordered as it has ever been.'

It would be hard for it to be otherwise, though, given his rootless existence over the past decade. London, Berlin, São Paulo – Cave has become something of a permanent traveller, despite an abiding love for his native Australia, one of those places (Ireland is another) people seem obliged to leave to find themselves. Why move so much?

'I guess so that I can have the luxury of being able to leave a place because I don't actually live there,' he says. 'I travel very light. I have books and records scattered with friends all over the world. I constantly buy the same record over and over again: I've bought so many versions of *Nashville Skyline* – I must be keeping Bob Dylan in . . . whatever it is that he needs keeping in.'

But what keeps Nick in whatever it is that he needs keeping in? How does he get by as a globetrotting fringe artist whose band members live almost as far away – Australia, Berlin, London – as it's possible to get? How does his art support his lifestyle?

'I make an extremely good living out of it, as far as I'm concerned,' he reveals. 'I make plenty of money, enough to do whatever I want to do. Usually, the records don't cost that much – we're not spending millions of dollars making them and having to pay that off. So I feel like I make a lot of money,' he says, adding wryly, 'I just can't stop the stuff coming in half the time!'

Nick laughs, an unusual sound.

'It's a terrible, terrible situation to be in! I don't have any property, and I don't have a car, and all my travelling gets paid for, so the money just goes into a bank account and earns interest.' He chuckles. 'So if anyone out there needs any money . . .'

It's strange to hear this famously melancholic person chuckling away, but Nick claims he has a fine sense of humour – it just depends on his situation as to whether it shows itself.

'When I'm in Australia, for instance, I laugh all the time,' he reveals. 'One of my major problems with people in other countries is that they don't think I'm funny and I don't really find them very funny – but as soon as I get back to Australia and get with my own kind, I feel I'm understood a bit more, because I have an Australian sensibility towards things. I laugh continuously there, belly-laughs and stuff.'

Andy Gill, *Q*, May 1992

The Return of the Saint

James McNair

It's five minutes to eleven on Sunday morning in Brompton Road, London SW3, just past the Victoria and Albert Museum and up the hefty wooden portals of the Brompton Oratory. A Catholic mass conducted in High Latin is about to begin.

Inside, all is ritual, serenity and intercession, an atmosphere redolent of *The Name of the Rose*. Heavy-laden candelabras form a city of tiny lights. A pipe organ slowly empties its long metal lungs as a procession of holy men trundle in as if on castors. There's a silence, then a baby burbles into the cavernous quiet. The congregation are seated, unaware that they have a rock star in their midst.

High in the altarpiece, cherubs recline on clouds set in skies of kingfisher blue, whilst underneath, against a backdrop of golden finery and white marble, stands the priest. The hypnotic pendulum swing of the censer frees the mind, releasing delicate puffs of incense smoke like dry-ice for the righteous. The scent of frankincense slowly shins up the nostrils of Nick Cave's blunt nose.

The choir begins to sing, their a cappella incantations beautiful and mysterious. Each note dies, then ghosts on in two seconds of natural reverberation. The congregation are expectant, focused. The first reading is taken from Luke 24, in which Christ returns to His loved ones . . .

Some months later and a few tube stops further north, Nick Cave and I take our pews in the rather less salubrious setting of the Portobello Café. We commune over coffee, Cave reclining with legs crossed in a voluminous armchair, fag as prop. He's come straight from the airport, having just flown in from Amsterdam.

With evening falling in Notting Hill, much of the light in the spacious upstairs room comes from the open fire. Its yellow-white flames are reflected on the lenses of Cave's Eric Morecambesque glasses. It is not, however, quite the right moment for a 'Wey-hey'.

'Very often people are driven towards a spiritual life through the failings of their personal life,' Cave muses. 'In the Brompton Oratory I was thinking about a particular girl that had left me, and found that the church wasn't a lot of help. I went along more for the event really, for the Catholic mass in Latin. When I go to church I have to take so much of it as metaphor, and I find it very irritating. The sermons are often pathetic and untrue, based on terrible misrepresentations of the Bible.

'But I like the order and ritual of a church service, the way it facilitates some kind of spiritual meditation. It gives me an elevated feel about the mundane. I'm more aware of things. It would manifest itself in the way I behave towards other people. There's so much mystery and beauty within the word of God, and what becomes the sermon is often just an awful demystification of that. For me, this whole business is very much a journey that I'm doing on my own. The very foundation of my spiritual belief is doubt about the whole thing. I haven't had any great epiphanies. I just feel it's my duty to educate myself about the concept of God.'

At eight years old Nick Cave was a choirboy at the Wangaratta Cathedral. At art college in the mid-'70s, it was the Renaissance and Gothic religious paintings which excited him most. His ten albums to date with the Bad Seeds are saturated with Biblical imagery, and the title of his 1989 novel *And the Ass Saw the Angel* (which sold a respectable 50,000 copies in paperback in the UK) was taken from Numbers, Chapter 22.

Lapsed heroin addict and alleged misogynist he may be, but when it comes to God, Nick Cave has read the book, and thoroughly. But what kind of rock star prefers church to MTV Awards ceremonies? And what specifically has led Nick Cave to the Brompton Oratory? If there's a crisis, it's not in his career. The formerly self-styled King Ink may still have his raven barnet, but the further he's wandered from his Gothic roots, the more successful he's become. Consider the *Murder Ballads* album – on *Top of the Pops* with Kylie; *a deux* with PJ Harvey – which has become his biggest seller to date, shifting around 800,000 copies worldwide. Not bad when you consider that it was ostensibly an exercise in genre-specific songwriting: a somewhat throwaway record cobbled together in the studio to buy time for an infinitely more personal and intimate work.

That was *The Boatman's Call*, Nick Cave and the Bad Seeds' forthcoming album, due for release in March. Sparse, stark and unrelentingly honest, the record seems likely to become the career milestone for Cave that *Blood on the Tracks* was for Dylan. And it's on this new album that Brompton Oratory slots into place, one of the twelve confessional songs which intimately portray recent events in Cave's private life.

It seems that there are several songs on the album which concern the mother of your son Luke, Viviane Carneiro, and others about PJ Harvey . . .
Well, hopefully the songs work in some kind of way without having to worry about the 'who' of them.

Yes, but inevitably people will ask who those particular songs are written about.
People will ask, but I think there's enough said in the songs. I did my best to articulate for myself what went on as accurately and clearly as I possibly could,

and I think I did that quite well. There were some things going on that I wasn't aware of at the time, so there are inaccuracies in the songs – and I can only talk about this in the most general of terms – but as far as I'm concerned they tell the truth about what went on as I understood it at the time. 'Far from Me', for example, documents the slow deterioration of a relationship, and the song was written throughout its duration. It starts quite beautifully and ends quite bitterly. There was something significant about writing that way at the time, and about actually getting it right. In the past I've fallen prey to tendencies to write things that simply sounded good or rhymed well, though they didn't convey what actually happened or what I actually felt or meant.

'People Ain't No Good' seems to relate the collapse of your relationship with Viviane.
Well, yes it does.

In the last three verses there's some lyrics which say: 'But that's just bullshit/ People just ain't no good.'
It's a comment on people's morality. I'm not saying that people are *bad*; I'm saying that people aren't any *help* – that ultimately, we're no use to each other. What I'm trying to put across on this record is that we have each other, and it's really not enough, but it's all that we've got. And there's a religious side to this record too. I don't believe that God is there to make us feel better, to intervene and change things. God is there as a higher entity beyond our questioning. We're given brains and hearts and wills and each other, but in the end it's just not enough. We're locked into our own worlds, and our own obsessions and problems. We can get support from each other, but there are things that happen that just can't be fixed.

And you felt you'd reached that point with Viviane?
Well, I think most of that's there. I was pretty straightforward with the stuff about Viv, and I've been exposing our relationship in one way or another on record for years, so I don't think it's really fair to open it up anymore than that in interviews. I write about it because that's what I have to write about. I think Viv understands that to a certain degree, and so she accepts what . . . she puts up with what I write. But I don't think it does any of us any good to talk about this kind of thing in interviews.

There's always been conjecture about the women you've been close to and their representation in your songs; Anita Lane is associated with the tracks 'Lucy' and 'Six-Inch Gold Blade', and some people recognised Viviane in 'Lament'. It's clear that 'West Country Girl' and 'Black Hair' from the new album are about PJ Harvey . . .
And 'Green Eyes' is about Tori Amos, the line about the 'twinkling cunt' particularly . . .

Are you taking the piss?

No, it is. She sews sequins into her pubic hair.

You have first-hand knowledge of this?

Yeah, absolutely . . . I've never really been asked before who songs are about, not until this album. People work their way up to the big question about Polly Harvey by talking a little bit about Viv, who no one's actually interested in at all, because there's no copy in it.

Did you have any misgivings about identifying PJ Harvey so clearly or detailing your relationship so intimately?

I don't know that I did.

A 'West Country Girl' with a 'heart-shaped face', 'widow's peak', 'black hair' and 'lovely lidded' eyes?

Well, I don't know. I just wrote some stuff and it came out that way.

'Are You the One That I've Been Waiting For?' discusses the idea of the perfect love, the perfect partner. Do all relationships have their shelf-life?

I don't know. These songs were written over a period of time. Some of them are very optimistic, some aren't. I'm not an authority on relationships. I'm not an authority on much at all, I don't think. I'm simply trying to write the songs in the best way I can, and each song is very much tainted by the way I feel at the time of writing. So there are no ultimate points being made here about love, or about God, or whatever . . . I have felt distrustful and bitter about relationships, and that's there on the new record occasionally.

You've been working with Mick Harvey for around twenty years now. Does he still play a key role as a sounding board for your ideas?

Not really, no. There are occasions when someone in the group will turn around and say that they think a song's not very good, or that they think I'm slightly misguided about something. There was one song which I'd written for my kid which was going to be on the album – a pretty sentimental piece of crap, actually – and Blixa [Bargeld, one of the Bad Seeds' guitarists] took me to one side, patted me on the shoulder and said, 'Why don't you spare the world this particular masterpiece and give it to Luke as a gift when he's a little bit older?' Ha ha. I was pleased that he said it. I can get very angry when I'm allowed to gnaw away endlessly on an idea which actually isn't very good.

I do like to record all the songs that I write, though, because otherwise I forget them and they get lost. For me, it's a way of making concrete a memory or a feeling which can become tainted, or which the future often dismisses in some way. And that's particularly true where relationships are concerned. I know that there are songs where I've felt a particular way about a particular person, and when I've recorded them that's down there in black and white, although perhaps two months down the line I can't conceive that I could possibly have felt that way. So sometimes later when all is bitterness, I'm reminded that there was actually something good there once.

For years Mick Harvey was the one who was able to reassure you about the quality of your songs.
Actually, I think nowadays I spend more time reassuring everyone else that the songs are okay. On this album there are certain issues that I'm dealing with lyrically which are possibly quite hard to swallow for certain members of the group. I'm dealing with things that are ultra-personal, and certain religious notions. There's a polemic there, a statement being made, that they simply don't agree with. This is becoming more and more clear, although it hasn't caused any friction between us. Before, I would use religious imagery in a fairly vague, colourful way and it was tolerated. I mean, it still is, but I know that there are things which I say in these new songs which some of the band just don't believe. I've had to persuade them to stand by the songs, to see them through to the end – and they have. But they've made it very clear that these are *my* particular views. They're not Mick Harvey's or Blixa's.

So really this is the closest you've come to an out and out solo album?
In a way, yes. All of the songs were written very much on my own, and I was very much absorbed in my own world at the time of writing them. Blixa would be saying, *[puts on German accent]* 'So why am I here then, why am I here?' And I'd be saying, 'You're here because I like the economy of your guitar playing and the fact that you don't feel the need to play over everything.' It's ironic that it's the largest band photo we've ever had on an album, but there's hardly any instrumentation on it. Everyone in the band suppressed their ego for the greater good of the record. Apart from me, of course, ha ha. My ego runs riot, as ever. The album was recorded quickly, so it retained some of its freshness in my mind. The idea was to preserve the rawness of the demos, and some of the songs were actually only re-recorded for academic reasons, to get separation between a vocal track and a piano track so that the songs could be mixed properly.

You have been portrayed by friends as someone who has always had a natural rapport with kids. There's a line in 'Where Do We Go Now But Nowhere?' about a child being startled by the crack of a drum and pressing his tiny fingers into your hand.
Actually, I'm describing a time when it was carnivale in Brazil; we were watching a parade and I was holding this little Brazilian kid's hand. What I was trying to say was that the feeling of his fingers pressed into my hand kind of prefigured the birth of my own son in some way . . .

I suppose Luke was a natural choice of a name for your son . . .
Yeah, there were only four to choose from, really *[smiles]*. He just really loves me

and accepts me, and that's a great feeling. He doesn't question who I am. Yet. I'm able to be myself with him, and that's very liberating. And I've found too, that over the last couple of years I've become very connected to *my* father, which is something I hadn't really thought about that much since he died. *[He was killed in a car accident in 1978.]* Being with Luke I find I remember my father a lot more. As a father the only reference point I have is my own dad, and I feel now that I'm able to do all the great things he did for me with my own son. Also I feel that I'm able to repair some of the mistakes that he made with me. I see it as a kind of evolutionary process from one father to another. I'm a slightly refined model of my own dad. I'm very much like him in personality – self-interested.

You'll be forty this September. Do you mourn the passing of the years?
I feel like I've reached forty and I still don't know anything. I'm still struggling with relationships. I feel that one should accumulate some knowledge about how they work, and how one can go about making them work properly. I'm still constantly baffled by the situations that I find myself in. So it's not like I'm entering middle-age thinking that I can relax, because I don't feel that I have life sussed out in any way at all. I think there are certain social skills which I didn't learn properly because I was preoccupied with other things. So far I've invested an enormous amount of time and energy into writing and solitary activities, and I've come out of the whole thing with somewhat retarded abilities where relationships are concerned.

When the author Martin Amis reached forty he described the awful realisation that girls in the street now looked straight through him, that their eyes didn't 'snag' on him anymore. Surely that's one problem you won't have to face?
I don't know, ha ha. I never had the feeling that girls did that anyway, and I've never felt that I was that attractive. Martin Amis is a good-looking guy. He has a certain charm.

James McNair, *Mojo*, March 1997

From Her to Maturity

Jennifer Nine

All they wanted was the usual holiday snap of hell. But there was a human being standing in the way.

Let me explain. We are in the gardens of the Rodin Museum in Paris, standing in front of the sculptor's massive, slate-black masterpiece, *The Gates of Hell*. Nick Cave, rail-thin and besuited, bounds up the steps of its platform until he's looming right up against those bleak, twisted portals that point to some human-forged abyss of godless night.

Knowing what I used to think I knew about Nick Cave, it's the perfect photo opportunity. Though only if you're unaware of *The Boatman's Call*, which is both the most astonishingly, fearlessly gentle record of his long and brilliant career and the most considered refutation of elements of his own back catalogue by any artist I can think of. But if you did consider only that seductively savage back catalogue, you'd figure there'd be no songwriter more suitable to be captured on film in front of an inferno: Milton's, Sartre's, the Old Testament's – take your pick.

As it happens, the Dutch tour group behind us, clutching their cameras and craning over Nick's angular shoulders, give no indication they know who he is. So the *carpe diem* moment passes unseized.

Anyway, this isn't the sculpture Nick wanted to show me.

'It's up this way,' he says.

And then, as though it were the most plausible thing in the world, Nick Cave takes my hand. My hand, not knowing quite what to do, scrabbles back. And we go up the stairs into the museum, creaking on our thirty-something knees as children clatter around us, until we reach a cabinet in a corner.

Nick crouches almost double to show me what's inside. A small, seemingly unfinished pieta grave; in rough plaster, in which an agonised, recognisably human Christ on a brutally truncated cross is enveloped by the rounded, pitying form of a naked Mary Magdalene.

Nick Cave onstage at the Town and Country Club,
Kentish Town, London, 12 October 1986.

'That's my next album,' says Nick simply.

I think this is what's known in the trade as A Clue.

Though it's not the first clue, in fact, or even the twelfth. That honour goes to the dozen rich, warm and meditative songs on *The Boatman's Call*. It's still Nick Cave – that velvet baritone, those effortlessly articulate lyrics, the elegant accompaniment of the gifted Bad Seeds.

But it's not a Nick Cave record like any other. Held up against the previous output of a man known, in both the Birthday Party and now, for mayhem-filled performances and a lexicography of gleeful savagery, it's quieter, more melodic, more vulnerable. More human. You might even say, it occurs to me as we dawdle over tea in the museum's outdoor café, that it's not even the work of the same man.

You'd be hard pressed to deny the visceral beauty and musical influence of Nick Cave's recorded output. At the same time, you'd be hard pressed not to notice that this brilliance has frequently been a vehicle for some of the cruellest, and most seemingly misogynist, scenarios in music. This is, after all, a man whose last album *Murder Ballads*, all rollicking penny-dreadful carnivals of violence, led less respectful critics to ask why the previous eight albums didn't bear the same name.

Condemning Nick Cave for the frequency with which women get stabbed in his songs mightn't be the most cogent of critiques, but it's one I haven't been able to talk myself out of so far. And, given that Nick claims to remember everything ever written about him in the English music press good or (especially) bad, he probably knows it too.

And, as I'm humbled to realise, I'm greeted with a generosity and graciousness rare in any man or artist, let alone Saint Nick. We drink the tea he offers to pay for. We make little jokes and laugh at each other's.

Nick tells me, 'There's a hole in my life called football, a football-shaped hole,' and we giggle like truants escaping from Lad World. He smiles, sadly or maybe just tiredly; he tells me he's sober now but almost winces at the thought that I might ask a supplementary question. So I don't.

He pats a passing wayward child – about the age of his six-year-old son Luke – but jokes that having a child has made him more irritated by other children, rather than less, even if he has 'infinite patience' for his own. And then he tells me astonishing things.

'No, I never thought I'd be able to carry an album on vocal strength,' he confirms of the sparse settings of *The Boatman's Call*.

'I've always lived with the fact that I can't sing, but in fact it's not actually true. It's just that often I'd not been in any condition to sing. And I guess with this record and with these shows, it requires a certain restraint and sobriety to pull it off. It just doesn't work any other way.'

Some people will always think a loud noise is more exciting than a yearning, vulnerable one.

'Well, I've always been of that school,' he admits. 'I've done that to protect myself, I think, over the years. Now I wonder what I was trying to protect myself from. There was an incredible amount of bluster, and a way of using words in order to hide behind them, to obscure what I was actually saying. To use characters, and storytelling – this was all a form of protection. It was a world I'd invented which I could escape into; my own little mythological world full of stock characters and a certain type of woman, with certain personalities and pursuits. And I think that this particular record is stepping out of that; just making a record about the way things are and have been over the last couple of years. Without hiding behind metaphor.'

He pauses and looks straight back at me. 'It's quite difficult to talk about it. I feel quite exposed about it. But it's kind of a relief as well . . .'

In the past, some of what you've written has seemed incredibly contemptuous of women, I say carefully. There's no hesitation in his reply.

'Well, I feel that . . . I feel bad about that, actually. I feel that I've misrepresented women in my songs and I've actually misrepresented the way I feel about them. I invented a type of woman that I used artistically in order to dump all my ill feelings and suspicions on. And that's actually not the way I feel about them.'

So, what would you take back?

'You can't take back what . . . no,' he shakes his head. 'But I do feel the need to apologise about some of it. There was deliberate perversity and vindictiveness in a lot of what I wrote. I wrote a lot of stuff for the wrong reasons, I think, in order to hurt people. Used the fact that I could make records, so that other people could hear what I thought about particular people.'

It's a great platform.

'Yeah,' he nods. 'You can get up there and . . . and they just have to be the object of your vindictiveness; quietly sit there and take it.'

Which is great for boys, I say doubtfully.

'Well, a lot of women responded to it, strangely, very positively,' Nick counters. 'Or maybe not positively,' he smiles a little. 'But they were attracted to it in some way.'

Women write letters to serial killers, too.

'Yeah,' says Nick, nodding. 'Yeah, that's right.'

Has that platform ever been used on you?

'Oh yes,' he nods. 'And we're playing a song live now which is some sort of, uh, penance for me – "Stranger Than Kindness" – which is a song [ex-girlfriend and Mute artist] Anita Lane wrote about me. Seems to be,' he shrugs. 'And it's a very pissed-off song, but very beautiful, too. So yeah, I have been the subject of those kind of songs.' He pauses. 'And I'm sure there's more to come, too.'

He doesn't say where those might come from. It's commonly thought that the songs of failed and star-crossed relationships on *The Boatman's Call* which are not about Cave's ex-wife Viviane might be about a West Country Girl named Polly Harvey. No, I don't mention her name. No, of course he doesn't, either.

You've always surrounded yourself with creative women. Have you ever felt you neglected their creativity in favour of your own?

'Yes. I guess a lot of the creative women around me suffered through the drive I had – were consumed by it, in a way. Anita, especially, is an incredibly talented person and gave a lot of ideas. Gave them to me; she was very generous. And after a while, that seemed to become her role. To give over herself to me while I just raged forward. I didn't do it deliberately,' he adds. 'I guess the pattern of my past relationships has been that I've met very strong women and, through the course of our relationship, have exhausted them in some way. And it's something I've had to face up to: why is this happening?'

'I'm in a fairly unusual situation now of being, um, single,' he adds suddenly. 'And that, for me, is pretty much the first time since I started all this . . .' He waves a hand. 'So, maybe that gives me some kind of opportunity to look at what's going on.' Nick stirs his tea. And begins again.

'I've painted a picture of past relationships, a pattern, but there have been newer relationships where I have invested a lot of time and interest and care, and put my whole heart into it. And then found that it availed me of nothing. And I was left with – um . . .' He looks away. 'Well, I was left.'

He laughs the smallest, saddest laugh I've ever heard. 'And that is a difficult lesson. That all the love you have, sometimes it just isn't enough.'

So, love can't move mountains after all, I mutter.

'I believe it can,' he replies. 'It's just finding out a way to do it.'

I assume the women these songs are about can see themselves in them. Not because you put their home addresses in, or anything . . .

'No, journalists put their home addresses into them,' Nick laughs, a little bitterly.

Didn't it make you feel vulnerable knowing that we would?

'A lot of those songs are written specifically for a person or . . . began as poems to a person,' he explains, delicately hovering around the word 'person' like it's a haven of privacy in this most unprivate of conversations. 'And then I thought, I can't just allow that to be a poem, I'd better put some music to it and stick it on a record. But they did begin as letters or poems, to a particular person, in order to . . . to show that person how I felt about her.'

Did it work? Nick sighs almost imperceptibly.

'It worked, in its way. But all the songs are different; they're talking about different times within a relationship. I mean, it's my form of communication. I'm not very . . . I find it quite difficult to communicate in other ways. Or I don't feel that I'm actually getting it right. But I can sit down and write about it, and I feel I am getting it right. At the time it seemed like the right thing to do, to write these songs and to record them and sing them. I don't regret it now, because I love the songs. But they are private messages to people. To a person . . .'

Nick Cave turns forty this year. Though, even in the sunlight, I still think he looks like a little boy in his father's suit.

Did you ever think that age would alter things?

'I've always been terrified of burning out. I mean, I've looked at other people and seen what happened.'

And you have been known to stay up late yourself.

'I have stayed up late in my life,' smiles the man whose visceral performances were frequently thought to have been part of the classic more-drinks-more-chemicals superhuman rock shtick. 'But I don't have that fear anymore. Not that I don't think I'm going to burn out, but it doesn't worry me so much if I do. I think I have a kind of realistic enough grip on things to know when to stop.'

At twenty-five the idea of being a burnt-out case might seem appealing.

'It never appealed to me. The thing about being young is that you think you're the final product in evolution. You are invincible. And nothing can hurt you. And people don't count.'

Ah, the solipsism of youth.

'Yeah. You can say I said that if you want,' he laughs. 'Though I can't even pronounce it. And that's fantastic. But I've had a kid and I understand I'm actually not the be all and end all of everything. I mean, it's something that young people quite rightly don't have to deal with and that's a great thing. But I do feel kind of more insignificant now. Though I still run to what I do, and hold it up and say, Look, I know I've done all this stuff, but look, I also did this. I made a record.'

Do you worry about being alone when you're old, through not having been good to the people around you?

'I haven't been that bad,' he chides, gently.

Do you feel like a grown-up yet?

'I dunno,' he shrugs, then laughs. 'Do I appear like one? I find it very easy to come down to my son's level. That's the secret of child-rearing, and I find it particularly easy to do. I think that's something my father and other fathers had difficulty doing – to be childlike.'

What about adolescence?

'Well, there's that,' he grins. 'I'm trying to rid myself of my adolescence, and I think I'm doing a kind of reasonable job of it now. But that took quite a while. I don't like being adolescent, I don't like adolescents. I don't really like young people, actually. I mean, I spent forty years getting away from young people, and I'm quite happy for it. With my music, I feel I'm talking to people my own age,' he says frankly. 'I don't feel I'm talking to the youth of today. They may respond to it in some way, but . . .'

Would your eighteen-year-old self have agreed with your views?

'Probably not, no,' he admits. 'Would have been horrified. And if he was sitting here now listening to me talk, he'd probably gob on me or something. But there you go.'

Are you frightened, or interested, by the way bodies decay as we get older?

'I'm kind of interested in where I'm going in that respect,' he says. 'I quite like the things about me that set me apart from being young, physically. And I'm looking forward to accumulating some more,' Nick Cave smiles.

'I always find the knee drops are really easy, it's just the getting up that's increasingly hard and embarrassing! I guess the idea, in a metaphoric way, is to dispense with knee dropping at a certain age. No, I still manage to sort of stand

and waddle around the place,' says the man who'd need another four stone to be 'filled out', let alone waddle.

But some fans still want you to be that brilliant adolescent.

'I don't want to be,' he says firmly. 'I don't want to be what I was. I'm tired of what I was. I mean, you'll see at tonight's show; we're doing a very different sort of thing.'

But perhaps people who remember your illustrious past will say, 'I liked it better when I thought he was going to beat the fuck out of the audience.'

Nick shrugs, and then smiles mischievously.

'Yeah. But they've been saying that for years.'

And then Nick Cave walks back past *The Gates of Hell*, and out of the Rodin Museum, and into the Paris spring.

Jennifer Nine, *Melody Maker*, May 1997

The New Romantic

Ginny Dougary

If you didn't know what Nick Cave does, you would be hard-pressed to guess. In the past couple of years, he has delivered a religious broadcast on Radio 3, contributed to the *Times*'s Op Ed page, alongside John Major, with a column on what Easter means to him, penned an introduction to Saint Mark's gospel in Canongate's bite-sized versions of the Bible, with writers such as A.S. Byatt, A.N. Wilson, Louis de Bernieres, Fay Weldon and Will Self, and been a visiting lecturer at an academy of poetry in Vienna; in three days time, he will be giving a recital on the love song at the Royal Festival Hall, and he is director of this summer's arts festival, Meltdown, on the South Bank. He has been the subject of a biography, the author of a novel which attracted some glowing reviews, including one from the *Daily Telegraph*; he has written film scripts and appeared, as himself, in Wim Wenders's *Wings of Desire*, and as an actor in a number of less memorable films. It's an unusual curriculum vitae, especially for a rock star.

Cave appears to have entered the ranks of the great and the good without really trying, and certainly without much fanfare. As a gifted writer with an abiding interest in literature, religion and art, it is perhaps not surprising that Cave has harnessed himself to projects beyond the narrow perimeters of pop. But how many of his fellow musicians could command comparably lofty platforms from which to broadcast their views, or the licence to experiment from within the portals of such august institutions? Cave is not, after all, a well-connected Brit but an Aussie outsider.

What is surprising is that he remains a marginal figure in the music business, albeit mega in those margins. When Cave and his band the Bad Seeds played at the Royal Albert Hall some years ago, both nights sold out; five hours after the box office opened, the tickets for Cave's solo show at the Royal Festival Hall had all gone. He is – what people often fall back on when describing an artist who is difficult or difficult to place, and Cave is both – a significant cult figure.

But why isn't he huge? His love songs on *The Boatman's Call*, Cave and the Bad Seeds' most recent album of fresh material, were a revelation to me when I first heard them a few months ago: sweet and melancholy, stripped back to the raw emotion and sung with the voice of a wayward Elvis Presley. I am not alone in thinking they are up there with Van Morrison and Dylan; everyone to whom I've played them has the same reaction. 'The guy's a genius!' they say, and 'Why haven't I heard the songs before?' The singer, of course, is partly to blame. He may have appeared on *Top of the Pops* with Kylie Minogue, for whom he wrote the murder ballad *Where the Wild Roses Grow* – and what a strange pairing that was – but the success of the single was a commercial deviation for him. He wrote it, not because he wanted a Top 20 hit, but because he liked to play with the tension between the darkness of the material and the lightness which Kylie projects. He is quite clear about his desire to conduct his life and career on his own idiosyncratic terms. In 1996, for instance, he was shortlisted for an MTV Award for Best Male Artist – but asked the organisers to withdraw his nomination. 'My muse is not a horse,' he attempted to explain in a letter, 'and I am in no horse race and, indeed, if she was, still I would not harness her to this tumbrel – this bloody cart of severed heads and glittering prizes.'

While he clearly had a lot of fun spinning his excuse – he sounds as arch and overblown as the Scarlet Pimpernel – the gesture can hardly have endeared him to the powers that be in the international music scene. Cave's habit of disappearing in foreign cities for years at a time – Berlin for much of the '80s; São Paulo in the early '90s – has not helped to build a serious profile in this country. And, of course, there have been some more self-destructive habits along the way.

Our first encounter is in Amsterdam, where Cave is performing in a kind of lit-rock festival at the Paradiso, billed alongside various artists with out-there names like Furry Green Lamppost. The Paradiso used to be a church and is one of the legendary venues, where everyone has played from Janis Joplin to the Rolling Stones and the Sex Pistols; in the late-afternoon gloom and empty, it looks tarnished and slightly seedy.

On the stage, Cave's elongated form is hunched over the piano like an up-ended U. He is wearing a skimpy V-neck sweater and with his eyes closed and his face pointed skywards, he could be a twelve-year-old boy. Since he is, in fact, forty-one, in the looks department at least, he is a disgracefully good advertisement for bad living. After an hour or so of faffing around with the sound engineer, Cave comes over to join a group of us.

Away from his piano, Cave towers over us but doesn't stoop. Walking back to the hotel at some pace, I clock the familiar wings of bat-black hair, the white face, blue eyes and cupid's pout. In his scuffed shoes, a fake fur collar adorning a long black coat, he has a certain theatrical – Aubrey Beardsley meets Withnail – a thrift-shop elegance. His people keep telling me what a great time it is to interview him. Why? He's so happy. He's so open. He's so well. He's in love.

Before the gig, there is a dinner for Cave and his friends in an old-fashioned seafood restaurant. It's a strange, slightly strained event. Everyone would like to talk to our host, but since he exudes all the hail-fellow-well-met bonhomie of a Howard Hughes, it does not make for an easy flow of conversation. Among the guests is Cave's new paramour, Vivienne Westwood's erstwhile muse, the model Susie Bick – who appears to have made liberal use of her boyfriend's hair-dye.

Bick is exquisite. She has a porcelain face, phosphorescent green gaze and a breathy, cut-glass little voice – rather like a posh Una Stubbs. With the *dansant* frock, antique clasp-bag and demure manner, she feels distinctly unmodern. She and Cave sip mineral water and smoke a great many Marlboro Lights. I ask him whether he's suffering from pre-concert nerves. No, he says, slightly bullishly. Then he grins and admits, 'Well, yes, actually – I am.' Moments later, as if to comfort himself, he folds Susie into his arms and kisses her. We all look away. But for some reason it's not embarrassing, just rather sweet and unaffected.

There's a commotion on the steps of the Paradiso, and a sign on the heavy wooden doors informing the crowds that the gig is SOLD OUT. Cave takes to the centre of the stage and starts to read his introduction to Saint Mark from the small book in his hand. The piece is long but the Dutch tend to speak English fluently, and Cave seems to carry them. As befits a former place of worship, the atmosphere is solemn, even reverential. Of course, it is equally possible that the fans have been stunned into silence by the oddness of this incarnation. Cave's voice is rising, clear and loud, and his body rocks as he describes his early love of the Old Testament, with its malign God and presence of evil so close to the surface, 'you could smell its mad breath, see the yellow smoke curl . . .' Give him a backdrop of cornfields and a southern twang, and he could be Flannery O'Connor's crazy-eyed preacher in *Wise Blood* (a book Cave knows and loves).

And now there are murmurs of recognition and approval from the congregation, as Cave says, 'But you grow up. You do. You mellow out . . . You no longer find comfort watching a whacked-out God tormenting a wretched humanity as you learn to forgive yourself and the world.' In his pre-teen choirboy days at Wangaratta Cathedral, he tells us, he was singularly unimpressed by the Anglican Church: 'It was the decaf of worship,' he sneers, 'and Jesus was their Lord.' And on he goes, via references to Holman Hunt and the odd Latin and Hebrew quote, to explain how Christ came to illuminate his life – through the Gospel According to Mark – 'with a dim light, a sad light, but light enough' . . . and on and on, accelerating as though wary of imposing upon our patience as he reaches his triumphant conclusion: 'Christ understood that we as humans were forever held to the ground by the pull of gravity – our ordinariness, our mediocrity – and it was through his example that he gave our imaginations the freedom to rise and fly. In short,' he stares out into the dark, 'to be Christ-like.' It's hardly rock'n'roll, but they like it.

Cave may have grown up, but he is still a perverse cove. His desire to move and shock – the function, he believes, of art – remains intact. Perhaps a religious reading is the '90s equivalent of bashing his fans over the head with a microphone. 'To get up and speak about matters like that is pretty much the last thing you can annoy people with,' he confirms. 'Because in my business God has a very, very bad reputation. He needs to get a new spin doctor . . . and I'm the man for the job.'

The rest of the set goes well. Post-Mark, the proceedings still have a gospel feel. The audience mouths the words to the songs or joins in. People sway arm in arm; a number of them weep. As Cave sings his anthem of disappointment 'People Ain't No Good', a young man plucks my sleeve, tears streaming down his cheeks, and tells me how the song speaks straight to him, confronting him with how badly he has treated his estranged brother and how he must make amends.

When he was a child, Cave tells me back in London, he and a mate would get driven miles out into the bush by his mate's dad, who would deposit them with a six-pack of beer and a couple of shotguns and instruct them to kill as many living things as they could. The boys were twelve at the time. Cave is the father of a seven-year-old son, Luke, and he's been thinking that was a pretty rum way to handle kids.

First novels have a reputation for tending towards the autobiographical. *And the Ass Saw the Angel*, Cave's fictional debut, would not appear to conform to that pattern. It is an extraordinary story – both compelling and repellent – of Euchrid Eucrow, the mute surviving twin of a grotesque alcoholic mother and a sadistic father, who is the outcast and antichrist figure of a warped religious community. It is full of Old Testament imagery welded onto the imagination of a serial killer, informed by a love and knowledge of the literature of the American Deep South. The novel is littered with the carcasses of small birds and creatures, captured or shot, which makes one think that those trips into the bush and the ensuing carnage must surely have made an imprint on the child's psyche.

Cave's writing has impressed some of the most respected young guns in publishing. Jon Riley, who bought the paperback rights to *And the Ass Saw the Angel* for Penguin, struggled to persuade his superiors that the acquisition was a good idea. Penguin stumped up £25,000 for the rights. Since its publication in 1990, the paperback has sold 75,000 copies and continues to sell steadily.

Richard Beswick, editorial director of Little, Brown, whose authors include Beryl Bainbridge and Gore Vidal, says of Cave's writing: 'Most literary novels look linguistically impoverished compared to his. If I'd been publishing fiction at the time, I would have jumped at it.' Instead, he commissioned a biography of Cave: *Bad Seed* by Ian Johnston, which has also enjoyed healthy sales – about 30,000 copies – since it was published in 1995. 'There's a very good crossover audience for Cave amongst literate rock fans,' Beswick says, and less reverentially, 'There's also substantial sleaze and some great photographs of him rolling around on broken glass.'

Cave arrives bang on time for our meeting, dressed smartly in a grey suit and white shirt. The rendezvous is in the library – appropriately since much of our conversation is about books and writing – of one of those discreet, old-fashioned hotels which seem to be popular with the rockerati. There is an interesting tension, a word he employs a lot, between his manner: still amiable, as it was in Amsterdam, and his body language, which is guarded. Before we get properly stuck in, Cave tells me about his mental filing cabinet in which are stored all the names of the journalists and critics who have offended him – which is less intimidating than it sounds. What people tend not to get is that Cave is funny, with that laconic, deadpan wit shared by larrikin Australians from Bob Hawke to your outback cattle drover. After his attempts to give me a preview of his forthcoming gig, for instance, he assumes a baleful expression and drawls, 'Thousands of people send their tickets back.' Knowing how seriously – and quite rightly – Cave takes his writing, I ask him somewhat tentatively whether he wishes he had been as rigorous in the editing of his novel as he was in his new songs. I preface the question by asking him if he minds me making a comment about it. 'Yeah. You can make a comment,' he says darkly, 'I'll log it in there,' tapping his high forehead.

During the years in which he wrote the book in Berlin, Cave's lifestyle was chaotic, to put it mildly. Rock hacks used to lay bets on who was most likely to die of an overdose onstage first, Keith Richards or Nick Cave. At one particular low point of his addiction, Cave resorted to dealing heroin and was thrown out of the room in his shared apartment when it became a shooting gallery. Writing the novel is what Cave believes kept him from going under. I ask him if there were any times during his work in progress when he wasn't off his face? 'Erm, no,' he says, 'but that suggests that you don't know what you're doing and you're wandering around in a stupor. I was taking speed a lot, and the thing about that drug is that it keeps you totally in the moment. It doesn't allow anything else in. I think I would have written the book anyway, I would like to say – and it could well have been a better book. Part of its obsessiveness and the way I was living at that time was to do with that.' Cave's tiny room was transformed into a sort of fetishistic aide-memoire; the walls were covered with a mixture of religious and pornographic images and a wig of a young girl's hair. 'It became a very similar world to the one I was writing about in the book,' he recalls. 'It was very tangible and different, populated with the people that I'd invented. It was a place I retreated into . . . It afforded me some relief.'

I ask him whether he considers that his writing, his art, is at the centre of his life. 'I think that attempting to strive at some kind of happiness in my life is more important,' he says. 'And I have to say that I feel happy quite a lot.'

Would you say that's your natural disposition?

'No, I don't think so . . .'

Is it because you're in love?

'Yeah, now I can never remember being sad,' he says, mock-mawkishly. 'But even despite all the disasters and catastrophes and the debris around me, I always got my sense of fulfilment from being able to write and come up with things that I felt good about and that if I hadn't had that artistic endeavour, I don't think I would have been allowed to survive.'

Allowed?

He sighs and shifts around in his seat. 'Oh no, I'm going to sound like Glenn Hoddle . . . but I feel I've been protected in certain ways by other, other . . .' he looks into my eyes, 'by God.'

So you link your creativity to God?

'Yeah.'

You think it's a God-given gift?

'Yeah.'

You talk about being in the presence of God. What does that feel like?

'Despite what's gone on in my life, I've always felt it. I just had a different concept of what it was. For a long time I felt it was a malign presence, and now I see Him as benign,' he clears his throat. 'It feels like a sense of being protected.'

There is a clear interconnection between the defining patterns in Cave's life: his drug addiction, his spiritual faith, his belief in his own creative powers, his touchingly transparent desire to hold on to the idea of true love, his attachment to artistic outsiders, and his complicated relationship with his father. There may be an element of self-dramatisation in the version Cave presents of his life story to me, but he seems to think that he was born a bad seed – shall we say – who has had the good fortune to be redeemed by a compassionate God. At one point, he says that if he had discovered heroin when he was a child, he probably would have taken it. He was one of four children, with two older brothers and a younger sister, and discovered that the most effective way of getting attention was to be a troublemaker. It is quite hard to picture him as a choirboy. At twelve, he and his gang of friends would drink themselves sick on cheap sherry. At thirteen, he was expelled from Wangaratta High School for attempting to pull down the knickers of a sixteen-year-old girl; her parents tried to press charges of attempted rape. By the time he left his new school, Caulfield Grammar in Melbourne, in 1975, Cave had formed his first band, the Boys Next Door, and discovered the joys of shocking his fellow pupils by wearing drag. On to art college, where Cave maddened his modernist teachers by decorating his workplace with prints of classical religious paintings. After failing his second-year exams, he concentrated on the band full time and hung out in St Kilda, the low-life area of Melbourne. By the time he was twenty-one – the year of the death of his father – Cave was already injecting heroin and speed. Colin Cave was a teacher of maths and English, and the director of adult education in Victoria. He was passionate about language and literature, and determined to pass that love on to his youngest son. In his Radio 3 broadcast, Cave recalls being ushered into his father's study to listen to 'great bloody slabs from Shakespeare's *Titus Andronicus*, or the murder scene from *Crime and Punishment*, or whole chapters from Nabokov's *Lolita*. My father would wave his arms about, then point at me and say, "This, my boy, is literature."' What Colin Cave really wanted to be was a writer himself. His son remembers seeing in his desk 'the beginnings of several aborted novels, all neatly, sadly, filed and titled'. When the boy was about twelve, his father asked him what he had done to assist humanity. When, stumped for an answer, the son turned the question back on him, Colin Cave took out a couple of short stories which had been published in magazines. 'And I shared in his pride as he showed them to me,' his son came to write many years later, 'but I noticed that the magazines were of an earlier decade and it was clear that these two short stories were tiny seeds planted in a garden that did not grow.'

Fuelled with enthusiasm, the young Cave went off to write what he admits was bad poetry and worse songs; none of which had the desired effect of pleasing his father. 'At some point, we became very competitive. I believe it was when I started to have my own ideas about things, and he wasn't particularly interested in that,' he recalls.

Was that hurtful to you?

'Oh yes,' he says. 'I just wanted to impress him. I thought that he was what it was all about.' Cave's behaviour at home and at school – extreme by the standard of even the most difficult adolescent – put further strain on the relationship between father and son. His mother, Dawn, a librarian, whom Cave describes as a 'very brave, intelligent, sturdy woman who just gets on with things', has always been unconditionally supportive of him. His father, in contrast, was not. And although Cave can see, now that he is a parent himself, how unbearable he must have been – 'a self-made monster in his very home' – it has taken him a long time to forgive his father for turning away.

Colin Cave died in a car crash in 1978. The news came through when his wife had gone to bail their son out of St Kilda police station, for the umpteenth time, where he was being held on a burglary charge. It is hard to think of a more harrowing context in which to hear of the death of a parent to whom one is unreconciled.

'Because I was there with my mother when we heard, it was quite painful and after that I don't really remember anything,' he says. 'I can remember going home in the car with my mother, and then . . . I don't remember the funeral or anything that happened afterwards. Pretty soon, I just left. I think the trauma makes you shut down until you're able to deal with it. Certainly, that's how it felt for me.

'I think that my father lost out on a lot of what's happened after his death, and I do feel a sense of regret about that. Considering that all I ever wanted to do was to make him proud of me . . . He died at a point in my life when I was at my most confused.'

In the years that followed, it must be said, Cave seemed no less confused. Wherever he lived – Melbourne or London or Berlin – he would be accused of glamorising heroin. Inevitably, in such a long interview, we talk about Cave's relationship – and it seems correct to call it that – with the drug. What really aggravates him is the way society demonises the drug-user. 'How are we supposed to look at junkies?' he asks. 'As the scum of the earth, so we can all feel better about ourselves? It's like the sex offender in prison; mass murderers can feel okay because at least they're not sex offenders. It seems like everyone needs someone under their heel . . . I was a heroin addict because I couldn't stop taking drugs. In fact, I didn't want to stop taking drugs. I liked taking drugs. That's my own choice, really, and I don't think I did glamorise it. I wasn't much of a glamorous figure back then, to be honest.'

Certainly, there doesn't sound anything very glamorous to me about all the times he lay sick and shivering, wrapped up in a blanket on a mattress on the floor. Or the state of mind he must have been in to write lyrics with a bloody syringe while travelling on the London Underground. (He doesn't much like it when I remind him of that episode either.) And it can't have been the last word in glamour to have to score in some dive every time you arrived in a new city. Or, indeed, to be a serial overdoser.

It is striking that what he admires about his cultural exemplars – from Van Morrison to the reclusive J.D. Salinger (whom he has invited, in a dangerous fit of optimism, to appear at Meltdown) to the Chicagoan outsider artist Henry Darger – is their refusal to run with the herd. 'I think the heroin addict becomes one in order to separate himself from the rest of society,' he says. 'It's a very masochistic act. For a long time it served me well, but there did come a point when it became intolerable. When it became clear to me and a lot of people that it was interfering with things that were ultimately more important to me – like my artistic aspirations.'

There was another impetus. In 1988, Cave was arrested in London for possession of heroin and agreed to undergo treatment for his addiction in order to avoid a prison sentence. He was not incarcerated in Priory-style rehab-deluxe but at a clinic in Weston-super-Mare which he describes as a brutal, shaming place.

'I don't think that just because you take drugs you should be made to feel like a degenerate,' he says, with feeling. 'When you go into a place like that, you don't really have much of your personality intact. You don't go there because everything's okay.'

As far as the CV goes, Cave endured his two months at the clinic and has remained on the straight and narrow ever since. But there have been various hints to various journalists in the intervening time which suggest that this is not the complete picture. And he tells me that he has been to rehab clinics more to his liking since his sojourn in Weston-super-Mare. It is almost as though it is a point of honour for him not to perpetuate the myth that he hasn't touched hard drugs in the past decade. Plenty of celebrities wouldn't feel the need to be so honest, I say, why do you?

'I won't be bullied into taking drugs or not taking drugs,' he says. 'I'm not a repentant ex-drug addict. I feel I have every right if I want to take drugs to do so.' And do you? 'I don't actually,' he says. 'I'm not taking drugs at the moment.'

There is only one point during this exchange when my questions seem to upset Cave, and I see now – in hindsight – that the awkwardness of his answers may have had something to do with his struggle to keep on an even keel. He had always hoped to become an artist; painting for him was the pinnacle of the creative ladder and rock music was rock bottom. For many years – but no longer, he insists – he felt like an impostor, a practitioner of an art form he disdained. But when he talks about the artists he admires – the ones he would exhibit if he could at Meltdown – what seems to grip him is the effect on their art as their minds deteriorated. Over lunch, he tells me about Louis Wain, an Edwardian artist whom he collects; a painter of cats in unlikely poses, playing cricket or a church organ, and how as Wain's psychosis deepened, the faces of his cats began to dissolve and unravel on the page. And of Henry Darger, who was raised in institutions and stayed at home seeing no one and creating a world of conflict between good Christian girls, cut out of catalogues and blown up with a projector, fleeing from anti-Christian forces who are hunting them down. Cave says that what he admires about their work is the excellence of the execution and their 'terrible beauty'.

I say that I read somewhere that he sometimes felt the need to take heroin to dampen his creativity, which suggested, intriguingly, that it was his art which was dangerous for his health rather than the drugs. 'Well, yes . . . I go through cyclical periods of being very up and hyper, a feeling of incredible inspiration and a kind of super-capability – and with that comes,' a rueful laugh, 'a voice, and it's my voice, and it observes and chatters away and always has something to say – about doing the dishes, or whatever – and it just rattles on and on. I can feel my whole body changing and it's exhausting. It also affects my judgment.'

Have you always had this?

'It's difficult to say, because it's something that makes itself apparent when I don't use drugs.'

How about in your teen years?

'No, one of the ways – oh God – one of the ways I've dealt with that in the past is to . . . I know exactly what will shut it all up. Unfortunately, it's very difficult for someone who is a junkie to go and take heroin once. So these days, I would try and deal with that stuff in a more appropriate way.'

Like?

'I have to . . . I have to . . . ration the kind of things I allow myself to get excited over in order that I sleep, which is the other problem with it. It would seem if I get involved in certain things creatively, it can lead to this sort of cycle . . . I also go through periods when I don't do much and don't feel inspired, and I don't feel very good during those times either.'

I ask him if he is a manic depressive, and he sighs and groans and rubs his hands through his hair. Why do you think you find this such a difficult area to discuss? 'Because,' a long silence, 'I'm not sure why.' Because it's scary? 'It is, actually, to be that way. It is quite scary.'

Do you think you're going nuts?

'It's just that I've not had much experience with it, and I'm trying to go through it without doing the drugs. I don't really know if I'm . . .

'I can't label it, and I don't want to do endless interviews about being a manic depressive – "Are you up or down today?" If I understood it better and that was the way things were, I could come out and say that I was bipolar – or whatever they call it. I'm not a doctor or a psychiatrist, but I do know they're discovering more and more forms of manic depression, and medication to cope with that.'

The most beautiful song for me on *The Boatman's Call* is 'Into My Arms'; the one Cave chose to sing at his good friend Michael Hutchence's funeral. The first two verses start with the things he doesn't believe in – an interventionist God, the existence of angels – and the last one deals with the redemptive power of love. Part of the strength of the songs is the nakedness of the emotion, unmasked by metaphor or allegory. It's all there for everyone to see: his love affair with Luke's mother, Viviane Carneiro, the Brazilian fashion stylist who was the reason why Cave transplanted himself to São Paulo, and its painful end; his doomed romance with PJ Harvey in 'West Country Girl', with her black hair and heart-shaped face and broad accent. I wonder, again, why he had felt the need to be so open; to paint the pictures so vividly.

'In order to write a worthwhile love song, it needs to have within it the potential for pain or an understanding of the pain of whatever you're writing about. I don't think they allow themselves to be written until I've fully experienced what it is I'm writing about. They wait patiently to be finished.' One can only hope, in that case, that the Songs of Susie will remain incomplete. He says, when I ask him, that he has never been married but likes the idea of it. And that he would like to have more children. And that, yes, he is in love and very much believes that she is the one (that he's been waiting for) . . . 'But I do have a past and I do have recollections of the way things go.'

Are you waiting for disappointment?

'When things go well, I'm often surprised and expect that it will be taken from me in some kind of way,' he says. 'But I'm not feeling like that at the moment. I'm feeling very happy.' I point to the scar on his cheek – which looks like an errant dimple – and he tells me it was an old domestic wound: 'I was stabbed in the face with a vegetable knife.' I wonder, thinking about the scar, whether his relationships with women have tended to be confrontational.

'In the past, I've had extremely volatile relationships in that way . . . but I think that there have been influences within that – alcohol and drugs – which exacerbate that kind of behaviour,' he says. 'What's going on at the moment is that I really value what is there, and I feel that I have some chance of making it work, which I've never really felt before . . . and with anything of value, you take care.'

When I ask him what makes him happy in life, he says: 'My son, my work, my girlfriend.' He's been with Susie, this time around, for six months – and is staying in her Chelsea home until he moves into a house he has recently bought on the river. Luke continues to divide his week between his mother, who lives in West London, and his father – but Cave admits that now he is living with Susie it makes things a bit more complicated. He has another son, Jethro, more or less the same age as Luke, who lives with his mother in Australia. When I ask Cave whether he has a relationship with this son, he says that he does, and that 'it's great' and 'he's coming here, actually, to live for a year'. Will you see a lot of him? 'I will, yeah.' So, soon, life is likely to get considerably more complicated.

He says that he's a hands-on dad and was a great nappy-changer. How did you find that? 'Interesting. Scary. Overwhelming.' Until recently, when Cave was living on his own, Luke used to share his bed, and now 'he's been booted out of it. So that's been one of the great wrenches.' He seems to take his parental role pretty seriously; he's there for the swimming galas, and speech days, and all the cringe-making stuff like the Dads' Egg and Spoon Race. But what they like doing most together is talking. I imagine Luke lying in bed, struggling to stay awake, while his father tells him stories of far-off places, and good and evil, and bewitching damsels with emerald eyes and ebony hair, who rescue poor travellers who've lost their way.

At the end of our lunch – during which Cave eats heartily – he asks me for the time and jumps up, stricken, when I tell him. 'Oh God, if I don't go now I'll be late for Luke,' he says, looking like the twelve-year-old I first saw. 'You know what it's like in the playground; I'm terrified of getting into trouble with the teachers.' His father, I think, would be proud of him.

Ginny Dougary, *The Times***, 27 March 1999**

Let There Be Light

Jessamy Calkin

Warracknabeal is a small town 180 miles north-west of Melbourne. It would probably be overlooked in the great scheme of things, apart from one significant fact: it is the birthplace of Nick Cave, singer, songwriter, author, who with his band, the Bad Seeds, has achieved enormous acclaim in the UK and heroic status in Australia. In fact, in a recent issue of the magazine *Australian Style*, he was awarded – along with (even more implausibly) Kylie Minogue – the title 'Australian of the Century'.

Cave has plans for Warracknabeal. He has commissioned a statue of himself atop a rearing horse, and hopes to erect it in the town square. And not just any old statue; this will be a life-size bronze made by sculptor Corrin Johnson, the man responsible for two Christian martyrs above the main entrance to Westminster Abbey, and the man who constructed the Princess Diana Memorial.

The statue will be cast in Britain, shipped to Australia and then driven across country to Warracknabeal. The Australian director John Hillcoat is making a documentary about it: the statue's trip in a U-Haul, the attempt to get the mayor to agree to it, the unveiling, the flock of limos and the velvet suits, the disgruntled locals. There will be a plaque, of course, which will read, 'Birthplace of Nick Cave'.

Is he serious? Well, that is the question. Nick Cave likes to ride a very fine line with his humour, which is dark and convoluted and heavy with irony. He likes to provoke and to subvert the obvious. It is a principle which can be equally applied to his new look. He describes it as New Labour: a cross between Tony Blair and Tony Montana (*Scarface* is one of Cave's favourite films). Today he is wearing – and let's not underestimate this – a toffee-coloured cashmere checked jacket; a brown woollen tie purchased at Selfridges; an almost imperceptibly striped white cotton shirt, a pair of dingo-coloured soft suede loafers. He is also wearing a pair of jeans, and they are from Gap.

Which is ironic, considering that a few years ago Gap asked Cave to appear in

Nick Cave onstage at the Kilburn National, London, 14 July 1988.

one of its advertising campaigns, and he replied with a letter: 'Dear Gap. I might put on a pair of your jeans if you were to pay me £1 billion, but even then I would have serious reservations. Signed Nick Cave.' And now he has to buy his own.

In the beginning, in Cave's wardrobe, there was a pair of leather trousers and a T-shirt saying 'Jesus'; there was a carrier bag full of flowery see-through shirts more often than not made out of his girlfriends' dresses; there was a green suit with trousers so tight that when he was strip-searched at an airport once he couldn't get them off; there were cowboy boots so pointed that the toes curled up completely, like elves' shoes.

In the late '80s there were cardigans, white patent-leather loafers and loud checks; a few years later there was a baby-pink Take That T-shirt for the video of 'Stagger Lee'. And running through this collection was an endless array of elegant suits and implausible ties. Cave has been described as 'the tapeworm that ate Elvis'. Gap just didn't fit into this sartorial equation.

But the main reason for this spurning of Gap is that Cave doesn't do advertisements, or allow his music to be used for them. He was not tempted by the sanitary towel manufacturer that wanted to use his song 'Red Right Hand' for its television advertisements. If he were to lease his music out for commercial gain, he says, his muse would desert him.

'I get letters from people telling me they got married to "The Ship Song",' he says, 'or that they buried their best friend to "Into My Arms", and I don't want them to look at the TV and see that they buried their friend to a Cornetto ad or something. I feel some sense of responsibility about that, even though they wave enormous sums of money at you. That's where my muse puts her foot down.'

We are sitting in Cave's office in Chelsea and his muse is all around. His muse, the creative impulse, whatever you like to call it, is what separates him from his contemporaries, what elevates him to the heights of the truly great songwriters, what keeps him sane – though in the past it has nearly driven him insane – and what has probably saved his life. It sustained him through days of starving and freezing in London squats in the early '80s with his first band, the Birthday Party, through endless touring with the Bad Seeds, through hangovers and overdoses, through addictions and clinics, through rootless years in São Paolo and Berlin. It was a lifestyle that could have claimed much lesser constitutions and warped much lesser spirits than Cave's.

'I think I have always had a pretty strong creative impulse,' he says carefully. 'And that has probably saved me from abandoning myself completely. I just don't think I would have allowed it.' But it is a dark gift of the gods and Cave is a driven man. In the old days he would write all the time, anywhere – lyrics on scraps of paper, in countless notebooks. He would even cart around carrier bags of books and papers covered in his spidery writing. For three years in Berlin he laboured over his novel, *And the Ass Saw the Angel*, tapping away on a manual typewriter in a cubbyhole in someone's flat. Sometimes he would wake up the next day with letters imprinted on his face from where he had slumped, asleep, on to the keys.

But now Cave has tamed his creative impulse; he has disciplined it for many reasons. When he starts writing, he says, it's almost as if a physical change comes over him; he feels very disconnected from everything, lost in his own world, and it can sometimes take hours for him to reconnect. 'It's almost like a chemical reaction. I feel different in my body – something changes, and I feel very isolated and estranged from things.'

So these days he is very organised; he has become a nine-to-five man.

It was here, in his office, from nine to five, that he wrote his new album, *No More Shall We Part*. 'I'd gone through a bit of a slump after *The Boatman's Call* [his last album]. I wasn't blocked but I felt a bit disgusted with the whole thing and I didn't really feel like writing. A couple of years later, I wanted to write again and I needed a place to concentrate in, so I got an office. And it has just grown into a place of retreat. It's a very protected environment, completely about my work, and I really like it here.' It is part of a large industrial building in Chelsea, divided into units, and there is a photographer working beneath him who frequently complains that the plaster is raining down on him from the ceiling. It is just Cave's fierce foot-tapping while he plays the piano.

The office is a large, cold room, dominated by a Napoleonic camp-bed thoughtfully placed there by his wife, Susie, and a 100-year-old Steinway piano which was a wedding present from her parents. There is an antique desk covered in bottles of Evian, ashtrays, piles of books (*Pascale's Pensées*, a poetry anthology) and an iMac, at which Cave is peering, keen to get back to the task in hand, which is writing a film script for his friend, John Hillcoat. It is set in the outback.

The name 'Samuel Stoat' is visible on the screen. 'Stoat: Flies? Don't worry about flies. You kill one, Charlie, and a dozen more turn up for the funeral.' Samuel Stoat is one of the film's main characters: a filthy, big-nosed, long-haired, bad-complexioned man with a beautiful voice – based, so Cave tells me, on Tony Cohen, the Bad Seeds' wild and wildly talented engineer.

Cave eyes the tape-recorder quizzically; he has always hated interviews, although recently he has become much more adept at them. 'In fact, I only talk in quotation marks now. It's the other sort of talking I can't do.'

The trouble is, he says, that journalists seem to think they have to ask him certain questions – you know the kind of stuff. Drugs. Murder. God. 'People think I'm a miserable sod but it's only because I get asked such bloody miserable questions.'

Whereas he'd much rather talk about, well, lighter things. Like fashion. So how do you like women to dress?

'Miserably,' he yawns. 'No, I have a thing about knees actually. I do like the hem of the dress to . . . glance upon the knee.'

Smart?

'Yes, smart. I like a dress that's tight in the body . . . and shoes that are not too high – but I like a heel that flexes the calf muscle.'

Hats?

'I'm not big on hats. Although Susie did have some kind of hat on when I first met her – a Philip Treacy creation – which I thought was kind of fantastic . . . with a tiny veil and little black feathers.'

In the summer of 1999, on the day of the eclipse, Nick Cave married the English beauty Susie Bick. Susie, thirty-four, is epically sweet and endlessly feminine. She is the kind of girl who always serves tea in china teacups with roses on and lights scented candles everywhere; her curtains are made of velvet; the furniture is covered in ribbons and lace; she wears pale-pink cashmere and summer frocks; and she is all green eyes and black, black hair with skin like cold white marble.

They met, says Cave, at the Natural History Museum, under the tail of the brachiosaurus. At a fashion show, then?

'Er, yes.'

And did you fall in love with her straight away?

'I did, yes. I thought that she was the most beautiful woman I had ever seen in my life. And continues to be. Even elbow-deep in baby shit she looks pretty good to me.'

Did you feel a sense of destiny that you haven't felt before?

He grunts a little, looking pained. 'Something very different has happened with Susie. It's the realisation at forty-three years of age that a relationship isn't something that just sort of blazes with fire for two months and then hits the decline and carries on downhill until the whole thing lies exhausted in the gutter. I've discovered that things go up and down and you can actually work through things and love the person more, stuff like that – it's quite extraordinary.'

Do you think it's because you've got older? Or you've met the right person?

'It's because it's the right person. I've found someone who really likes being with me. She thinks I'm really great. And just likes me the way I am . . . I think.'

They now have twin boys, Earl and Arthur. Although they own a houseboat in Chelsea, for the moment they live in an ordinary terrace house in an ordinary street in south-west London. In the sitting room a fire burns; there are pictures by Cave's favourite artist, Louis Wain (the mad-cat painter) and a piano with its middle keys worn away.

Sometimes when Cave comes home he feels a bit disorientated because Susie tends to move the furniture around a lot; it's one of her eccentricities and her husband speaks fondly of it, sings fondly of it, in fact, in a song called 'The Sorrowful Wife'. But today he is sitting securely on a bottle-green damask sofa reading a newspaper, an item which he never used to even glance at, but which now, he admits slightly sheepishly, gets delivered daily. 'Tell me,' he arches an eyebrow. 'Do people read the whole thing?'

He has enjoyed the newspaper experience, he says, seeing where everything fits in the world, piecing together its politics. 'I think people just assume I'm a kind of cretin about things like that. Or that I have no interest, that I'm just locked away in my little world, tapping away at the typewriter.'

And to a certain extent they would be right. It has very much been his own world. In the early days, Cave's lyrics revolved entirely around a world he had created, a world full of retribution and desire and violent, vengeful gods; obsessive, poetic tales of love destroyed and innocents smote down. They were epic, literate stories coiled within a song.

It was the Old Testament Nick. Now Penguin is publishing his collected lyrics, more than twenty years of work, and Cave recently had to proofread them. It was the first time he'd seen them like that, all together on paper, clinically divorced from the music, and though he was in many ways impressed, he was also shocked by how fixated he'd been on a particular theme in song after song.

By *Let Love In*, released in 1994, it had all become a bit more personal, and by the time of *The Boatman's Call*, three years later, the lyrics were agonisingly intense, eviscerating in painful detail his breakup with his Brazilian girlfriend, Viviane Carneiro, and his short-lived, emotive affair with Polly Harvey.

'My lyric writing reached some sort of hysterical crescendo about the time of *The Boatman's Call*, reporting what was going on in my life in the most melodramatic way; ordinary stuff magnified to heroic proportions. And I find it very difficult to listen to that record now because of that.' He thinks that, in many ways, it is quite a beautiful record and that he'd probably like it if he hadn't made it himself. 'But . . .' he screws up his face, 'sometimes it sounds like the moaning of a dying insect.'

No More Shall We Part is, lyrically speaking, more open to the world. Cave's songs seem to have a higher intelligence about his life. The album has its surreal touches – Cave must be one of the few people who can get away with beginning a verse, 'I'd given my nurse the weekend off . . .' – but it is a beautiful record, full of sad melodies. It is in many ways a love letter to his wife; she certainly fares better in it than his previous girlfriends have in past records. And the one constant through all of Cave's albums is his love songs.

He has even lectured on the subject. 'The Secret Life of the Love Song' originated at the invitation of the Poetry Academy in Vienna in 1999. 'The peculiar magic of the love song,' he wrote, 'if it has the heart to do it, is that it endures where the object of the song does not. It attaches itself to you and together you move through time . . .' He delivered the lecture and then went on to teach fifteen carefully selected aspiring writers for a week-long workshop on the love song.

'I have very clear memories of being about twelve years old,' he said in his lecture, 'and sitting, as you are now, in a classroom or hall, watching my father who would be standing up here, where I am standing, and thinking to myself, "It doesn't really matter what I do with my life as long as I don't end up like my father." Now, at forty-three years old, it would appear that there is virtually no action I can take that doesn't make me more like him. At forty-three years of age I have become my father, and here I am, ladies and gentlemen, teaching.'

Nick Cave grew up in Wangaratta, a large country town in Victoria. His father was a teacher of English literature who went on to become director of adult education in Victoria; his mother was a school librarian. Cave spent most of his time outdoors, hanging out by the river, jumping over train tracks, tying up his younger sister, that sort of thing. He and his friend Eddie Baumgarten would be driven into the bush by Eddie's father, issued with a six-pack of beer and a shotgun and told to shoot anything that moved.

'We shot rabbits,' says Cave wistfully. 'Rabbits with myxomatosis that couldn't see us coming so we would walk up and shoot them, executioner style. Poor bunnies.' When they were twelve, Nick and Eddie started the Triple A club (Anti

Alcoholics Anonymous); they would get local taxi drivers to buy them drinks then hole up in a garage somewhere, get drunk and throw up. It was Eddie's sister, Anne, who introduced Cave to Leonard Cohen, and they would sit in the dark, listening to *Songs of Love and Hate*.

Constantly in trouble at school, Cave was sent to boarding school in Melbourne; later his parents moved there and he became 'a day scab'. At school he met Mick Harvey, his long-term collaborator, and they started a band. Cave's father – who had planted the creative seed in his wayward son by introducing him to good literature – was beginning to wonder what on earth he'd created and, as Cave grew older, he found himself competing with his father in a way that wasn't entirely healthy. 'I would look for things he didn't know about, holes in his knowledge. I would read up on lots of obscure French literature and take it to him and say, "Have you read this?" But he was pretty clever, my father, and he would always win and I would walk away with my tail between my legs.'

When Cave was nineteen his father was killed in a car crash, a tragedy which he learned about at the police station where he was being hauled over for some minor misdemeanour. After his father's death, says Cave, he just took off and didn't stop or look back for twenty years.

What do you mean, took off?

'Left. Just sort of blasted forth, out of Australia. I didn't really feel anything for a long time, I just took off. It was as if I couldn't stay still. It was the suddenness of it, and the fact that things were really incomplete and very confused for me at that time.' People who have an absent or dead father often have remarkable motivation, an insatiable drive. 'I'm sure that's true of me. It was as if I could never do enough.' It's only now, with children of his own, that he feels better able to understand his father.

In London, Cave's band, the Birthday Party – who were wild and poetic and apocalyptic and mad – was signed by the revered Daniel Miller to his newly formed label, Mute Records, in 1983. Six weeks later, they split up and Cave and Mick Harvey created the Bad Seeds. 'At the first Bad Seeds gig ever, nearly twenty years ago,' says Miller, 'I remember having my breath taken away. Both bands were like gangs in a way, but the Bad Seeds seemed like a gang with a massive purpose.' Warren Ellis, who now plays violin with the Bad Seeds, also remembers meeting Cave around this time. 'I first met Nick in a Melbourne house I used to frequent. One of the women living in the house wouldn't allow anyone else to sit in the chair he had sat in – I was very impressed by that.'

Eleven albums later, credit must go to Harvey for keeping the Bad Seeds together all these years, both musically and practically. An arranger and very talented musician, in the old days Harvey would play virtually everything in the studio (and indeed onstage, at one time or another): drums, keyboards, guitar, bass. He attributes the longevity of the Bad Seeds to the fact that the band don't see much of each other because they all live in different countries and that almost all of them have their own separate projects, musically. 'And,' says Harvey laconically, 'we don't have that problem of democracy that other groups have. We're all perfectly entitled to our opinions, but if Nick really wants to do something, he'll do it.'

Having known Cave since their schooldays, Harvey says that although their relationship has changed over the years, Cave hasn't: 'He's always been an egotist, he's always craved attention – and he's still like that. He's always been very creatively driven, with quite high ideas about what he could be, he's always had this wild streak, and he's always been very generous and lovable.'

But outwardly, things have altered. The crazy, drug-fuelled days are over and have been for some years. Cave is calmer, more open. 'I'm doing pretty much what I want to do, and there isn't that horrible sense of panic that I used to have about everything. I used to feel that I was just clinging on to something, which was primarily about my work, but also about the relationships I was in. I felt that I was hanging on by my fingernails to everything, and that it was all just slipping away.'

The high esteem in which Cave is held culturally has enabled him to broaden his interests. In the summer of 1999 he directed the Meltdown Festival at the South Bank Centre, putting together ten days of music and performances from his favourite artists, from Lee Hazlewood to Les Patterson.

In 2003 he will be musical director of an extravaganza to be put on by the Sydney Dance Company. Musically, Cave is neither mainstream nor superstar (the Bad Seeds have never done particularly well in America) but in the particular niche that he occupies, he is very significant indeed. His concerts always sell out and his albums continue to sell substantially, long after their release. Despite an acrimonious relationship with the press in the past, acclaim for Cave's albums has grown stronger and stronger, with some critics rating him alongside Dylan, Van Morrison and Leonard Cohen as a songwriter. Among his contemporaries he is unusual in that, from a very promising start, his work has just got better and better with age.

Bob Dylan sought him out at Glastonbury in 1998 and wandered over to tell him he liked what he did ('It was as if God came out of heaven,' Cave said later); earlier, Dylan had even allowed Cave to add to the lyrics of his song, 'Wanted Man'. On his last album, Johnny Cash paid him the compliment of covering Cave's song, 'The Mercy Seat', and Leonard Cohen said of Cave's version of 'Avalanche', 'I really like it. He really goes out with it, makes the song alive. Not that I've ever abandoned it. I've always felt good about that song. Or bad. Whatever the feeling is.'

The Bad Seeds' bestselling album was *Murder Ballads* (1996). It sold a million worldwide, partly because of the single 'Where the Wild Roses Grow', a duet with Kylie Minogue which reached the Top 20 in Britain. 'It started as a joke,' says Cave. 'It wasn't supposed to be an important record, and it sold way more than anything we've ever done. It was almost a hit,' he adds worriedly. It is a dark collection of droll little songs, like 'O'Malleys Bar', in which a psycho wanders into a bar and shoots everybody. *Murder Ballads* was a comic opera of a record, and mostly it was taken in the right spirit, except, predictably, in America, where one journalist asked Cave, 'What are you going to do next, an album of rape ballads?'

A few days later, in a studio in Battersea, south-west London, a video shoot is being set up. 'As I Sat Sadly By Her Side' is the first single from the new album.

John Hillcoat, who has directed many of Cave's videos, is in charge. It is a song about seeing the world in two different ways. A row of mirrors has been set up to reflect the projected footage: multiplied images of planets exploding, roses blooming, kittens fighting and a carousel out of control, creating a kaleidoscopic effect. The strains of the song and its plaintive vocals are all around, along with a regiment of technicians, assistants, cameramen and hair and make-up people.

In the middle of all this stands Nick Cave. It is cold and he is wearing a rather incongruous item, a sort of blue-and-white padded jacket like you might find at a yacht club.

'It's very you,' says one of the technicians.

'Isn't it,' says Cave in a deadpan and slightly camp way. 'I'm a chameleon. Like David Bowie.' He takes the jacket off to reveal a black suit and stands there, only slightly self-conscious, with his awkward gait and big hands, overblown gestures, furrowed brow and his funny little tapping dance.

Later, his nine-year-old son, Luke, comes to visit the set and stands watching in his school blazer, swaying slightly to the music. He looks very much like Cave, although his colouring is that of his mother, Viviane Carneiro, who split up with Cave several years ago but still lives in London with Luke.

Having children, says Cave – who is a very hands-on father – makes you feel connected to the world. To Luke, having a famous father means that his dad is invited to his school in west London to take part in the Week of the Voice. The idea was that he should educate the children about rock'n'roll – along with Bruce Dickinson from Iron Maiden, whose son is in the same class. Dickinson, it has to be said, holds slightly more sway, having been on *Top of the Pops*, 'while I'm just some gloomy old git who sits at the piano moaning on about this and that . . .'

Luke, says Cave, has never really known his father do anything else and is quite bored by the whole thing. He prefers Green Day, a recycled punk band. Sometimes, in the car, Luke will say, 'Listen to this, Dad. Did you ever play real music like this?' And Cave will reply, his knuckles whitening on the steering-wheel, 'No, son, I never played music like this.'

Next month the Bad Seeds are going on tour again, and although Cave won't be doing anymore kneedrops (years of doing them have taken their toll on his knees, and his spine has suffered slightly from the backflips he used to do onstage with the Birthday Party) he sees no reason why he can't go on performing live indefinitely, 'as long as I can do it with a certain amount of grace'.

In the past, he would cling on to things in the fear that they might evaporate. Now his life has attained some sort of order. He has just a handful of friends ('Why is that?' he asks. 'What's wrong with me?') and he has his family and work. When pressed, he says he has no guardian angel. 'But I have something which seems to be a marriage of my conscience, my muse and God – and maybe it's all the same thing, I don't know. But I feel protected by that.

'That and the missus.'

Jessamy Calkin, *The Daily Telegraph*, 17 March 2001

Nick Cave: Renaissance Man

Robert Sandall

These days Nick Cave is an early riser, up at 5:00am. Well before most of the other residents of the genteel seaside town on the South Coast where he and the family moved in the spring of 2002 have so much as boiled a kettle, Cave is striding off to a rented studio he calls his 'office'. On one side of the room stands an old upright Yamaha piano, on the other a desk with a word-processor, an ashtray and a profusion of papers and books, prominent among which is a well-thumbed copy of Roget's Thesaurus.

Between these two work stations Cave divides his solitary day, pausing at lunchtime to grab his regular penne napolitana from the Italian at the end of the road. He brings it back and eats it at his desk, then resumes: sketching out tunes and lyrics for the next album, writing down fugitive thoughts for future essays or songs, adding to a film script commissioned by his friend the director John Hillcoat, smoking roll-ups, sometimes, quite often, even, just sitting. 'For a lot of the time you don't do anything,' Cave explains. 'It's intensely frustrating.'

What comforts him is the thought that 'the idea that you're destined to burn out isn't necessarily true'. Until about five years ago, when he met his wife Susie and finally gave up shooting heroin, he admits that he had 'bad working habits. I was always surprised when another album eventuated.' Now that he has realised that 'inspiration is important but it's not the only thing', he applies himself more steadily. He recalls the novelist John Steinbeck's crack: 'I used to work six days a week but I couldn't stand it. So now I work seven,' and says he sympathises; although a five- or six-day week is his lot at present, because there's Susie and their two-and-a-half-year-old twin boys, Earl and Arthur, to attend to. 'And they do have an uncanny knack of disrupting the flow of things.'

Maybe. But at this point Nick Cave's highly idiosyncratic flow looks pretty unstoppable. Since he moved back to Britain from Berlin at the end of the 1980s he has recorded ten albums and repeatedly toured the world with his band the Bad Seeds in support of them, published an internationally acclaimed novel and two volumes of lyrics and miscellaneous writings, starred in the feature film *Ghosts of the Civil Dead*, which he also co-scripted, curated the 1999 Meltdown alternative music festival on the South Bank; oh, and sired four sons. He has turned up singing a duet with Kylie Minogue on *Top of the Pops*, written for the comment page of *The Times* on what Easter means to him, delivered a religious talk for BBC Radio 3, 'The Flesh Made Word', and given public lectures on the art of the love song.

On the face of it, Nick Cave is one of the squarest pegs ever to have been jammed into a round hole. Nowadays he sits comfortably alongside the artists he most admires, Neil Young, Leonard Cohen, Tom Waits and Dylan. When Bob came up to him at Glastonbury in 1998 to compliment him on his work, Cave says he was stunned and slightly embarrassed: 'I thought, Now just go away, don't say anything else,' mindful no doubt of the fact that he has covered several Dylan songs in the past, notably 'Wanted Man' and 'Death Is Not the End'. Few would have put money on Cave surviving to earn such an accolade twenty years ago. When he was fronting a noisy post-punk band, the Birthday Party, he looked all set to crash and burn. But despite his best efforts, he didn't, emerging instead as a songwriter and storyteller of doom-laden intensity and mordant wit; a staunch upholder of the traditional ballad which he freights with melodramatic violence and Biblical terror. He sings at times like a particularly sonorous Scott Walker grappling with a special and rather peculiar relationship with the guy upstairs. Mostly though, he sounds like nobody other than Nick Cave.

He does what he wants, when he wants to. 'I go through periods when I don't have any money, but it doesn't seem to make that much difference,' he says quizzically. Even now as a forty-five-year-old father with responsibilities – four sons by three separate relationships, two of which he conducted simultaneously, with the result that his oldest boy is only ten days older than the next – he says that he never makes plans for the future. He claims to have a 'reasonably steady income', thanks partly to demand for his songs to be used in films. But opportunities to raise quick cash by licensing his songs for adverts he has always rejected. He says he was once tempted to let a cheeky New Zealand-based sanitary towel manufacturer use 'Red Right Hand' in a TV ad, but held firm. 'Some of these songs are precious to people. I don't want to see them in an ad.'

In a three-way conversation with a couple of other uncompromisingly ornery types, Shane MacGowan and Mark E. Smith, recorded for the *NME* in 1988, Cave interrupted Smith's rant about how much he hated touring etc with a simple question: 'So why don't you just stop?' At which Smith, never normally stumped for a rejoinder, fell silent.

His view of the pop establishment, which still tries to claim him as its own from time to time, was best summarised in the announcement he issued declining an MTV nomination in the Best Male Artist category in 1996. 'My relationship with my muse is a delicate one at the best of times and I feel it my duty to protect her from influences that may offend her fragile nature. She comes to me with the gift of song and in return I treat her with the respect I feel she deserves – in this case, this means not subjecting her to the indignities of judgement and competition. My muse is not a horse and I am in no horse race and, indeed, if she was, still I would not harness her to this tumbrel – this bloody cart of severed heads and glittering prizes. My muse may spook! May bolt! May abandon me completely.'

There are a several unusual aspects to this rail-thin, whey-faced crooner of jet-black ballads, not least his uncanny resemblance, in both utterance and appearance, to the film character Withnail. He hardly ever uses swear words. He thinks long and hard before speaking, sometimes politely rejecting questions on topics he says he has covered elsewhere, or are too personal, with the result that the interviewer often feels like an interviewee. Some days in the past he has talked openly about, say, the sequins Tori Amos sews into her pubic hair, of which he has claimed first-hand knowledge. Other days he keeps schtum about his more colourful escapades. You never know when he will go stern and clam up or when his face will suddenly crease into a broad grin.

But the strangest thing about Nick Cave is that he is in many ways a product of his upbringing. The bookishness he inherited from his parents. Colin and Dawn Cave both worked at the local high school in Wangaratta, the provincial capital of Victoria, a hundred or so miles north of Melbourne. Mother was the school librarian, dad taught English. Of their four children, Nicholas, their third born, showed an aptitude for language and was duly rewarded by his father, an aspiring writer, reading to his twelve-year-old son from the classics of world literature. Dostoyevsky's *Crime and Punishment* made such an impression that Nick later named his band the Birthday Party after one of the scenes in the novel. 'My father was interested in the nitty gritty of writing, how to construct sentences, the effectiveness of alliteration.'

Cave has talked and written a lot about his complicated, antagonistic relationship with his father to the point now where, out of boredom or embarrassment, he prefers to avoid the topic. Instead he insists he had a happy childhood, 'with the freedom that people living in safe communities can have, in a time when the values of good and evil seemed to be more clearly defined'. He was, then as now, close to his older brother Tim, who loved music and introduced him to English prog rock. He also got into to old blues and country and discovered a curious affinity for easy listening, particularly the voice of Karen Carpenter.

The places he grew up, like the river in Wangaratta 'where most of my childhood was played out', is, he insists, always the river that features in his songs. He says his interest in the Bible stemmed not from his father, who never went near it, but from his experience as a ten-year-old choirboy at Wangaratta Cathedral. Adolescence, he claims, was a breeze, hanging out in Ned Kelly country. 'We would roam around the countryside shooting rabbits, drinking beer, doing all the things country boys do.'

But there was more to it than that. Cave 'left' Wangaratta High at thirteen after allegedly pulling down the pants of a sixteen-year-old girl and was sent away to a boarding school in Melbourne. There he befriended the son of a vicar, Mick Harvey, with whom he formed a rock band. A club called Anti Alcoholics Anonymous was another of his rebellious initiatives. Harvey has said that he thinks back then young Nick was a compulsive attention-seeker, hurt by his father's increasing absorption in his own studies, like his paper 'Ned Kelly: Man or Myth?' Whatever, before he left to study fine art at Caulfield Tech, Nick Cave already was what the world would later applaud him for being, a hell-raiser.

Art schools in Australia in the mid-1970s were not the same enlightened places that encouraged a generation of English artistically inclined rockers to experiment with sound and images. Cave says he 'wanted to be a painter, and I was dedicated to it, though I didn't do a lot of it, unfortunately, because I was dedicated to sitting in the pub talking about it with my fellow artists as well'. He admired, and has since learned to imitate, their industry: 'The thing about them was that they worked all the time. They got up in the morning and no matter how crapulent they were, they started painting. I was always impressed by that.' Impressed but at that time anyway, unmoved. At the end of his second year the only painting he handed in for assessment was a surreal piece in which a circus muscleman was depicted gazing up a ballerina's skirt. In the light of this, and of his continued involvement with a rock band, in the summer of 1977 he was asked to leave, 'which I never quite got over, I have to say'. His mother, he recalls, was equally distressed.

As the era of punk rock dawned in Australia, Cave's drift away from the path envisaged by his educated, middle-class parents accelerated. His raucous punk band, Boys Next Door evolved into a more theatrically noisy outfit, the Birthday Party, whose version of Screamin' Hawkins' 'I Put a Spell on You', accompanied by frenzied back flips from the singer, went down a storm with Melbourne's punk crowd. In the studio Cave would sometimes sing through a telephone, a trick he employed in imitation of the Cleveland art punks Pere Ubu. In concert, a mayhem of barely controlled violence led to one hapless punter getting kicked off the stage by the bass player and sustaining broken ribs. The band were avid drinkers, before and after gigs, and were consequently well known to the local police. When two of them were arrested for urinating out of the back of their moving van by a traffic cop convinced they were masturbating on a public highway, they missed the gig altogether.

By 1978, booze and sulphate were no longer enough to keep the twenty-year-old Nick Cave entertained so he took to buying $50 bags of heroin in Melbourne's port district. Thus began a love affair with the needle that was to last, with minor interruptions, for twenty years. Its onset coincided with a tragic, traumatic event which he now declines to discuss. On the night of 11 October 1978, while Cave was sitting in a Melbourne police station charged with various drunken misdemeanours, his father – the man who had taught him to love literature and writing and who couldn't understand what on earth his talented boy was doing making that unintelligible racket with the Birthday Party – died in a car crash.

For much of the next ten years it was hard to tell whether Nick Cave was heading up or down, though he was clearly headed somewhere. Bored with playing to 'the same 200 people in Melbourne', early in 1980 the Birthday Party flew to London, where they and their girlfriends shivered in a one-room basement flat in Earls Court for a while, puzzling over how 'dead' the post-punk scene here was. The song that finally got them moving in 1981, 'Release the Bats', was by no means typical of their challengingly jerky style; it was intended as a joke. But there was something about a tune naming bats, roared by a man called Cave who wore his long black hair teased violently upwards, which strongly connected with the emerging youth cult known as 'Goth'. 'We thought they were barking up the wrong tree. But we were in no position to pick and choose. A little bit of attention, perhaps wrongly applied, was better than nothing.'

Cave's memories of what happened next are, at best, hazy. 'I'd like to help you out there,' he says apologetically, 'But I'm not too clear about dates.' Small wonder. By now his drinking and his heroin habit were spiralling, and overdoses, enthusiastically reported by a prurient rock press, were becoming commonplace. After one gig at London Poly, Cave collapsed and was showered with banknotes by a disgusted promoter. He even once managed to pass out while being searched in the customs hall at Heathrow. But through it all, he and the band played on. 'I'm not sure the drugs made much difference,' he says thoughtfully. 'For twenty years I was on drugs all the time. I mean, it wasn't like there was a day with and a day without that I could compare.'

Moving to Berlin, one of the junkie capitals of Europe, hardly addressed the drugs problem; but it did enlarge Cave's artistic horizons. Initially, it just provided added opportunities to shock. After recording in the Hansa Studio, site of a former Nazi dancehall, the Birthday Party issued an EP with a barbed-wire swastika on the cover. But in other ways Cave was tiring of his reputation as a wild man. 'You'd be looking at the audience, they're all leering back at you, and you know they want you to do a back-flip. So you do one and feel like an idiot,' he told a journalist.

Within a year of meeting Blixa Bargeld, leader of the German industrial noise band Einstürzende Neubauten, at a disco near Imola, Cave was starting to think beyond the Birthday Party. Neubauten, the epicentre of a radical art scene based next to the Berlin Wall in the crumbling Kreuzberg district, were intent on destroying every convention of rock by 'playing' power tools, machinery and bits of scrap metal in a ferocious re-statement of avant garde notions of *musique concrète* or 'found sound'.

This appealed strongly to Cave's arty, confrontational and iconoclastic instincts. After Blixa and his gang leapt, fists flailing, to Cave's defence ('as they are wont to do') the night when a bunch of angry radical feminists invaded the stage, a firm connection was established between two men who agreed that rules were there only to be disobeyed. It wasn't so much that he enjoyed the sound of Blixa, with microphones on his chest, being thumped by a fellow band member; or listening to a similarly wired dog eating offal off the studio floor. But he admired the underlying spirit. 'I was much more conservative in my musical tastes. But I liked the way they turned their radical principles into something soulful and human. It was soul music.'

In a reciprocal gesture, Bargeld accepted Cave's invitation to play the electric guitar in his new band, despite the fact that the guitar was an instrument he had previously and very publicly scorned. 'I hate the symbolism of guitars, the guitar hero, so I shall try to do everything differently,' Bargeld announced when Nick Cave and the Bad Seeds were finally convened in 1983. Their name, tinged with filial guilt, was biblical, derived from Psalms 58, verse 3. To the added dismay of many of his old rock'n'roll fans, Cave's new songs were more narrative, lyrical and slower. To the bafflement of all but a few of the close friends and family who turned out for the first gig in Melbourne on New Year's Eve, he titled the show, after his late father's paper, Nick Cave: Man or Myth?

Unlike the Birthday Party, the Bad Seeds were conceived as a part-time outfit whose members were scattered around the world and often involved in other projects. So, by now, was Cave. Two friends from Australia trying to make their way in Hollywood, Evan English and Paul Goldman, had asked him to write a script for a low-budget movie they were trying to get off the ground: 'Because no one else that we knew could write.' The script of *Swampland* soon foundered for lack of funds and a clear plotline, but Simon Pettifar of the Black Spring Press, who had seen and admired Cave in the Birthday Party, was interested in what he saw as a maverick writing talent. Eventually it was decided that Cave would rewrite his script as a novel. 'Simon bought me a dictionary and a Thesaurus and off I went to Berlin to write the novel,' Cave states, matter of fact. And why the Thesaurus? 'It's my most used book and my most loved book. I use it to write with all the time. Don't you?' This is not a rhetorical question. It turns out that Cave's fascination with unusual words has led him, over the years, to compile his own dictionaries, in his own way. He explains that if he ever had cause to look anything up he would copy down all the entries he did not recognise on the two pages in front of him. (He likewise scours this conversation with occasional 'is that the right word?' inquiries.)

What with the Bad Seeds and the druggy distractions of Berlin, the novel took him three years to finish. Initially he tapped away on his typewriter in a tiny room on Yorckstrasse in a flat occupied by the Bad Seeds drummer Thomas Wydler and a German family. Surrounded by an avalanche of books and pornographic postcards, he became detached and uncommunicative, unhappy of the female attention he automatically attracted if ever he and Blixa went out. His old fondness for amphetamines would keep him indoors typing for weeks at a time. A girl named Elizabeth Streicher briefly tried and failed to interest him in marriage and her nice flat, but she found that Cave was more interested in shooting up and driving around off his face in her Opel car.

In Berlin's artistic circles, this sort of decadent behaviour was well received. 'Nick is dealing with his preoccupations as if he is trying to get rid of them,' said the movie director Wim Wenders 'He's almost trying to exorcise them.' And he duly cast Cave and the Bad Seeds, as themselves, in his film about Berlin, *Wings of Desire*.

But art and life proved uneasy bedfellows, and by 1987, Cave's life was a complete mess. The flat he had borrowed from a wealthy German friend,

Nick Cave on the road from Rio to São Paulo, 16 February 1994.

Christoph Dreher, had turned into a shooting gallery and Dreher was tiring of coming across strangers slumped in his toilet. He had run up large drug debts; and his stormy, on-off relationship with his girlfriend since art school, Anita Lane, was suffering from his recent liaison with a German secretary called, improbably, Bunny, whom he moved in with for a while. Lane tried to be understanding, as she had in the past, but her patience was finally wearing thin. The English rock press had also turned on him – and he on them – with the result that journalists got threatened. One was physically attacked in Amsterdam, and features appeared with headlines like 'A Man Called Horse'. The editor of the *NME* even accused Cave of 'promoting evil'.

After he fled Berlin and returned to London in 1988, he touched bottom.

Even Mick Harvey, his oldest friend and the only member of the Birthday Party to join the Bad Seeds, said that Cave's drug abuse was finally taking its toll on his work: 'And that's when it had to stop, because up until then it hadn't.' Convicted of possessing a gram of heroin he finally went into rehab in Somerset and emerged claiming, incorrectly as it turned out, that he had kicked the habit.

Rehabilitation of a different kind followed. Critics across the board began to praise not just his music but his writing, sometimes even his 'vision'. Culled from his interest in the Old Testament, the Delta landscape of the old blues musicians (which to this day he has never visited) his love of melodrama and his painstakingly acquired grasp of arcane vocabulary, Cave's lyrics and prose were nothing if not different. A collection of his writings, named after the Birthday Party's song 'King Ink', played well mainly with rock cognoscenti. But the novel *And the Ass Saw the Angel*, which came out in hardback in 1989, won acclaim from reviewers unaccustomed to lauding the literary pretensions of rock star junkies. *The Daily Telegraph*, no less, declared: 'it is as if a Faulkner novel had been crossed with *Whistle Down the Wind* and narrated by a stoned blues musician.' *The Daily Mail*, mouthpiece of middle England, conceded that the reader would 'be startled by the scale of its originality'. *The Scotsman* observed that 'it reads aloud beautifully' and concluded that Cave had written 'a genuinely nasty book'. The tale of Euchrid Eucrow, a bastard mute slowly sinking into a swamp somewhere in the Deep South, recounting his woes in passionately archaic idioms, seemed an unlikely candidate for the bestseller lists. But, helped by numerous public readings from its author, it went on to sell over 100,000 copies worldwide.

While Cave's career at last moved steadily forward, his life careered less steadily to and fro. In 1989 when the Bad Seeds played São Paulo, he met a fashion stylist, Viviane Carneiro, and fell more or less instantly in love. Two years later he was living in a suburb of the city, unable or unwilling to learn Portuguese, and about to become a father. So far as the world knew, the child Luke, born to Nick and Viviane in May 1991, was his first. In reality, Cave already had by another Australian woman, a son, Jethro, who had arrived just ten days previously at the end of April. How Cave juggled these affairs he prefers not to say but by the mid-1990s he was living back in London with the two boys, ('both of them are wonderful kids') and, somewhere in the vicinity, the two mothers. Cave's talent for reconciling opposites in his work evidently held him in good stead when it came to managing this awkward situation. Jethro now lives in Australia with his mother, but for a while sightings of Cave, a spindly apparition dressed for a Victorian melodrama, wandering around Westbourne Grove holding the hand of a small boy – was it Jethro or Luke? – were common.

Despite, or maybe because of all this domestic upheaval, his music got stronger. As his head cleared, Cave became more serious about his singing. He still has mixed feelings about his deep, dark brown voice. On the one hand it isn't what he regards as a natural rock'n'roll instrument, and he blames its low burnished timbre for obscuring his black sense of humour. 'I'm a person who laughs aloud at slapstick in the cinema. And I think a lot of my songs are slapstick in a way.' But fond as he has always been of easy listening, he has worked on his own vocal delivery. 'I took one singing lesson from a famous gay instructor who told me the way to sing is to feel that you're having three fingers thrust up your anus.' He paid his sixty pounds and left, never to return. He says it took him 'a couple of records' to realise that there was some quality to the voice, but 'I do sing in a more controlled way now. From the anus.'

The album that took him to another level, and remains his best seller, was *Murder Ballads*. It appeared in 1996, by which time Cave had started seeing PJ 'Polly' Harvey, a person he later alluded to in a song, 'West Country Girl', but whom he says he is no longer in touch with. His decision to record a collection of songs based entirely on grisly fictional slayings seemed to have been partly inspired by Harvey's Mercury-nominated album *To Bring You My Love*, a record full of Gothic tales with a hefty body count of its own. But Cave demurs from this assessment.

'I'm not familiar with her music. I was always more interested in . . . other things, actually. I'm not interested in contemporary music per se.' He mainly listens these days to Nina Simone, and the Dylan canon. Young upstarts like PJ Harvey need not apply. Beyond singing the track 'Henry Lee', Harvey, he insists, had no creative input into *Murder Ballads* whatsoever.

More important to the success of the project was its other star contributor, Kylie Minogue. Her vocal on 'Where the Wild Roses Grow' was widely interpreted as a camp joke. Cave looks thunderstruck at the notion. 'It was in no way a joke or a cynical exercise. I've always loved Kylie. She's an Australian. I think she's a great pop singer and thought it would be an honour to have her sing one of the songs. When she came in the band and I were justifiably in awe of this woman. I'm always impressed by people who do things fast.' Kylie did the job in two takes, the first being a shade too frilly for Cave's purposes. Released as a single, the song was his first and only Top 30 hit. _____ USEFUL TERM

The following year, 1997, marked a watershed. In February he issued *The Boatman's Call*, generally regarded as his finest effort and the one where he revisited and polished the piano technique he first acquired in Wangaratta aged eleven. In September he turned forty, and a couple of months later was devastated to learn of the death, in a hotel room in Sydney, of his friend Michael Hutchence. It is tempting to suppose that Cave and Hutchence were simply drug buddies, in the way that he and Shane MacGowan once were. But the relationship between the two most famous Aussie rock stars in the world had another dimension: they jointly owned a café on Portobello Road. At Hutchence's funeral Cave sat at the piano and boomingly intoned his song 'Into My Arms' – a curious choice for a Christian burial opening as it does with the line, 'You know I do not believe in an interventionist God.' But the effect was, as it often is with his performances, mesmerising. So much so that he was asked to repeat it three years later at the funeral of Hutchence's wife, Paula Yates.

Finally deciding to give up all drugs may have had something to do with Hutchence's death. It also coincided with his meeting a high-born model called Susie Bick at a fashion show in the Natural History Museum – a love match he eulogised in a recent interview in *The Erotic Review*. 'It was a happy accident that I met her at that time and it certainly helped me to make the decision to give up drugs,' Cave says, casually adding that he 'could write the Michelin Guide to detox centres but I have no desire to talk about it'.

He says the process was 'long and messy' and what with that and marriage and the twins, it took him a while before he felt fully creative again – hence the four-year pause between *The Boatman's Call* and 2001's *No More Shall We Part*. But he's back up to speed now, and knocked off the recording of his new album *Nocturama* in a week in Melbourne during a Bad Seeds tour of Australia. The only slight cloud on his horizon now is that he has to go and talk about himself to journalists whose reports, good, bad or indifferent, he generally finds painful to read. 'I tend to bring out a certain prose style in some writers. Purple. Is that the word?' We agree that it might well be. 'Okay. Very purple.'

The problem is that he doesn't like accounting for himself, or his work. 'I have no interest in telling people anything other than what I give them through the music, which is something I do intuitively. I don't listen to my own music. As soon as it's mixed, and I get this . . .' he disdainfully holds up a copy of *Nocturama*, 'I lose interest in it. It's just another record. It's something I send out, that's no longer mine.'

But it is, all the same, classic Nick Cave – and not the gloomy old Goth of popular repute either. From the lush piano ballad, 'Wonderful Life', which opens the album to the wigged-out fourteen-minute rocker 'I'm on Fire' that closes it, *Nocturama* is a fine portrait of the artist as a lively old goat. 'Dead Man in My Bed' offers an unmistakably droll reflection on the strains of marriage; and the single, 'Bring It On', boasts one of the strongest anthemic choruses he has ever written – helped on its way by the serrated rasp of his old mate Chris Bailey, vocalist with Australia's greatest punk band the Saints. Recorded as it was mid-tour, the whole thing crackles with the energy of a band who knew this stuff well before they went into the studio. As twelfth albums go, it sounds remarkably fresh. As indeed do most of the other eleven. Yet bizarrely for an artist whose albums have all sold upwards of 500,000 each and whose entire catalogue ticks over nicely, Nick Cave says that he has no sense of achievement. He is glad his mother feels proud of him, 'because it didn't look to her like it was going to happen for a long time', and he is happy to see all the brothers, sister and cousins who turn up to see him play in Melbourne. But the words are his real pride and joy, the music still a bit of a sideline. When he reviews his career he compares it, not to that of other musicians, but to the Bible.

'I used to read the Old Testament a lot in my twenties and then I made a transition to the New Testament.' Though he is not a Christian, and has always found the rigmaroles of church 'toe-curling', he finds the word of God, with all its joys and terrors, inspiring and believes that alert listeners will detect this is in the songs.

'I know about writing. I don't have any of the insecurities about writing that I do about music. I always felt like an impostor in the whole thing, like I'd fallen in the wrong job. I suppose I do have a vague unsteady pride in what I've done over the years. There's some good stuff in there, although it's not for me. It's not my cup of tea.' He cackles and rolls himself another cigarette. It's time for Nick Cave to go and rejoin Susie and the twins, and when the kids are down, sit and read a good book; maybe even *the* good book. And then to bed.

Robert Sandall, *The Word*, March 2003

Nick Cave: The Songwriter Speaks

Debbie Kruger

Nick Cave is a spiritual man, so I decided the best way to start was with a confession.

'I was a complete Nick Cave virgin,' I said boldly. 'I'm not sitting here before you having spent twenty years falling at your feet. It was a real experience for me to learn your work. I went through a journey.'

'Oh, good,' he responded. 'And why hadn't you listened to it before?'

'I never went in that direction,' I admitted. 'I think the kind of music that I was into might be the kind of music you would abhor.'

'And you thought that I was a miserable bastard and you didn't want know,' Cave said, eyebrows raised.

'Something like that, yes.'

He nodded. 'Well, I know deep down that I will always be kind of marginal and that my music isn't going to be universally liked, that your average person, whatever that may be, is not going to really take to my view of things. But it's the only view I have; it's not something that I can do anything about. And I happen to be very fond of my view of things, so I don't have any desire to do anything differently. But I do understand that it's not for everybody.'

'Would you want to be for everybody?'

'No. I guess I don't really want to be for everybody.'

And so it was that in May 2004 we spent three pleasurable hours talking about his songwriting. With the intermittent sounds of neighbourhood traffic and seagulls in the background, we sat together in his 'office' – an unkempt one-bedroom flat in Hove, Sussex, on England's South Coast – after first meeting at his home around the corner.

During the interview the phone rang a few times; usually it was his personal assistant, checking that he was okay, wondering why I was still there. One call was from his elderly aunt from Melbourne who was in England and visiting him this weekend. Cave was extremely relaxed. It was his first day off in months, having worked relentlessly in Paris and London on his new album, *Abattoir Blues/The Lyre of Orpheus*, and the flat-come-office was in good need of airing and cleaning. But it was quiet, private and comfortable for Cave, who liked to take many long thoughtful pauses when answering questions, and who laughed and made me laugh a lot.

Has the way you write songs changed since the earliest days?

Yep. I've always worked hard at it, but these days, at least for the last five years, I work a very strict routine with songwriting. Which comes to a degree with a lifestyle change as well. Getting up early, coming into this room and staying here till about five o'clock. I do that every day that I'm not on tour or making records or doing other things. And I guess that's something to do with some notion that the muse is unreliable.

So you have to be on standby for it?

Yeah. To walk in and be prepared. And so this office to me represents periods of incredible frustration and also amazing periods.

Does it get easier, the process of connecting with the muse?

You have less doubts. The way that I write is I have a project to do, and I come in and do it. I say, 'Today I'm going to start writing songs for the new record.' Invariably there's a three-week period of not being able to write anything, and it's a deeply frustrating period. But that becomes less and less so simply because I know now after fourteen albums that eventually it comes. And I can see very clearly the way that it comes. With one song that's often about not being able to write anything, but a couple of lines suggesting something else for the next song, and this sort of thing grows until you can cut the front ones off, and then start, and you've got some substantial songs.

So the first one is just like warming up?

Yeah, and it's usually very tentative and frightened and conservative. Really not knowing what to write about. But I find that if I'm writing for a particular project, then the songs begin to feed off each other and they begin to suggest the next song.

You're never flooded with inspiration between projects? You might just be walking along with the kids and an idea for a song comes to you?

No. I'm taking everything in and my inspirations come from everywhere. They come from the good and the bad and the beautiful and the ugly and deeply flawed things and extraordinary things. They come from watching really bad movies, from watching really great movies, listening to really bad music, great music, I find everything is either telling me what not to do or what to do. So you absorb stuff without really realising it.

But you're not taking notes?

I'm not taking notes. And it's almost a rule of thumb that I don't work outside this office. I feel that I give a large amount of my time to this; I work it as a job.

A job which I love. And it's also necessary not to be thinking about it. It's not as easy and as cut and dry as that, obviously. But I don't think creatively in the company of other people. I don't think creatively with my children. My mind doesn't work in the same way as it does when I'm alone here. I need solitude, I need the phone not to ring, I need friends not to visit.

You've said that you filled the void in your life left by your father's early death by writing. While you've written a novel, plays and film scripts, why have you focused most of your energy on writing songs? Is the song a more powerful form of art?

Yes. It's because music is right up there at the top of the ladder in regard to the effect that they can have on me. As opposed to the effect that a movie can or even a book can have on me. I love the immediacy of music, the reliability of a song, that you can play it again three weeks later and it still does the same thing to you, and the mystery of the whole thing. I don't know why one note alone is just this kind of idiot noise but you put another note next to it that suddenly can turn into something that can change your life.

I suppose there's something in the fact that my father always considered rock music to be right down the bottom. Like it was something not even really worth wiping your shoes on. My father drummed that literature and poetry were the great spiritual aspirations of mankind. I always felt like I was doing the wrong thing with music; I should have been doing something more worthwhile. Until it suddenly dawned on me that I was. That actually music to me means a hell of a lot more, it reaches a deeper part of me than books that I've read.

But your work is poetic and literate.

Well it is, yes. I try to combine the two. And I do hope that my father would be able to see what I did now and review his opinion.

How do you think your father would view your lyrical work now?

I think he'd be jealous.

Jealous of the quality or of your success?

Both. *[laughs]*

Do you hold your body of work up as a worthy example of literary achievement?

On a good day, yes I do. On a bad day definitely not. The whole thing with writing and making music is that when I'm in the moment with it I feel like a different person, I feel like what I'm doing is the greatest thing not only that I have done but that has ever been done. It's this extraordinary feeling. I get the same feeling performing live onstage, that it feels like I'm exactly the kind of person that I always wanted to be. Unfortunately when I go offstage or when I finish a record and it gets sent back to me and I have it in my hands, it's very anticlimactic. I realise I'm just this guy like everybody else. But the feeling that I get in here, when I feel like I'm really doing something that's great, is beyond any other feeling that I get.

So when I talk about coming in here and I do it as a job I don't mean that in any demeaning way to what I'm actually doing. It's not a cynical activity. One of the reasons why I never listen to my music back or never listen to live recordings of what I do is because of this terrible fear I have that I won't be able to regain that feeling once I actually look at it.

When Johnny Cash died, you wrote in a tribute piece that you lost your innocence with him at the age of nine or ten, and previously you had no idea about rock'n'roll. You said, 'I watched him and, from that point, I saw that music could be an evil thing, a beautiful, evil thing.' Why evil?

I think at the time, as a young kid, I suddenly realised that it could represent something other than the stuff that my mother and father were playing, which was not of any particular interest to me; it was classical music basically. Just in the same way as my kids relate to evil things. They want to dress up and they want to be the bad guy. That's pretty much what I was getting at, that music could be done by the bad guy. It could be great, much more exciting.

Was that then the beginning of your lifelong fascination with iniquity or had you already been aware of it through your relationship with the church?

[sighs] I'm not sure if I have a lifelong fascination with iniquity. *[laughs]* A lot of my songs, probably all of my songs are dramatic in the sense that they have a beginning and they have an end and they have a narrative curve, and often a moral at the end and a verse that sums up what I've been talking about. I've been writing that way for a long time; it's just the way I think about things. In any movie or in any story there needs to be conflict, or else there isn't a story. And I think that works in my narrative songs.

But your subject matter has been on the nasty side as opposed to the happy fluffy side.

I don't really relate to the happy fluffy side. In the music that I like I relate to tragedy and to sadness and to violence, to aggressiveness. I find that exciting and I haven't ever thought about that or questioned that. At the same time I find certain songs of praise very exciting as well, but a song of praise or a good uplifting song is usually suggesting an evilness by its absence. What I'm not interested in is songs that don't address that at all.

You've said, 'All love songs must contain duende.' Deep sorrow. If a love song, or any song, is never truly happy, how do you account for the heartfelt joy in the songs of, say, Stevie Wonder, some of the Motown songs, or a song like 'Wonderful World'?

I think that 'Wonderful World' is putting forward almost a polemic, that it is a wonderful world. It's saying we are all suffering, and we may see this world as a bad place, but I'm here to tell you that it's a wonderful world, the dark sacred night and the bright blessed day, and to look for these kinds of things. And I think that's a very beautiful thing, but in some way it's the springboard to the notion that it actually isn't a good world.

So a song like Stevie Wonder's 'For Once in My Life' is suggesting the fact that the rest of his life isn't happy.

There you go, yeah. For me music is a good thing. It's not a bad thing. In the world that we have today, which seems to me so destroyed and exhausted by the horror of it, to be able to get up and play music is a good thing, it doesn't matter what you're singing about. I really cling to that, that what I'm doing is a positive, life-affirming, God-driven thing to me. It doesn't matter what I'm writing about. It's a great thing to be a musician; it's a great thing to be a songwriter. And it's a very pure thing, and to somehow have a deep understanding of the purity of it and not do things to violate that.

How does a songwriter summon deep sorrow? Does one have to have experienced it?

Everyone's experienced sorrow. I don't think I've experienced it anymore than anyone else. I don't ever consider myself to have been an unhappy person. I've had troubles like anyone else, so I don't know.

It's interesting that in the joy of your marriage you wrote a song called 'My Sorrowful Wife'.

Well, you met her.

She looked pretty chirpy to me.

She is chirpy. But there is a sadness that lives in my wife, that I've noticed. That I noticed from the start and I found deeply attractive.

Do you think it's a brave thing to focus on that sadness, where an average songwriter might have written some glib happy song about being newly wed?

I wouldn't want to demean our marriage. *[laughs]* I'm reluctant to talk about this a lot, the sorrow thing, because I don't like the idea of putting myself as a miserable sorrowful person who sits around and mopes. Because I'm absolutely not like that, I never have been like that. But I find that the basic words that can be used to express sadness, and also to express violence, are much more interesting than the words to describe happiness. It comes from there.

There is a fine line between despair and humour in much of your

work. Have you felt misunderstood?

Yes. Humour is really important to me. Always has been, and I guess more and more so. In that it helps provide some kind of levity when you are writing quite a despairing lyric, and people don't just dismiss it as, 'God, I really don't want to have to listen to that kind of thing!' Most of my comic songs, if you want to call them that, are pretty sorrowful states of affair underneath the whole thing. And I like that, that the first response is to laugh. It's laughter in the dark inevitably. But I also just really enjoy it; it's entertaining for myself here alone to write stuff that I'm smiling about when I'm writing it.

Does it concern or bother you if people don't get your sense of humour?

It doesn't really. It does bother me that people dismiss what I do because they're under the impression that I'm just this . . .

Lugubrious.

That it's just this miserable shit. 'Oh, I don't listen to that kind of stuff.' Because of what they've read about it. When in actual fact they could quite possibly enjoy it.

If you wake up and you're particularly happy, it's a beautiful day like today, and you walk down here, where does the sorrow come to you from?

It's irrelevant. My moods, such as they are, seem to have nothing to do with my circumstances whatsoever. It's really to do with the writing and the use of words, and rhyme. If I can sit down and write a line, then put another one next to it and it rhymes beautifully, it echoes back and forth in the right way, and it can be deeply sad, it can make me happier than anything, I can feel extraordinarily happy about that. It has nothing to do with my emotional state, what I write. I can be real happy and write a sad song. I only have to sit down and play an A minor chord. It just puts you in that kind of frame of mind; musically, that chord suggests all the sorrow in the world.

Do you intend the music to convey mood and atmosphere equally to the lyrics, or is music mainly there to serve the lyrics?

I think one of my problems recently, in the last three or four records, the music has taken a secondary place. This new record that I've made, I've had a completely different songwriting process than the last ones in order to rectify that. It was much more band-orientated, it allowed them to be involved in the writing of the music. They had some stake in it, as opposed to just doing the songs that I've brought along. And that's improved things immensely.

I found No More Shall We Part a very musical album.

It's not that the songs were musically uninteresting; it's just that I felt that the band hadn't been able to flex their muscles in the music. In particular that record, actually. This new one, which is a double album, it's very different, in the sense that it's much more powerful and much more convincing musically. Within the playing. I'm not talking about the chordal structures or the songs themselves, but in the playing of it.

And that's an important component for your writing, the band's involvement? When you sit in here and you sketch out a song, just you and your piano, that's a complete song, is it not?
Yeah, it's important for me to be able to know that the song that I've just written works at its most basic level, which is sitting and playing it at the piano. That I can take it back home to my wife and say, 'I wrote this.' I don't say, 'Well, when the drums come in here, it's going to be good.' It's good, I could play it at a party – not that I would, not that I go to parties – but it works on that basic level. Which is a great thing. But going into the studio, some songs didn't get taken from that basic level.

Is that because they were so complete?
Yeah, because they sounded convincing in that state. So that the last record, I had three other members of the group and I went into a very small studio in Paris and said, 'Right, we're going to write songs.' I didn't have any lyrics, I didn't bring any chords, anything. It was just, 'All right, you're going to help write them as well.'

When did you write the lyrics?
I went back and wrote the words for the music that we'd come up with.

Do you do a lot of rewriting?
This record I did. This record I kept coming back and working away at them. What tends to happen to me is that songs can often start off with untruths or things that are inauthentic, or you've read something and you like that, and you write it up and then you rhyme it and then you suggest something else. But you have these lines in here that aren't really your own. A song that's written quickly often can have that kind of stuff left in. You forget whether it's meaningful to you or not. It just sounds all right on the page. And those lines really come back to haunt you, when you're playing live and you're thinking, 'Fuck, why didn't I get rid of that?'

Is there a line in a song that you perform regularly that you wish that you had changed?
Yeah. There's a song, 'The Loom of the Land', which has, 'The elms and the poplars were turning their backs.' Which I thought was really nice. And then I was reading *Lolita*, and it said, 'The elms and the poplars were turning their backs,' and it's like, oh right. I read that and wrote it down, stuck it in the song and didn't go back to sort that out.

But people borrow from each other all the time.

People do borrow all the time; people do steal all the time. And I don't really have any problem with that. But I don't like the idea of someone reading *Lolita* and going, 'Oh. How often has he done that?'

Do you overwrite? Do verses get discarded?

Yeah. A lot gets discarded. I had to edit a lot on this new record, I was really pushing to get the songs shorter. Which I succeeded sometimes and didn't other times. You become very attached to stuff, and sometimes you write a lot of sprawling songs, it's obviously got three verses too many in it, but it's like, 'Oh, I don't want to lose that one, and I don't want to lose that one . . .' But I do try and edit stuff down to keep it.

What does the piano offer you as a songwriting tool?

The A minor chord. *[sniggers]* I love the piano. I wish I played guitar. I know I'd write totally differently. Each year I vow that I'm going to learn the guitar and I never do. But the piano's a deeply soulful instrument, a sad-sounding instrument. It sounds really good on its own. And the piano certainly has an influence over the types of songs that I write. I've always written on the piano, or I've not written on anything at all, just sung the bits.

Was 'The Mercy Seat' written at the piano or did that actually come to you away from the instrument?

That was written in the studio. That was just a bunch of words and I came up with that slowly descending chordal thing. Mick came up with the verse chords and we stuck them together. That is a really good song and it can be played in a thousand different ways and I don't think we've ever done a concert where we haven't played that song. It's like what I was saying before, that song works; if I just sat down and played it now and sang it, it works perfectly well on that level. And that's a testament to a good song, as far as I'm concerned.

Many have commented on the long repetition of the chorus at the end. Repetition has been a common structural device in your writing, through to and most notably 'Babe, I'm on Fire' on Nocturama. What's the purpose of repetition within a song?

It's a musical thing as much as anything else, in that you can just keep shifting it up a notch each time and I have a band who can do that. It's like Spinal Tap, taking it to eleven. You can take it to twelve, thirteen, fourteen, it just keeps rolling on, and I love being able to do that. And having a basic structure within a song to be able to do that. Especially once you don't rely on a chorus to get in the way of that.

When did you start reading the Bible closely for your own gratification rather than because you were instructed to?

When I was about twenty-two.

Do you draw your Biblical references off the top of your head, or are you constantly re-reading it and looking for new inspirations there?
I go through periods. And I'm not reading it to get stuff out of it for my lyrics; it's not like a Thesaurus or lyrical tool. I read the Thesaurus for that.

You read the Thesaurus?
Yeah, it's sad, but I do sit and read the Thesaurus. Because I love words. I just think, oh God, what is that? And look it up and it means this and I find that really exciting. About the most exciting thing in the world. *[laughs]* And I've always been like that. I can remember being eleven or so and picking up an Edgar Rice Burroughs Tarzan book and reading something about 'the lazy lion waving his tail spasmodically', and I thought, God! I've always been really turned on by that.

A Thesaurus is like a map.
Yes. It's just such a wonderful idea and adventure.

And the Bible you read for pleasure?
The Bible I read for spiritual enlightenment, I would say. I read the Bible these days to be reminded that the words of Christ are actually to me the right message. And in this world the words of Christ have been so violated and hijacked and used for deeply unrighteous political purposes that it's important for me to go back to the Bible and remind myself that I'm not absolutely out of my mind to be thinking that Christ has something worthwhile to say. That's why I read the Bible these days. But it is an incredibly beautiful book.

Do you read the New Testament now more than the Old Testament?
I've always been more interested in the New Testament. Apart from very early on. The Old Testament to me really has been nothing more than an extraordinary kind of storybook with wonderful tales. But the New Testament spoke in a very different way to me.

I'm interested in your focus on antiquity, creating characters and stories from the past, in preference to contemporary settings.
I tried to create an alternate environment or arena in which these stories could play out, that was a kind of hybrid of different things that I was interested in. But I think it's become less that way over the last records. I've got the word 'Frappucino' on the last album. *[laughs]* 'I woke up this morning with a Frappucino in my hand.'

That's contemporary.
Yes, very. There is some sport in putting in a very contemporary thing. There's a rather pleasing jarring effect to have some of these elements suddenly come into a song that feels pastoral or timeless and adds a kind of ugly jerk into the times that we actually live in.

You described love songs as the idea of 'the cry of one chained to the earth, to the ordinary and to the mundane, craving flight, a flight into inspiration and imagination and divinity'. Did 'Into My Arms' exemplify that?

I wrote that particular song under very difficult circumstances. I wrote a few songs like that, but that one I wrote about three days into some drug rehabilitation clinic. You were allowed out of the clinic if you went to church, and I had gone to church that day, it was a Sunday, and I'd come back and I was feeling very ill, and sat down and wrote that very quickly, and I didn't have anything there to play it on, I had the melody in my head. So even though that particular sojourn into rehabilitation didn't work, *[laughs]* at least I got a good song out of it.

And had you taken that flight?

Well, I certainly felt that I'd done something worthwhile. Doing that meant more to me than why I was actually in there at the time, put it that way.

You said that through the use of language you wrote God into existence. Is writing always a link to divinity?

It's one of a million things you can do that's a link to divinity. Living is a divine act in some way, and I feel the idea of divinity is something that reflects the good in us and that can be claimed in all sorts of different ways. I don't think that you have to be involved in creative things to have a link to divinity, or that I'm doing something particularly special. I think you can get that same link sawing a piece of wood or looking after your children or being an accountant if it's something that you feel is rewarding to you and elevating.

Not all songwriters feel divinely inspired when they write songs.

Why I'm being hedgy about this is 'divinely inspired' seems to suggest that you sit at the piano and God comes down, and it's not like that at all. It's just most of the time numbingly hard work.

Why is the love song 'the truest and most distinctive human gift' for God? Does God need gifts from man?

I think it might be nice for Him, don't you?

Some songwriters believe songs are gifts from God. From the divine, from a higher power.

I think it's a bit of each. I think that in some respects if we didn't do things that in some way glorified God, God wouldn't exist to us. That it's these things that breathe life into Him.

What's your feeling now about 'Mutiny in Heaven'? If you listened to it right now in this room, would you reconnect with the place you were at when you wrote it?

I know very well when I wrote that song. That was basically a bass line that the band played to and it sounded great in the studio, but I hadn't written anything for it. We had one day to go, and I was sent home to write the lyrics for it. And I stayed up all night and came back and sang all this stuff over the top of the bass line. And Rowland Howard, who was the guitarist at the time, said, 'Well where do I play in this? All it is is just this fucking singing all the time'" Blixa Bargeld was in the studio at the time visiting, and he goes, 'Oh, I could put something in there.' And he did these wonderful bell chords that he does through it.

I love that song. I couldn't write a song like that anymore. I couldn't hold true to some of the viewpoints and I couldn't be bothered writing a song like that anymore. But for when it was done and the age I was at, I thought it was really good.

How did 'The Ship Song' come to you?

I think what happened was there was another song on a record that we made before that, which I didn't have all the lyrics for when it came time to do the vocal. I can't remember what song it was. So some of the lyrics I just pretended to sing stuff, ad-libbed, incomprehensible mumbo jumbo, not even words, just mumbled, meaningless nonsense. But then the *King Ink* book was being put together, a complete collection of my lyrics, so I had to come up with the words. I didn't want to write, 'Woah yeah, come on, baby, get down, blah, blah blah,' or whatever nonsense it was, so I wrote 'Come sail your ships around me' instead. And then later on I was looking at the printed lyrics and thought, 'God, that's good, you know, that's a nice image.' It reminded me of *Gulliver's Travels*, of a giant being circled and subdued by a fleet of tiny ships. I thought that that line deserved a better song. So I worked on it a bit and wrote 'The Ship Song'.

As your most covered song, does the fact that other artists want to sing it validate it for you in any way?

Yeah, very much so. I mean, depending on the artist, obviously. I'm always happy for people to cover my songs. Because it's enormously flattering.

By the stage of Let Love In you were saying that you were drawing far less, if at all, on outside influences and relying on your own power to influence yourself. But I did find that 'Nobody's Baby Now' was reminiscent of Bob Dylan. It could sit really nicely alongside 'Just Like a Woman'.

I wouldn't mind that.

It didn't surprise me that Paul Kelly had done a version of it.

Right. Way back I was asked to write a song for Johnny Cash. It was the beginning of these American Recordings where he was getting different people to write songs for him, and he asked me to write a song, and that was the one that I wrote. And after I thought, 'Fuck it, I'm not handing that over. I really love that song, and I'm going to do that.'

As you wrote it with the intention of Johnny Cash singing it, was it something different than you would have ordinarily written for yourself?
Possibly. One of the things that I really enjoy and value and find to help enormously is when I'm asked to write music for people, or asked to write songs for films or whatever. A case in point is with Wim Wenders. He would literally ring me up and say, 'I'm making a new movie, it's about this, I want a song about time.' And I'd go, 'All right, I'll have it to you in a week.' And would come in and write something. It's not for me, it's completely for him, so I feel a complete freedom to write whatever I want to write. I feel suddenly that it's not totally my responsibility. Because it becomes a craft thing. Purely craft.

Is that where the Thesaurus comes into play more than ever?
The Thesaurus is always in play. And it's the same with other sorts of writing. Scriptwriting. I was asked by Johnny Hillcoat, 'I want you to write a song about bushrangers.' Which I have no particular understanding of or great love for, they're just Australian bushrangers, we all love 'em, but I didn't have any particular fascination with them. But I just found it very easy to do, to write things for other people. Very freeing, and you learn a lot by doing that. You go other places that you would not normally go.

Again, it's like this notion of a map; you're following paths.
It's also that Nick Cave and the Bad Seeds have always been a very insular set-up. I don't have much to do with other musicians, I don't hang out with other musicians, I don't talk about music much. It's always felt very much to me about coming into an office and working away on my own. And the times that I'm dragged out of that can be immensely rewarding. I did road songs for Marianne Faithfull for her new record, the music to three songs for her, and then went into the studio and recorded them with her. And certainly you learn enormous amounts of stuff doing that, watching the way someone else does something. You find yourself suddenly growing. That happened recording with Johnny Cash, and that's why it's interesting to read your book, because you find out the way other people go about things.

When you were with Johnny Cash, did you actually talk about songwriting?
He did. I was too busy polishing his shoes, you know. But he had his way of recording, which was actually quite similar to mine, in that I don't think he's the kind of guy who likes to do fifty takes of something, he just wants to get it done. And he was quite ill, so it had to be done now or not at all.

Are you often in awe like that or is that quite a rare thing for you?
Well, I'm not often in awe, but when I am in awe I'm in awe. We just did here in Brighton on the weekend this Leonard Cohen concert. That was really interesting because it was a lot of different singers singing Leonard Cohen songs.

And Leonard Cohen songs are done in a particular way; you always know they're Leonard Cohen songs, even though the musicians change and the musical styles change. It was really interesting to see how brilliant these songs were in the sense that they could be done in any form. These songs are just extraordinary. And there's so many of them. But that was nerve-wracking, because I ended up getting 'Suzanne'. It was the one song I really didn't want to have to do.

Why? Is it too great a song?
The pressure. The pressure's too much. [*laughs*] It's so easy to fuck up; it's actually a really difficult song to sing.

You've also recorded the work of other writers, especially on Kicking Against the Pricks. Why has it been important through your career to perform and record covers?
It wasn't an important thing to do before we did that, but we certainly benefited so much from the *Kicking Against the Pricks* record musically that it turned out to be really important. We just did it at the time for something to do. We felt that there were certain expectations about our music that it could benefit us if we destroyed those expectations. But it proved to be very valuable because we found out we could play all different kinds of music. And so that opened things up a lot.

It was a great selection of songs. I found the inclusion of 'By the Time I Get to Phoenix' interesting. It's an unconventionally structured song for Jimmy Webb, being that it has no chorus. Is that what appealed about that song, were you paying tribute to Webb's overall mastery in pop songwriting, or was it more about that theme of a relationship ending, as all must do?
It was all of those things. There were certainly versions of it that were great, that influence that version possibly more than the original. Isaac Hayes did his twenty-minute version of it.

By which time he actually got to Phoenix.
Well, he does a long explanation about what women are actually like; it's very funny. How men have just got to go out.

So what did you take back with you into your own songwriting from the intense focus on other writers' work?
It was mostly that I learned how to sing in a different way on that record. I discovered a quality in my voice that I didn't realise was there, and it was to sing softly up close to the microphone. That there was something that was actually quite attractive about my voice, which I had absolutely no idea of before. And that consequently allowed me to write different sorts of songs, where they could be pulled back.

When describing the process of writing 'Far from Me' you said: 'I find quite often that the songs I write seem to know more about what is going on in my life than I do.' What other songs depicted or foretold your life beyond your own awareness at that time?
There's a comical element to that whole conceit, that the songs are ruling my life.

I didn't think of it as songs ruling your life, more just life imitating art, maybe.
I don't know if I could think of another song like that. There are songs that I find quite difficult to extract from the events around the song and I find quite difficult to perform on occasions. I can just about perform that song now and see it as a song about a failed relationship without the actual relationship itself hijacking the song, and I'm kind of back there. Not that I have any particular bad feelings about that, but it's just that I'm singing it about a particular woman and situation that I don't have any particular feelings for anymore. And in some respects I see that as the failing of that song. That I can't lift it out of that, because it is so specific. But I'm sure that for other people it's probably the beauty of that song.

Is it necessary for somebody listening to the earlier songs to have knowledge of your personal relationships, inner and external conflicts, your addictions, beliefs or literary influences at those times to fully understand them?
I would hope not. If it is then it's what I'm saying: there's a certain failure in the songwriting. You don't need all that. And it has been something I've been very conscious of and that I've been trying to pull away as a character so that the songs can breathe a little bit more. That this character that I'm supposed to be suffocates a lot of these songs. It feels like that to me.

So I guess there's been, on some subconscious level, a certain amount of effort to make my life appear as uninteresting as possible. So that there's just nothing to talk about anymore. I actually feel I lead an incredibly interesting life. It's not all about being in this office; I have so much more in my life. But it's stuff that no one's really interested in talking about. So it's great.

Notwithstanding Kylie Minogue's considerable contribution, did you ever see 'Where the Wild Roses Grow' as a commercial hit?
No.

It must have amused you to think what all the people who bought the* Murder Ballads *album on the strength of that single would have made of it.
Yeah. I was on *Top of the Pops* two weeks running with Kylie, trying to fumble my way through the song. I remember being in a toy shop getting a toy for my son and this little kid coming up to me in a Power Rangers outfit, and he goes, 'Are you that old guy that was on with Kylie Minogue the other night?' He was just this

little kid but he really loved the song. And I'm just like, [*under his breath*] 'Oh fuck off you little bastard.' [*laughs*] But it suddenly occurred to me that these people may even be buying the record, and it deeply troubled me.

'Are You the One That I've Been Waiting For?' on The Boatman's Call, was so simple and guileless lyrically. Was it more difficult for you to write than your long, complex, literate story songs?
I think that's very beautiful, that song, and I was really pleased with the lyrics. I remember writing it in a taxicab on the way to Michael Hutchence's house, for some reason. It's easier for me to write a narrative than one that doesn't have a denouement or an end. I'm hardwired to write narrative type songs because there's a logic to that, in the whole structure of the song. You know when the song ends, it ends the way a story ends. I find those particular songs, the ones that are really narrative, like on *Murder Ballads*, really easy to write. All I do is get two characters, give them names, stick them in a song, and off they go.

And kill at least one of them.
And yeah, [*laughs*] one kills the other, and you say it's not a good thing at the end and move on to the next one. But just on that point, a lot of these narrative songs, I don't know what the story's going to be. It's not like I've thought of the story and I'm going to put it in words, it's very much about inventing a character and the scenario and letting it play out. The songs write themselves in some kind of way. The other ones seem strange for me to write.

Because they're so exposed? Because you're the character?
It might have something to do with that. But I'm the character in a lot of them, even in the narrative ones. Not so much the *Murder Ballads* record, but a lot of the deeply personal ones are still narrative. 'Far from Me', that's still a narrative song with a beginning and an end. They are harder to write because I don't really know how to end them, they're just this chunk of stuff and I don't know where they should stop. I suppose they should stop at four minutes, or something like that.

Is that what you do then? You let the structure guide you?
Yeah, I write three verses or four.

'Love Letter' on No More Shall We Part is something very grand, like the best of Webb or Newman or the grand popular music composers. Were you pleased with that song?
Yes. I like that, it took a very long time to write, and went through all different sorts of versions. I remember a friend of mine coming up, I'd been living at his house in Ireland, working out there, and he heard me play it live a year or so later, and he said, 'God, that song turned out really well. 'Cause when you were playing it at my place it sounded like the worst fucking thing I've ever heard.'

So it did go through a lot of versions. But it had the basic chorus, 'Go get her/ Go get her/ Love letter/ Love letter.' I like that song.

Can I name some of your songs we haven't mentioned yet and get your responses to them? 'From Her to Eternity'?

I guess it's one of my favourite songs that I've written, as a piece of music, especially, and have great joy in playing live. We stopped playing it for a while and brought it back in on the last tour and lyrically and musically it propels forward. I remember writing that sitting up in bed with Anita Lane; she helped me write that. And conceiving this notion that the object of desire is being up on the next floor, and all of the connotations of that. I thought the recorded version of it was extraordinary; I'd never heard anything like Blixa's guitar in that song, and I've never heard anything like it since. From anywhere. It's just so out there. It's so powerful, but it's basically piano driven. I heard an early Górecki piece or something like that, done on the piano, which sounded incredibly similar to it, years later. But it just has this magic about it.

'Deanna'?

'Deanna' was written about Deanna, based on 'Oh Happy Day', and I like that one too, actually.

I was interested in the contrast between the melody and the lyric.

Yeah, it's got a jaunty rock'n'roll piece of music but it's a dark lyric. At the same time it to me really sums up that relationship that I had with that particular girl, which was a really fun youthful relationship where anything goes. Lyrically it talks about that excitement of young love without any responsibilities, where you feel you could just do anything. That's not necessarily anything good, it's anything bad as well. *[laughs]* Deanna on the one hand really likes it, but on the other hand every time she says her name's Deanna they go, 'Oh, are you *that* Deanna?'

'Tupelo'?

'Tupelo' is based heavily on a John Lee Hooker song. It welds the mythic flood of Tupelo, which he talks about in his song, with the Elvis thing.

How do you feel about that song now?

Well, it used the John Lee Hooker song as a kind of springboard for something else so I'm very much aware of that, and I'm aware that I took full songwriting credit for it. *[laughs]* I was talking about that earlier, that you kind of wish now that you had have been a bit more generous in that respect. It's a good song, some great lines in that: 'The sandman's mud' and all that spooky stuff.

Do you have lines in different songs that you relish the opportunity to sing?

Well, there's verses. I'm particularly proud of the first verse of 'Nobody's Baby

Now', which takes so long to get to the point. I like the way that stretches for so long to get to that line. It reminds me of 'Tupelo Honey', the Van Morrison song, about all the tea in China, talking about getting the ship and putting all the tea in it and taking it out into the sea and dumping it into the sea, and you realise he's working on that line. It's just such a beautiful idea to expand on this cliché.

'The Weeping Song'?
'The Weeping Song' was written very quickly. I wrote that in Brazil, walking from the place that I was living down to the bar, and that came out of nowhere, with very little thought. And there's a narrative thing going on. 'The Weeping Song' isn't actually one of my favourites.

I was interested on that album, **The Good Son,** ***in the whole notion of calling a song a song – 'The Weeping Song', 'The Ship Song', etcetera. Do titles come to you easily?***
No. Obviously in some the title's already there. But I think that was a bit of both. It was that I didn't know what to call 'The Ship Song'. It was just these lyrics and everyone kept calling it 'The Ship Song' and then, 'Well, we can do that with a few of them' type of thing.

'Papa Won't Leave You Henry'?
I like that song a lot. That was another one written in Brazil. It's this sprawling lyrical thing. We were playing that as a very slow ballad on a different chordal structure altogether, which then became 'Darker With the Day'. It had a different melody, but very slow and it made for a very haunting thing. That song was composed over a long period of time and something that I would sing to my little son, Luke. It was kind of a nasty fucked-up lullaby.

Whether you're in London or Hove, Berlin, Brazil or Melbourne, does your physical environment affect what you're writing?
I'd like to say that it didn't, but actually I think it really does have an enormous effect. Living in England, which was a place that I hated to be but have spent an enormous amount of time in, I found I looked outside. The world that I was creating was not English, it was something else. And through living down here, I started to understand England and started to love certain aspects of it, which have definitely crept into the writing. A lot of the songs I think are very English, especially the pastoral side, the vegetation, the kind of animals that are in it, and the flowers, all of that stuff to me is very English. But it's an England that I don't really know much about, it's an England that I know more about from reading poetry. I enjoy setting songs up in these English pastoral settings that all seem to be on the point of collapse in some way. I'm interested in that old notion of England as the fair England, being some kind of New Jerusalem, almost like heaven. The ancient notion of England and the rolling green hills. And to use that for a stage where other things happen within it. I like the tension that's set up with that.

So England finds its way into your work now more than Berlin and Brazil did at the time you were writing songs there?

Berlin had a huge influence over me simply because it was a lifestyle influence; it was a place where we got some kind of recognition. We lived in London for a long time and people just thought we were this whacked-out band from Australia and didn't take us particularly seriously. But when we went to Berlin they didn't have these prejudices; they just liked us. So we suddenly got some positive attention and became part of the Berlin arts scene. But I wasn't interested in my songs becoming German.

You can't live in Brazil and it not have an impact. I mean visually, everywhere you look. It's so different and so beautiful and so horrible and such incredible extremes. For the first year in Brazil I was just constantly looking around me. I was living in São Paulo, which is a big nasty city. But within that there were both sides of the coin there all the time.

How Australian do you think your songwriting is?

I think in some respects it's very Australian, because many aspects of the kind of world I've created are just pilfered from other lands, so that I've created my own setting and world for my songs to play out in. I have enormous love for much about Australia. The countryside, the bush and all that stuff. But there's bits of America and bits of England, and I've created my own unique land. I think that's quite similar to a lot of Australian cinema, to Australian songwriting, Australian society. It's largely a kind of hybrid, mongrel society.

Debbie Kruger, Expanded chapter from *Songwriters Speak*, 2005

Old Saint Nick

Barney Hoskyns

On *Abattoir Blues*, the cheerily-titled first half of the new double album by Nick Cave and the Bad Seeds, there is a song called 'There She Goes, My Beautiful World'.

In it a number of august figures crop up: Marx and Gaugin, Larkin and Dylan Thomas, Vladimir Nabokov and the dissolute Earl of Rochester, Christian mystic Saint John of the Cross and punk junkie Johnny Thunders.

Talk about bathos: how in all seriousness can one compare the co-writer of cold-turkey classic 'Chinese Rocks' with the 16th-century author of 'The Dark Night of the Soul'?

'Well,' Cave says with a slightly sheepish smile. 'The song is just asking, How did these people do it? How did Johnny Thunders write "Chinese Rocks", which is one of the great drug songs. Obviously there was a certain humour to including him in that list, but I think I've got a certain talent for pulling those lines out on occasion.'

I ask Cave if he recalls an infamous afternoon many summers ago when he and the former New York Doll actually met in a drug-infested flat in Paddington, London. Against all odds he does.

'I don't remember much about it, except that his hands were in unbelievably bad condition' he says. 'But I wouldn't trade that moment for anything.'

You won't be altogether surprised when I tell you that it wasn't music that brought these two rock icons together. Nor should you be too astonished that the younger musician almost overdosed after reboiling the cotton the elder one had used to strain his hit. Such was the scale of Thunders's heroin habit at the time.

Ah, the long cold summer of '82: blood on the walls, *Astral Weeks* on the turntable, Cave's band the Birthday Party in ever-more desperate straits. Life as a junk-yard: a bunch of diseased Aussie Goths playing death-rattle jazz-punk horror-rock while all around them lay flouncy haircuts and synthesizer whimsy.

Of all the singers from that era you'd have bet on enjoying a long career of cult status and 'respectable album sales', Cave would have commanded very long odds indeed. Johnny Thunders eat your junk-blackened heart out: you couldn't see Cave making twenty-five, let alone thirty.

But here he is, sitting in a modish hotel in his adopted hometown of Brighton, forty-five years racked up on Planet Earth. He's still rake-thin, but the August sun has tanned his cheeks. On the mobile is wife Susie, former model and mother of twin boys Earl and Arthur. (There are two other, older sons. Both are from different relationships; both are worshipped by Earl and Arthur.)

'I'll be home soon,' Nick tells Mrs Cave. 'I've just got one more of these to do.'

Cave has never enjoyed the stale rituals of the interview treadmill. Most journalists, he says, come to him with a fairly stock notion of what 'Nick Cave' means.

'I can see sometimes with people who interview me that they're really struggling,' he says. 'They're not equipped to talk about the music, so you feel it drifting back to the past and they want something about all of that. I guess it must be, like, "Oh, Nick Cave's put out a new record, who's gonna go and interview him?"

'What I think is important to me, in regard to my songwriting, is trying to create some songs where you no longer have to listen to them and think, "How is Nick Cave doing at the moment?" Part of that is to create, at least within the media, the blandest possible lifestyle I can work out. There just ain't no story there. Because there came a point where it became clear to me that the weight of people's ideas of what I was would destroy me. And that was hugely problematic for my songwriting, I think. A lot of other things happened, but one of those things was, Let's try and pull all that back. And as far as I'm concerned, that's benefited what I'm doing tremendously. I know some people don't agree with that, and they would rather see the songs in that way. I mean, you like to listen to some of those Dylan albums and think, Christ, what was he going through at that time? On the other hand, I genuinely believe there's nothing to know about me. On some level, there just is no story that's really of any interest to anybody – except what I'm doing musically. And I think what I'm doing musically is unique and it's challenging and I'm really proud of that aspect.'

The new record, *Abbatoir Blues/The Lyre of Orpheus*, is the first Cave/ Bad Seeds album to be recorded with former Gallon Drunk frontman James Johnston, whose organ playing beautifully complements the melodic piano work of Conway Savage. It is also the first Bad Seeds record to be made without Blixa Bargeld, the eccentric and charismatic Berliner who for years simultaneously led the group Einstürzende Neubauten. Anyone who's seen the Seeds live over the last two decades will know that the dynamic between Cave and Bargeld was as integral to the band's chemistry as the Jagger/Richards yin-yang was to the Rolling Stones in their pomp.

'The Nick-Blixa relationship always seemed very theatrical to me,' says Jim Sclavunos, drummer and percussionist with the Seeds. 'It was like watching some sort of ritual or pantomime, like a little dance or stately minuet.'

Cave says he misses Bargeld: 'It feels sad that he's gone, and I do miss him a lot, and we parted very amicably. And he was a big figure in my life. But on another level it feels really good, because the band's been forced to change its methods. The whole sound shifted when he left. We still don't know what the effect actually is. He had his way as well, as a person, which was very different to all the rest of us – especially the Australians, who in many ways are neither here nor there with their opinions about things. He was like, "Where is my fucking vodka and where is this and where is that?" And refreshingly so. And I miss that aspect of the band: Blixa, you go and fucking sort it out!'

'Blixa's departure really changed an entrenched structure,' adds Sclavunos. 'It was a good opportunity for us to take a lot of the old songs and re-address them in a fresh way.'

Sclavunos was one quarter of a scaled-down 'micro-Seeds' that decamped to Paris earlier this year. 'There's always some sort of effort to do things slightly differently,' he says. 'In Paris we were trying to put songs together out of thin air, and a lot of stuff came out of those few days.'

Although Nick writes mostly alone, it's still important for him to feel that he has this gang – the Bad Seeds – around: 'There's definitely been a return to that sort of thing, and I think that that largely comes from the *little* band that I started playing with – a micro-Seeds. We're a working band in the sense that it's got nothing to do with records coming out or anything. When we feel like going somewhere, we're mobile enough to call each other up and decide to do that. But through doing that, I think we've just discovered enormous amounts of things musically, because we're not trapped into this massive musical apparatus. The Bad Seeds give something else that the little band could never give, but at the same time when you're playing you're stuck in your part – you can't just do freeform shit all over the place. We do all still live in different countries – France and Australia and America – but the whole thing's still fluid. And there's a real thing that it doesn't fucking matter if we do really diabolical versions of the songs as long as we attempt something different with the group. We did this songwriting session with the little group in Paris, and I don't think I've ever done that – gone in and said, "All right, I've got nothing, let's try and write some stuff together." And we said to ourselves, "It doesn't matter what the music's like, it doesn't have to fit into any kind of Bad Seeds type thing, so if we wanna do twenty-five-minute prog-rock explorations, we're able to do that" – and we did. And it just opened up all kinds of things up.'

On the new album, 'Let the Bells Ring' is about Johnny Cash, a central musical figure for Cave. 'There's only been one other person that I've felt that way, and that was Barry Humphries. In the same way I was fearful of meeting him. But as soon as they entered the room, it just felt good to be there. I got asked to sing with Johnny Cash, and the night before, I was thinking, "How do you *do* that?" By the time I got in the studio I was feeling like a fucking gnat. But as soon as he came in, it was like, "Nick!" And I thought, "It's okay, I can do this."'

In contrast to the fairly full-throttle *Abattoir Blues* – which includes the hummable single 'Nature Boy' – *The Lyre of Orpheus* is softer, more unplugged. 'Easy Money' is close to soulful and 'Breathless' could be a campfire singalong.

'"Breathless" was the last thing that was written,' Cave says. 'It was an attempt from my point to write a song that didn't have a twist at the end. It was a celebration of nature and divinity, and it had a buoyant melody. I mean, it still sounds sad to me, but I think that's just something that lives in my voice no matter what I do with it. To me, songs like that that are obviously written as celebrations of things always suggest the other side of it anyway.'

If last year's *Nocturama* reached back to the feral fervour of early Seeds, the new double is a generous blend of calm beauty and holy-roller intensity. (It even features a clutch of voices from the London Community Gospel Choir.) But why have the Bad Seeds always come across like quasi-criminals? Why the suits and ties?

'For me the Bad Seeds has always been about a group of men, primarily. It's about a group of men with a man's work ethic about things. The times that we've worked with women have always – apart from with Kylie – been very difficult. And I think that's because in my life, outside the Bad Seeds, I don't actually have these male relationships. Sometimes I feel like I've been accidentally put into the life raft that was for women and children. Which is fine, really, because I love women and children, but the Bad Seeds thing is a very male work-type thing. Everyone's personal lives are fucking left elsewhere and we just go to work. And I think we cleave to that in some way. We *dress* like we're going to work. We don't dress in Bermudas and flip-flops.'

Has Nick ever worn a pair of blue jeans in his life?

'I don't know. Maybe. I really don't like them very much. I would if I liked them.'

Does he get his male bonding in the Seeds?

'I don't know if that's the right word. We bond on a musical level, and that's where it happens for us. We don't go rafting . . . or skipping through the fields reciting poetry and sniffing each other's armpits – whatever men do these days. We turn up to work, and I think it's something that we all really value. We all have a very similar sense of humour about things. We all have this thing that we click on in our brains where it doesn't really fucking matter what happens. I think it's an Australian thing.'

Is Cave still an Australian?

'I certainly *feel* Australian. The way I write is because I'm an Australian. The humour, such as it is, is Australian. To me the Australian sense of humour is often about saying things that nobody – even the person who's saying them – knows whether they're funny or tragic. There is some kind of humour in that to us, and it's a unique thing that doesn't exist anywhere else. It probably just comes from a deep insecurity about our country and all of that sort of stuff.'

Even in the midst of chaos and degradation, the Birthday Party were always able to raise a chuckle. I suppose it was a kind of gallows humour. English junkies weren't able to do that.

'Well, the English take depression seriously, which I don't think Australians do. I think that my wife, to a degree, finds that annoying – that there are serious things, and yet I'll always have the last laugh about them. She's English and she doesn't see things in that way. She's like, "Things are fucked up." And I'm like, "Things might be fucked up . . . but anyway . . ." It's just hard-wired into the Australian psyche.'

Is that also true of Cave's beloved Saints, whose albums have just been reissued?

'There was something funny about the Saints, though I don't even know what that is. Another very Australian thing that they did was provoke their peers rather than the establishment itself. The whole punk-rock thing was going on, and they did things with brass sections. They came over to England, and there was just this fat guy with long hair – and people went, "Oh, is *that* what they're like?" When all that Right to Work stuff was going on, Chris Bailey would go, "Right to Work? Right to fucking *not* work!"'

Is Mick Harvey still an anchor for Nick after all these years together?

'Well, our relationship changes. We definitely have a work relationship, me and him, and it's always been that way. In the fondest way, he's a nuts-and-bolts type guy and he doesn't take any bullshit. In a constructive way, he tends to deflate certain pretensions. Certainly on some level, he continues to pull the whole thing together and oversee the workings of the group. Although in some ways, I think Mick may now be having the youth that he had stolen from him back then. He's a wicked drunk, Mick. Don't sit next to him if he's got a bottle of red wine in front of him.'

In a recent South Bank Show about Cave, Blixa Bargeld talked of ways to survive being a rock star. One way, he said matter-of-factly, was to 'notice that there is a life outside of being a rock star'. Has Nick achieved that?

'To an extent, certainly. I had to separate my work methods from my family, simply out of respect for them. I don't think it's fair on them to witness the creative process. It's ugly, and there's something kind of vulgar and demeaning about the whole thing. So I go off to an office and go through whatever I go through to write the songs, and I don't bring all that shit home with me – as well, obviously, as needing to be alone to do what I do. And I think by virtue of that I have managed to separate what I do creatively from my home life, which is incredibly devoid of my career. I don't allow records of mine to be played in the house. I don't think my kids are even that familiar with my music. For their sake I don't think they need to be privy to all that.'

Does Cave still regret the self-exposure of 1997's *The Boatman's Call*, born of the pain of splitting up with PJ Harvey?

'I think it's a really good record, and I'm really proud of it. I haven't listened to it since we made it, so I don't really know what I'm talking about, but I felt that some of the songs came from a place that was something I railed against through my life – that place of self-pity. And I think you can call me all sorts of things, but self-piteous wasn't one of them. I was always like, "Let's get on with it!" And I think that whatever happened around then knocked me for fucking six. And I didn't see it coming. And there's a couple of songs on there that came from this place, and it's not a place I'm particularly proud of. There was a feeling, to me, of "Welcome to my pain" that I found a little excruciating to me. Having said that, I think at least one of those songs, "Far from Me", is a really brilliant song. And it's just not something that I'd feel comfortable listening to – or playing. Sometimes we try to resuscitate it, but it never works.'

Where does this figure of 'The Sorrowful Wife' (from *No More Shall We Part*), the sad woman tending her flowers, come from?

'Well, it's about my wife and her rather sorrowful attempts to make things grow.'

Clearly the English countryside has affected Cave as a landscape. In some ways he *is* a 'Nature Boy'!

'I'm a nature boy in theory. To be honest I don't spend a lot of time in the countryside. I would dearly love to, and I often say I'm going to, but it's more in my mind. There is something very beautiful and gentle about my concept of the English countryside. To me it's about seasons, and Australia doesn't have seasons as such – it's just fuckin' hot or bloody cold, and the flowers don't turn in the same way. To me it's a really beautiful thing about England.'

Since his marriage to Susie Bick, many of Cave's songs have implicitly been about slowing down, taking stock of his place in the world. There's a lot of pastoral imagery – a lot of flowers and trees – in these songs. Does he feel more at peace with the world, and with himself?

'I don't particularly feel that, to be totally truthful. I feel that the circumstances of my life are greatly improved than they were five years, ten years ago, but whether I feel at peace . . . I really don't think that I've ever felt at peace. Except probably when I used to take smack, early on in the whole thing when it still worked. There was this feeling that I never had anywhere else that was just relief. I had that absolutely fundamental feeling that this was what I was meant to do. And I may well still be doing that, except that it just didn't work anymore. And I don't come from any moral high ground about that sort of thing. It just stopped working, so I basically stopped it. But this is not to say that I don't feel happy. There are times where I feel *really* happy.'

Isn't work – specifically, Cave's very driven regimen – sometimes just a substitute addiction?

'Well, one of the things that happened when I took smack was that all the voices – all this chattering fucking nonsense that used to go on in my head, all those nasty little voices – just went away. And those voices go away when I work, especially when I'm on a roll. They swap from "You're fucking second-rate, you're mediocre, you'll never amount to anything" to "You are the fucking greatest person that ever walked the earth, you are God's gift to music" . . . they flip over to that. And I know that neither of these voices is telling the truth.'

Does he think that on any level he's still trying to prove himself to his English-professor father, who died in a car crash when Nick was nineteen?

'Um, I think I've done that. I think I proved myself when I wrote my novel

[1989's *And the Ass Saw the Angel*]. He probably wouldn't have liked it, but . . . ah well, I don't know.'

Why has Nick never followed up *And the Ass Saw the Angel*?

'Because it would take two years to do, I figure. I've done the calculations. Three pages a day, take out Christmas and other holidays . . . and then the editing. I just haven't found two years to do it. And in any case it's not like I feel that writing a book is of a higher nature.'

Has the absence of the Father had anything to do with his search for God – the ultimate Patriarch?

'I don't know about that. But I feel that it's important to mention God in my songs, and to put forward my notion of what that is, because I'm sickened by what is being done in the name of God these days – that the concept of God has been hijacked by bullies and bigots . . . and *psychopaths*. And part of this is because they don't have a questioning view of God. It's narrow, it's locked-in, it's *right* – to them. Christ talked of these people at his most vehement, and he called them hypocrites and blasphemers. And I know it's unfashionable to bring up the name of Jesus Christ, but I feel duty-bound to do it.'

These are difficult times to live in, in the sense that one is caught between the two poles of dogmatic religious doctrine or a very irreligious, materialistic world that lacks a spiritual dimension – waking up with a Frappucino in your hand, as you sing on the new album.

'Well, I feel that that aspect is important, which is why I talk about it.'

Is great music inherently religious?

'I think a lot of musicians are believers, and it seems that if you're working in music it's quite a logical step to take. I feel that a lot of people would quite like to believe, or get the benefits and security of that belief, but find that it's an impossible notion to defend. And it is, in some respects – the existence of a benign God *is* an impossible notion. But for me that lives quite comfortably in the part of my mind that is about imagination and magic and absurdity and everything that there is no argument for. It's pointless for me to argue the existence of God, because I'll lose. In the end I just have to go, "Well, it's just something I feel, it's just this feeling I have." I've given up having those conversations.'

Over two decades since those crazed Birthday Party shows that usually involved 'Nick the Stripper' injuring himself, how does Cave now view the business of live performance?

'It feels to me the same, only I feel I'm better at it in that I get better as a singer. It's just a place where I can go and I can be that person that I always wanted to be. You feel God-like, and that's something I really value.'

God-like?

A guilty, almost boyish smile plays across Cave's face. 'It doesn't last very long,' he laughs. 'Once you come offstage you realise you're the schmuck you always you knew you were.'

Could Cave have imagined, all those years ago, that he'd have this amazingly even and consistent career?

'I had an unfair advantage – I had talent. And I've always worked hard, even in the thick of it. I always hung on to . . . not only a work ethic, but there was something that was more important than . . . whatever other activities I was involved in. And it's just a feeling I had when I was a kid, about making things, that I recognise and still get to this day. My own sense of validation or whatever it is comes from work, and I always had that as a child. It just . . . drives me.'

Barney Hoskyns, Expanded from *Dazed & Confused*, October 2004

Nick Cave: Raw and Uncut 1

Phil Sutcliffe

The William IV pub on the Harrow Road, West London. An upstairs room, darkish and leathery; Cave is in a dark suit. During the interview he picks at a kebab and rice lunch and doesn't get very far with it but nicks a few of my big chips.

His hair looks dyed on close inspection. He has an air both diffident and friendly. He stops to think at great length before answering many questions and the longest pauses tend to produce an 'I don't know' answer. He's quite responsive except in the area of his wild period, more willing to talk about drugs than acknowledge and discuss past violence.

I see in several interviews you're saying that the new album is 'a masterpiece' and 'a work of genius' . . .
I don't recall ever calling it either of those things. But it is a good record and good records are rare these days. I still like it. That's unusual.

When did you finish it?
Please don't ask me questions like that.

When questions are bad, are they?
Yes. Some months ago I finished it. We were rehearsing some of it yesterday because we have a tour coming up and it was a real pleasure to play this stuff. Felt really good. Some records they're all right to record but once you get them in the rehearsal studio you realise you're going to have quite a lot of difficulty presenting some of the songs live. And to me if you can do the song live it's a testament to a good song. And these were just rolling out of us at the rehearsal. So that was further proof that it's . . . a work of genius and a masterpiece.

There you've said it again. I thought it was un-English and bold to say

Nick Cave in his office in Fulham, London, 6 February 2001.

***those things and you'd probably had people shouting, 'Oy, big head!'
at you in the streets of Brighton.***
No, that hasn't happened yet. But it's an Australian thing too that. You're never
allowed to stand behind your work in Australia. You have to talk about it in a
slightly demeaning way. Otherwise you're considered up yourself. Australia's a
great leveller.

***Part of what's enjoyable about the new album is a return to a degree
of rowdiness . . .***
There is definitely a joyfulness in playing this stuff and making a bit of noise.
Very enjoyable.

***. . . as if following directly from the last track on* Nocturama, *a big
rowdy thing a good deal of quietness. Playing them consecutively, I
came straight out of 'Babe, I'm on Fire' into 'Get Ready for Love' and
it felt very much a continuation.***
Did it? I hadn't thought of that. It would be wrong to think we thought 'Babe,
I'm on Fire' was a successful track on *Nocturama* because I'm not necessarily
convinced about that so I wouldn't say I wanted to duplicate that on the next
record. *Nocturama* certainly set up this new record in the way that we recorded
it. *Nocturama* was recorded fast and spontaneous and we carried that on with
this record. Ten days. For a double. Maybe eleven.

That's a hell of a lick. Not quite early Beatles but . . .
Not quite but we're getting there. I think the songs are better on this one than
on *Nocturama*. More considered. I kept going back and back and back to the
lyrics until I was completely happy with them, until I'd edited out and chopped
away all those lines that aren't that good and don't really mean anything. So I'm
extremely happy with the lyrics.

Any examples of that kind of stuff that you improved?
I won't give particular examples but sometimes I write stuff that I've read in
books down in my note books and I don't put quotation marks around it, see a
line in a poem, think, 'Fuck, that's really nice,' whack it in a notebook . . . I do a
lot of that and sometimes you don't know what you've written yourself and what
you've taken from somewhere else. You put one of those lines in a song from
the notebook and three months later you're re-reading a book and you go, oops.
For example, in a song called 'Loom of the Land' there is a line about the poplars
turning their backs. I was re-reading *Lolita* recently for the millionth time and
there it was, 'the poplars turned their backs'.

Inadvertent plagiarism?
Well, I don't mind stealing stuff but occasionally it's, um . . . anyway I got rid of
that stuff on this album. *[grins]* Hopefully.

Definitely no lawsuits, not even from dead people.
Yeah. Um. Apart from 'You are my north, my south, my east, my west' which is from an Auden poem called 'Funeral Blues' and it's in 'Supernaturally' but I left it in because it's a deliberate – what's the nice word? – reference.

Right, you need to know about these things, you mean, it's the accidental ones that give you a jolt. Right. Speaking of 'Supernaturally', it also seemed to me that apart from the rowdiness of a lot of it there's more enigma and mystery about what you're saying this time – whereas you've often been more direct recently. I suppose all I'm saying is I don't understand all of the lyrics, but in a nice way.
Well the records I turn to again and again are the ones I don't completely understand. *Veedon Fleece*, for example, which I've probably played more times than any other record I've ever owned and it's probably my favourite record of any I've owned because of that. It's something that to this day I know I don't understand completely, I don't know how Van Morrison arrived at those lyrical decisions, but it always feels like there's more to learn from that record. I always feel I get a little bit closer each time I listen to it, as opposed to, say, *Astral Weeks* which is in some respects a more complete record, but something I feel I understand, that I know what it's about. *Veedon Fleece* I don't get that feeling about. It's constantly on my turntable.

There's been a lot written about you as office worker, that you go into a routine now. How did that start?
It started when I met my wife, actually. As soon as I started living with her it became clear to me that I wouldn't write anything under those circumstances – that I needed to be alone to write. Which I had been previously. I'd worked at home before. I don't feel that other people need to have the creative process inflicted on them. It's not something you do around the people you love.

Why would that be?
Because it's undignified. They shouldn't be subjected to the difficulties of creating something. The screaming and crawling the walls and tearing your hair out and cursing – everything that goes into actually writing a song. I feel there's something actually noble about coming home and it appearing like these things have just happened. Understand?

Feeling like a worker? Coming home and you've done a decent day's work?
Yeah. I do feel like I've done a day's work. Call me old-fashioned, but I think there's a certain nobility in a day's work. *[he lights a roll-up]*

In this office, do you distract yourself? Do you have a radio or TV? Or do you maintain strict discipline?
I have a desk and a piano.

A telephone?
Yes, a telephone.

Do you talk on the telephone for hours?
Sometimes. Well I used to. I had a friend who died recently and I used to ring him up every morning and we would talk for at least an hour every morning.

Is that the chap the album's dedicated to?
Yeah [Mick Geyer]. Since he's died I have more time to work but it's not quite as pleasurable because . . . you know.

What was he giving you?
Encouragement. I could put the phone down and play the piano and sing and say, 'What d'you think of that one?' And he'd say, 'I think that one needs a bit of work, Nicholas,' or, 'You're onto something there, mate.' Whatever. And I had a complete respect for his opinions.

I saw a credit to him on a previous album – did it refer to him as a 'guru'?
I think there's a flippant remark like that made. There's a credit on one of the records as a kind of co-producer. He was in the studio while we were recording most of the Bad Seeds albums. He was a friend but he was a lot more.

He was with you from your early days in Australia?
Yeah.

And do you think you can keep this office working up now that there's that significant change in the circumstances? I know you're choosing solitude, but it must be a lonelier place now.
It is a lonelier place. Yeah. Because he didn't actually work in music as such but he knew an enormous amount about music and he spent his time looking for obscure and delightful music that he would let his friends know about. I don't have time to do that and I don't have that same adventurous spirit with music that he had. In that respect there's a channel of information that's gone which was very much a part of my development.

But you are sticking to this office setting.
Yeah, I don't know how else to do it. I've done it six, seven years now. The idea of sitting around with your mates, strum a guitar and try to write a song appalls me.

You never did that?
No.

Even back to schooldays?
No, never.

Because your starting point is the lyrics?
It's both.

Brighton is full of journalists and when I mentioned to another journo I was interviewing you he said, 'Oh there's a friend of mine, a Nick Cave fan who lives in Brighton and he bumped into you in Waitrose and was therefore shocked because he doesn't associate you with ordinary life.'
[grins] Must have been somebody else.

You don't go to Waitrose?
No. He's lying!

The point is that you are operating this ordinary life and that's not how people think of you. But I also think it's very different from your idea of how an artist should be. To produce a quote from the late '80s, apparently you said, 'The idea of a calmer life frightens me more than anything else. It's inherent in my character to destroy that.'
I think it's ungentlemanly to throw old quotes at an interviewee.

Journalists aren't gentlemen.
Well, I'm not convinced by the Waitrose anecdote but I'll play along for the sake of your question. I see the idea of work, organised work as a creditable thing. I actually see it as a romantic thing and a noble thing.

The romantic thing? A factory worker will say, 'Fuck that, squire.'
Well, a factory worker, I assume, does something he doesn't particularly want to do. I don't. I go into the office and it's actually something I enjoy, something I'm totally involved in. It transports me in some way. And it also functions really well for me. I have written songs on beer mats and so on but I've always ended up taking those beer mats back some place to work the song out. I've always done that. Whatever was going on in my life. Throughout my life I've sat there with the collection of beer mats and worked the song out because I've always written in a very considered way. For better or for worse.

Mostly for better surely?
Well, you know, there were times in my life when I could have loosened up a little bit – maybe there was too much consideration going on and things could have felt a little laboured lyrically. But it's the way I write.

Could you name names on the stuff you see as laboured?
When Penguin were putting together the collected works they sent me the proofs and I read them from beginning to end and I definitely saw periods in there, which I guess correlated to things that were going on in my life where I was

thinking, 'Fuck! This guy needs a night's sleep! He could lighten up a bit.' But there were other periods I was immensely proud of. But there were times I was so involved in the English language that it took over somewhat. To no great effect.

But you don't want to be specific about when that was?
I couldn't. Different times.

The quote about the calmer life and your instinct to destroy it – is that no longer true or does it ring no bells for you anymore?
I don't really know what that means. The thing that I value most about my life in regard to my work is that I'm able just to get on with it in the way that I want to. I find it slightly irritating that I have to justify the fact that I have a family or work office hours as if it's bizarre or eccentric.

I'd say you don't have to justify it, but it is bizarre in the rock world.
Well, I'm working more as a writer. And I'm sure you know yourself you can't write a novel on a beer mat. Eventually you've got to sit down at your fucking typewriter and do the work.

Every novelist does that.
They put their hours in. Now, for a songwriter it is different. You can knock out a few verses, put a few chords to them and you have a song. I just happen to write in a completely different way.

You do seem to be in a right creative burst at the moment, which must be nice.
Good if you can get it.

The Andrew Male who talked to you for Mojo *a while ago said that one of the most striking things you'd said was that, at least in part, you'd taken some drugs to slow down or beat back an onslaught of stuff that was flying at you from your imagination, as if your imagination was almost overwhelming you and drugs were in part a defence against that.*
I think that's true. It glorifies it somewhat. And I don't have it anymore. But I felt besieged by absolute bullshit that went on in my head all the time. An endless stream of internal dialogue and prattle that went away when I took smack. It was just like I was delivered into this place of peace for a while. That was certainly one of the attractive things about it. Eventually heroin stopped doing that and just exacerbated the problem and so I basically gave it up, to cut a long story short. It wasn't quite that easy. It was quite a time ago, six years ago. And that nonsense seemed to have dissipated over the years. I don't have that problem anymore.

I was thinking that the imaginings were rather fine, that it was the

characters who people your songs who were yakking at you, that there was a teeming creativity. But it was actually more like radio scrambling.
Yeah, bullshit. *[laughs quietly]* Everything comes out of your head, of course, but I wasn't able to sleep and it accelerated. In periods where I would try to stop taking drugs it would get overwhelming and the logical thing to do was go and take drugs again because then it stopped. Anyway, I'm sure I'm not alone in that.

The way you're working now is also clearly about dealing with family responsibilities while working within the rock world – you talked about resenting justifying it, but I'd say back that it is unusual in your world, and that's partly because it is about family responsibility and rock stars are supposed to be above that, so to speak.
For me, family is of the utmost importance. I wouldn't have had kids if I didn't feel that way. It's simply too much to take on. There's a whole world that exists within that, that is, beyond anything I do workwise. I guess I feel that in some ways it is necessary to protect the family from the work.

I had a father who was larger than life. When he entered the room he was Godlike to us all but his personality took over and in some ways – I loved him very much – but in some ways his personality was so big that it sucked everyone else's away. He was very much about his work, what he did, and it seems important to me that I don't affect them in that way. That they are free to *[smiles and laughs]* blossom in the way they want to blossom. My kids don't even really know what I do.

The older kids too you mean?
Well, Luke is thirteen and he understands more now. He comes and sees me, he's around a lot more, but the little ones don't. They don't see anything.

They just see a dad going off to work and coming home I guess.
Yeah, but we don't do day trips to Waitrose, honestly.

Does it have a bearing on you now, that just like any worker, there is a living that has to be made for other people, not just yourself?
Do you mean money?

Yes.
There is that aspect to it. I'm vastly overpaid for what I do if you look at the hours I work. In that respect it's the best job in the world. And I don't actually need to work as hard as I do. All a rock star needs to do is put out a record every three years. That's all the record companies want them to do, because there's a whole marketing strategy that works around being visible then being invisible then being visible again; it's self-perpetuating and it makes good economic sense. In the Bad Seeds, we have a different view, and we have a record company that supports what we do – that we can make as many records as we like.

So your routine doesn't relate to the need to provide for your family in fact.
Yeah. To have to write thirteen songs every three years is not a lot of fucking work. Well, and go on a tour. No, there's no problems in that area, no pressing need to get in there and write, so that's different from the factory worker we were talking about.

To move to the deep past, what started you off towards being an artist?
I guess I always wanted to be a rock star. I wasn't that musical. So I thought maybe I could be a writer or a painter. I was quite good at painting and I had a lot of encouragement from an art teacher, so that became my chosen field. And then I failed art school and at the same time this band I was in – which had been definitely a secondary thing – started to take off and so I got involved in the music business which I'm really happy about! I am very happy about it, in fact.

But were you disappointed at the time?
I was outraged that I failed art school. I was fuckin' mortified that these professors could fail me. But I'm slowly getting over it. *[grins]*

You had a nice phrase, which I think related to your art phase rather than your music: you talked about discovering 'the joy of displeasing somebody'.
We had that twofold. We had that with the band. We were playing in Australian beer barns so that they could keep these places open and sell alcohol. We were weaned on being booed, people sitting there and shouting, 'Get off you wankers!' Because in some weird way we believed in what we were doing there was definitely something about that that felt really good. In art school it was a similar sort of thing. There were a couple of fairly conservative teachers there and some of us took great joy in painting the sorts of pictures that offended them.

Lots of penises and so on.
Yeah. I think here's an Australian thing that takes that a step further, which is going against your peers, what is expected of you within your peer group. Offending them. If you're working in rock you want to go against what's happening in rock at the time – rather than trying to offend your parents or society. I think that might be an Australian thing. Separate yourself in some way from your contemporaries and peers.

As long as you've got your gang too, so you get support and applause from them?
Yeah. Adolescent nature. *[laughs merrily]*

Did the joy of displeasing carry right on or was there a moment when you discovered the joy of pleasing as well?
Yeah, there is a joy of pleasing.

But reading your biographies and . . .

I mean displeasing people keeps you awake and it keeps you alert and it keeps a good healthy fuck-you attitude to things, and pleasing people can lead to a kind of complacency. I think I'm very aware of complacency, of becoming that way, and working hard not to be that way.

You see it as a current threat?

Yeah, I think you have to work hard at that. When you're in your mid-to-late forties, people consider you complacent even if you aren't. I think you have to work very hard at that, to try and keep things alive.

From those years and on through to even your thirties you do seem to be raging a lot – the joy of displeasing seems to be right up front in what you're doing.

[pause, grin] Could have been.

Tell us about getting into Johnny Cash.

It was from watching *The Johnny Cash Show* on TV when I was nine. *[Editor's note:* The Johnny Cash Show *did not start broadcasting until June 1969, when Cave was eleven.]* Seeing this man. Seeing something he was putting forward that I hadn't seen before. Up until then I was just listening to children's music. I saw and thought rock'n'roll could be about something else.

What did he sing?

Oh, all sorts of stuff. It was a TV series. And I've listened to him ever since.

What did you get off him at nine?

I got that rock'n'roll could be evil, it could be a bad thing; he seemed like a real bad man. Dressed in black. At the start of the show he stood there with his back to the camera, then he swung round and said, 'Hello, I'm Johnny Cash.' I think some people thought for him to do that TV show was a selling-out, but I don't think that's true. I think it was a brave thing for him to do. Generous.

Is there a line from there to your Murder Ballads? In starting off a line of feeling about music . . .

Early on we played Johnny Cash songs live – possibly in Boys Next Door, certainly in early Bad Seeds. On *Kicking Against the Pricks* there's 'The Singer'. We've done a version of 'Wanted Man', the song Bob Dylan wrote for him. Also 'Long Black Veil', which he didn't write but which is very much based on his interpretation of that song. There's a song we did called 'The Good Son' which starts off with the repeated phrase 'One more man gone', which I remember hearing Johnny Cash sing though he may not have written it. We've been involved with him one way or another throughout. He did a version of 'The Mercy Seat' and I sang with him a couple of years ago. He's been around.

Extraordinary that he got to you when you were nine and you ended up singing with him just before he died. What did you think of him, having meant so much to you?

Rick Rubin rang me up and said, Would I like to sing with Johnny Cash? I said, Yes. I was in the studio next day – I was on tour. I was a little early or Johnny was a little late, so I was there when he arrived and when he entered the studio he was blind and there were these steps he had to negotiate down into the studio so he was helped down – whatever the disease was he had it affected his eyes so that he was blind for several minutes until he adjusted to the light. He looked really ill. He was like, 'Are you there Nick? Are you there?' It was a very haunting moment. I couldn't understand how he was going to . . . but he was so warm and generous in every possible way and June his wife was the same and once he started singing he came alive. It was extraordinary. They asked me to come with a couple of songs, name anything we'll do it, and that was exactly right. You know this Hank Williams song? Yeah, yeah. The band starts it up and off you go.

What do you think of him as an artist then?

A great artist, and more, he's a great man. I think that comes across; that he's more than a great artist.

What is his greatness?

Oscar Wilde said something like, 'Only the mediocre change,' and there was something about Johnny Cash, a line that was consistent through his career. Basically he stuck to his guns throughout. Of course he had this voice . . . I find that really inspiring, that he was his own man and everything he did he made his own.

You said to Jessamy Calkin way back, 1981, 'I want to write songs that are so sad, the kind of sad where you take someone's little finger and break it in three places.'

[laughs] I don't think I can add to that quote.

Does it hold from all those years ago?

I dunno. I often prefer a quote on how it sounds rather than what it actually means. There's other things to write about. I dunno what to say. I do like a sad song. I do like a sad song. When did I say that?

Nineteen-eighty-one.

Well, there you go. I've always been miserable. It isn't just recently.

I'm very impressed with all the fighting you were doing back then.

What's that?

You seem to have been a very violent fellow for quite a long time, starting in school and going on through to fighting with fans in

Birthday Party days.
I fought a lot at school, but I was forced to. I was a boarder for one year and boarders always fought. Wars, physical wars with the 'day scabs', as we called them, but then I became a day scab myself the following year so I was in a very awkward situation. Caused a lot of problems with these bad boys. And, um, so I just had to fight.

Do you remember the big fight with Beaver Mills?
I do, yeah. *[laughs]*

Are you going to tell me about it?
There's nothing to tell. We had a fight. He was a little rat-faced guy and he carried a knife – that was his big thing. We had a fight. *[shrugs]*

And you won?
I think I won one of them. We had several.

A regular part of the entertainment at school.
Everybody fights at school, don't they?

No.
Well, I wasn't a very good fighter but I did have a certain spirit.

That you wouldn't be beaten?
I dunno. Schooldays. You fight.

Okay. Onwards into the Birthday Party. You seemed to be forever jumping into audiences and sorting people out.
Allegedly. There's not a hell of a lot to say. Was that a question? You'll have to do better than that. You'll have to ask me a question. I don't know how to answer that.

It seems that there was a lot of violence associated with the Birthday Party and that you would pile in and . . .
We were billed on one tour of Europe as 'the most violent band in the world'. We didn't put that on the poster but some promoter decided that was the way to fill the places we were playing. And a lot of people that came along didn't know the band; they just thought it was an open invitation to disaster. So there was conflict. We had an ex-marine who was a fan and became a friend of ours; his name was Bingo, big guy, and he used to keep an eye out and disarm the front row – backstage he would show us the iron bars and whatnot he had confiscated off people in the front row. In those early days there was a lot of aggression.

And you . . .
I'm not saying I didn't play my part in it, but there was a certain amount of self-

protection involved and being not a great fighter, uh, sometime you have to do pre-emptive strikes. *[grins]*

For instance?
You know, you have to get some of them before they get you. Take 'em unawares. *[laughs]* I think I've said enough about that.

Did you enjoy it?
Yeah, it was fun; we had a good time. We had a good time, yeah. Eventful. The shows were eventful. I guess after a while it became a little tedious, a little predictable, and I guess that's why the Birthday Party broke up. We had an audience who were coming along expecting us to be a certain way and as soon as we felt that happening, our natural inclination was to do nothing at all, move to the back of the stage and sing the songs – disappoint everybody! There is something to be said for disappointing people, going back to what we were saying before. To displease and disappoint it keeps you on your toes, keeps you alive.

There's a picture from New York of you jumping offstage to wrap a microphone cord round a woman's neck and scream at her 'Express yourself! Express yourself!'
[chortles] Yeah, we were having a good time. That particular night we were billed to play a concert and then the venue changed and we were still contracted to play. The clientele were different – a singles bar, and we were the wrong band for them. It just felt like the right thing to do. There were only about six or seven people in the audience. What are you going to do?

Back then when you were interviewed you were very negative about your audience: what was that all about?
Was I negative? I don't remember that? I think I thought there were people there for the wrong reasons, as I mentioned before. People who went along in order to fight the band. Which became tedious.

When did that change?
When the Birthday Party ended and we started the Bad Seeds. There were internal problems in the Birthday Party; it couldn't have survived, it would have gone into decline and I think we got out of it at the right time. We were becoming successful and we broke it up and changed it to something else.

With that change, how did you see your audiences? Do you have an objective in the way you direct yourself?
We present the songs the best we can. We have no control over whether people are going to like it. But I basically think we stick to our guns about things. We've been around for a long time and there have been periods when we've been hopelessly irrelevant to what's going on. We've played concerts or festivals and

it's clear we should be put out to pasture. But we hang in there. We've always hung in there. Sometimes we're popular and relevant and sometimes we're not. This goes back to what we were talking about with Johnny Cash. Certainly there were periods when he could capture the audience's imagination – on a much larger scale than what we do, obviously, but it's not dissimilar – other times he was hopelessly out of his time. But he didn't demean himself by attempting to stick with the times, and change his music and fly with the winds of fashion. He was just Johnny Cash and I deeply respect that about him and other artists like that.

So that's a fundamental objective of yours?
Yeah. *[laughs]* We just plough our own lonely furrow and people can like it or not.

When did you feel most irrelevant?
We did the Lollapalooza tour in America [1994]. It was fifty-three dates in a row. Grunge was happening and it was very difficult because people just didn't turn up to the stage to see us. We were no longer in control, we had to persevere. I personally found that extremely difficult.

Was there active hostility as there was with the Birthday Party?
No, people just went had their lunch while we played and then came back when we stopped. *[laughs]* I'm talking about kids. There wasn't one person there wearing long trousers.

But you played through it.
We couldn't pull out contractually. We would've if we could've.

A challenge to the ego.
It hardened us against America. It took us many years to go back. We decided we'd just play Europe and Australia and it was years before we went back.

Going back to the Birthday Party and that whole period, the general take has been that it was self-destructive, that it may be of a piece with people like Keith Richards making themselves a human laboratory. Do you see yourself as part of that or do those clichés have nothing to do with it?
The idea of being a human laboratory: I can understand that Keith Richards may have seen himself that way because for white rock'n'roll he was one of the forerunners of people taking massive amounts of drugs. By the time we were doing it everyone was taking massive amounts of drugs, so we weren't experimenting, we were doing something that was tried and tested a thousand times before us! I was a junkie. I was not particularly adventurous with drugs. I took heroin and I took speed. That was pretty much it. I didn't smoke pot. Oh, and I drank. I led a fairly conservative existence in the sense that I did that at home in my flat. The

Birthday Party weren't particularly tied up in all the rock'n'roll thrills; in fact it was kind of depressing, *[laughs]* the drug aspect. The first ten years were all right; the second ten years were nothing to write about; certainly no story there. But to me way too much has been made out of the drugs thing.

In what sense?

In the sense that everybody, as far as I knew, was doing it. When I grew up heroin in Australia was *the* recreational drug. Everybody did it. Everybody that I knew shot up heroin. And it was only when I came to England that I realised it was probably the most antisocial drug you could take. You were marginalised. You were on the lowest rung of the ladder. You were a junkie. Down there with the paedophiles basically. The worst thing you could possibly be. In Australia it wasn't like that.

In the NME *feature where you were talking with Shane MacGowan and Mark E. Smith in 1989, Shane MacGowan said: 'Nick, you're doing a Jung-style trip of examining your shadow, all the dark things you don't want to be. A lot of your songs are trips into the subconscious and are therefore nightmarish.' Any truth in that?*

[laughs] In a rare lucid moment! I don't know what that means either. I love Shane and I think that's a very charming quote. *[laughs some more]* I don't know what to say. Change the 'charming' to endearing.

I think that was the first time you met him.

Yeah, and I was a huge fan of Shane's so it was an absolute pleasure to meet him. It was a disastrous article. But a pleasure to meet him. We're good friends to this day.

He sticks to his guns too.

Absolutely.

Have you ever felt part of a community?

I'd have to say no. I'd have to say no because I live in Brighton and not long ago I had this twinge, this feeling within me, and it had to do with the place I was living in, Brighton, that I felt a part of it, that I actually cared about this place, that I cared about what happened in this place. I guess that was a feeling almost of *civic duty* creeping in – and it was utterly foreign to me. Utterly foreign.

What did you do about this burgeoning sense of civic duty?

Oh, nothing. But it was a feeling that I'd never felt before. Except that within the band there was always a very solid feeling and there still is, a very solid feeling of a group of men working together. Going out and working together. I think we prize that aspect of what we do. We're very careful not to disrupt that by bringing personal problems to the band. In that sense it's very much a working unit.

It's a community thing. And it was like that with the Birthday Party too. A gang mentality. An us against them.

And the mannish thing of not bringing the personal into the band?
Yeah, yeah. Well, in the Birthday Party I think those lines were blurred somewhat. With the Bad Seeds we communicate with each other through our work and I personally value that.

Those relationships are long, up to some thirty years. Through no end of chaos, no end of problems, some of these relationships have held through it all completely undeterred.
They're battered around in the process to some degree, but at the death we value what we're doing and we've learned over the years when to pull back and keep the mouth shut so that people can be what they want to be. It works in some kind of way.

You've said several times that you rate yourself as a father but not as a husband or a son . . .
Oh, when I said that, it was a particularly self-lacerating . . . I don't hold by that anymore.

What is it that makes you a good father?
Oh, I dunno. Like my parents I'm winging it day by day. That's the revelation about being a parent to me is I always thought my parents knew what they were doing and suddenly I realised that I don't know what I'm doing and they didn't know – you're fucking winging it! *[laughs]*

So the great godlike authority figure of your father who you presumed knew it all . . .
Yeah. And I find that it suddenly endeared me to my parents and reconciled me a lot. That you're not actually supposed to have all the answers. And who fucking wants all the answers?

One thing being a parent must challenge is one's egocentricity, and there is a particular egocentricity about being a creative artist, isn't there?
You can be incredibly selfish about it. It's a very selfish business to be in because you're spending much of the day examining yourself and plumbing the depths of yourself. Which, on one level, I find nauseating and not something I want to inflict on other people. It has to be done. If you're going to write worthwhile things a certain amount of that has to happen. But I don't see why other people that you love should endure that as well.

As an artist has it affected you, being deeply committed to various relationships?

Yeah. I think it's made me better. It's made me better.

In what way?
It's deepened me. You have to cast an eye to other people. You have to compromise. And compromise can actually be strengthening, I think. Where at times you have to stand down. You see there's something greater going on in a marriage than the two parts – does that make sense? – which is the marriage itself. I think that's a good thing.

Can you give any example of how that's reflected in your writing?
No. I've always written about love in different forms – I've written a lot about the beginnings of love, I've written about the ends of love, but there's this whole middle section that hasn't really been examined. I don't think it's really been examined in rock'n'roll music. Rock'n'roll is about bursts of positive and negative energy, and I'm kind of interested in that middle period and writing about that, seeing where that goes, where it takes me. Trying to find something there to write about.

Is it difficult?
It's harder. It's less dramatic. There's no story in it – or there's no beginning and no end. But it is interesting. For me. It may not be for anybody else. I'll give it a bash.

Love gets a fair kicking in your earlier work . . .
There's certainly a nice sense of drama in letting the whole thing explode. So, yes. It gets a kicking.

And there's no satisfactory answer.
To what?

The need for love and the impossibility of it. Is that how you felt back then?
I was falling in love every week.

You were a romantic soul at the same time as you were writing all those songs?
Very much so, and I had anything but a cynical attitude to love. I suspect what I thought was love then may not have been love. I don't know what to say.

It seems to me that the big change comes with* The Boatman's Call *and 'Into My Arms' where it actually says, 'I believe in love.' Was that a big shift for you?
Of faith?

In love.
It came out of a very wounded period. Experience. Some of it did. Not that song.

That record has the whole gamut; it has the beginnings and it has the ends. I think I've always had faith in the idea of love.

You declared it in that song . . .
I believe in love, yeah.

The religious side of what you write about: what was the starting point?
I was in the choir in the country town where I grew up, Wangaratta, so I grew up knowing about the story of Christ. And Biblical stories. And they were intriguing to me. They were spooky, violent.

What was your favourite?
I've always been interested in the story of Christ as such and that was what was pushed in this Anglican church where I was a choirboy. I didn't remain interested through my teenage years but in my twenties I started to read the Bible a lot; was drawn back in by these stories.

Did you believe when you were a kid in the choir?
I don't know whether I did or not.

It was the words, the stories that got you?
I don't know about back then, but yeah.

And then they got you again as a grown man?
I was reading the Bible in art school. I was interested in religious art. I found I had much more of an emotional attachment to religious art than I did to a lot of modern art, secular art. But I wasn't examining why, particularly. But I was reading the Bible a lot then, the Old Testament. Then I wrote the novel and I was reading the Bible a lot when I did that. Then I started reading the New Testament a lot and very closely and I was taken away by the life of Christ. Because he seemed, in the Bible, he seems very different to this Christ character who was being pushed at me when I was in the choir – a figure that was deeply human, fallible, and something one could almost aspire to, as opposed to the gods in other religions who seemed to be beyond us as humans.

What story made you like him most?
I guess the story that affected me most was the touching of the hem of the garment; Christ is in a throng of people pushed from all sides and there is a girl who has had an issue of blood for twelve years, and she reaches out and touched the hem of his garment. He stops and says, 'Who touched the hem of my garment?' Everyone says, 'Oh, we all were.' He says, 'No,' and turns round. She says, 'I did.' He says, 'You are made whole – go now.' It was that notion of being made whole which to me was a very human idea. That to be made whole is to be human; that was the human nature of him.

And you still read the Bible?
I do. I don't read it every day.

And have you been persuaded?
No, I don't belong to any church or organised religion.

You believe in God?
I do, yeah. But it's open, doubtful, sceptical.

How does the doubt and scepticism sit beneath the faith?
Because I'm a human being and I fluctuate from day to day. Sometimes I feel very close to the notion of God and other times and I don't. And that used to worry me. I used to see it as a failure in some way but these days I see it as a strength, especially put up against the more fanatical notions of what God is and where that can lead which is so evident today. I think doubt is an essential part of belief.

What did you make of Dylan's born-again albums, Slow Train Coming **onwards?**
I wasn't a Dylan fan from the beginning. I actually came to Dylan late in life and it was very much with that record *Slow Train Coming*. I did know some of his earlier records because my brother had them – *Nashville Skyline* was one. I always loved *Nashville Skyline* from my brother having it. I didn't see that in relation to anything else he'd done, I just loved it and I still play it a lot. But I had no overall concept of what Dylan was. Then I played that song, 'You Gotta Serve Somebody', the single off that album on the jukebox in some bar in New York, and just thought it was the most amazing thing I'd ever heard, then listened to the rest of that record. I think it's one of his great records no matter where you stand.

Why did it inspire you?
That song? The simplicity of it. Things changed for me after I heard that song. Not in regard to my belief. I'm not the kind of person who is affected by other people's beliefs and I don't want to know about other people's beliefs . . . but . . . it's just such a great song. *[laughs]*

But how did it not offend you? It's ferocious, it says, 'You gotta,' it points the finger . . .
I'm impressed by people who are committed to something whether I believe it or not. I'm also impressed by people who turn their back on all preconceived notions of what they are supposed to be about. I find that attractive no matter how great the folly. And Dylan does that. He confounds and frustrates and disappoints constantly. He's made a career of it and to me that's to his credit. I loved *Slow Train Coming* because it rages. It's incredibly mean-spirited, bilious, and I love that.

In 'O Children' you say 'the answer is short, it's simple, it's crystal

clear' – so what is it?

That's one of those things that keeps you visiting the record. If Van Morrison told me why he wrote 'I wish on a toilet roll' *[laughs]* in whatever song it's on *Veedon Fleece* I might stop listening to the record.

But you're starting to tell people now.

Well, maybe. But it's also saying we can't find it, we've lost it. I guess there's an element of preachification in that. But to me the song is very tender and heartfelt towards the legacy we leave out children. Bleak in a way. But it has a lot of feeling to me. I don't like being preached at and I never intend to do that. I don't feel I have the authority to do that.

Whereas Dylan does obviously.

Dylan's fanatical in what he does. He doesn't do things by half-measure. That's Dylan.

Nobody would accuse you of being a half-measures person, but there's a big difference in your approaches.

If I started to do that, it would take something away. The thing I value most about my work is that there's a certain amount of mystery about it. To me, that's more affecting than having someone point the finger at you and tell you, This is what you should believe, this is what you should support. But I do see it as my duty in some way to put forward my own notion of God and that even though that may be unfashionable or distasteful to some people I don't think it would be true to myself not to do that. Because it's a genuine preoccupation. Always has been.

Do you have a converse big idea for what music can do apart from breaking someone's finger in three places as you said in 1981?

What it can do?

Your own big ambition maybe . . .

I don't have a big ambition. I have the ambition to make another record. It only goes that far. I'm delighted when I make a record like this one which suggests so many things I can go and do with the next record. That's what I consider to be successful. Some records feel like dead ends. *Boatman's Call* was like that. I made it and I just didn't know what to do next. It took a long time to be able to work out where to go after that. But this one feels as though it opened up a lot of doors in many ways.

It took me a long time for me to see the value of music and the value of being in a rock band because I had a lot of received notions about where rock music was on the creative ladder – it came from my father and art school. There were the painters up here, my father always put poetry at the top of the ladder . . . it took some time before it dawned on me that I was doing something as worthwhile if not more worthwhile than some of these loftier pursuits

Why is it worthwhile, then? What did you come to see?

Because I found what music did for me, which was it that it had a potential which the other forms don't have which is to utterly change you from the moment you put on the song – within three minutes you can be a changed person, your whole body chemistry can change, your mood, your perspective. And I use music for that purpose. I feel a particular way, I put a record on and I know, I can guarantee that I will feel better.

What do you use?
Dylan or Van Morrison or Nina Simone – I have particular people that I use to make me feel better. It makes me better. And I don't get that from sitting down and reading a poem or a book. A book can widen my ideas about things and it can warm my heart but it's not like; *[snaps fingers]* it doesn't have that immediacy about it.

Oddly you've come to that conclusion in early middle age.
Yeah, because the defining moments in my life, like putting 'Gotta Serve Somebody' on in that bar, they're usually musical – talking about art, I mean – it's usually been music, a concert where my view of things has been totally changed.

Have you ever heard anyone whistling one of your songs?
Er, no.

Would you like to?
Oh I would, yeah. Walking down the street, yeah.

Why doesn't it happen to your music?
Well, I don't know that it doesn't. I think some of our music is immensely whistleable. Some of it. You can't whistle 'The Lyre of Orpheus'. But it would be nice.

It shows something.
Just it's got a good melody and I'm always happy about that.

I can't think of a round-off question, but I'm torn between Southern literature, the blues and your singing.
Singing.

Do you think you've become a good singer?
Oh. Yeah. You don't know how hard it is for me to say that, but yeah. I've always been bowed beneath the limitations of my voice and I've always felt that very deeply. But I like it now. I don't know why. Well, I do sing better than I used to, I have more control than I used to. I've accepted the fact that my voice will always sound the same way: morose, melancholy, lugubrious, plaintive. No matter what I do those feelings will always be there inside my voice. There are other singers who have the same problem – Leonard Cohen, Johnny Cash possibly. Saddled with a particular type of voice. But I've come to like it.

In performance, in the studio, do you prepare yourself at all?
I don't prepare myself at all. Tuning isn't one of my great talents. Intonation isn't one of my greater talents as a singer. But I do think I have a pleasing way of phrasing at times and I can be quite expressive. To a fault at times. *[laughs]*

You might go over the top?
It can become a little melodramatic. *[laughs]*

But when you let rip it's not that you've method-acted your way into it.
No, it just comes out like that.

And you've got a good ear? In the Birthday Party you would sing off key and I never knew if it's art or bum notes . . .
Oh, I think that was just weirdness. *[laughs]* I don't think there's many bum notes. But luckily the Bad Seeds play in a certain way and they can accommodate a certain amount of looseness.

Listening to you non-stop this week, I've never been so conscious of the band as a frame for the voice.
Is that a good thing?

Yeah, they're full of detail and yet it's all unobtrusive.
I think they have a natural desire to serve the song and it's a rare thing. They're quite happy not to play or go ding-ding twice in a song and sit down again. There's a lot of them so they can't be playing all over the place. But they do have that sense of economy. I guess they all come from punk rock so there's never been that problem about the lead guitar . . .

26 October 2004, Lounge at the London Outpost Hotel
The movie: does it relate to your dad's interest in Ned Kelly?
It's called *The Proposition*; it's set at the end of the bushranger era in 1888 – do I need to explain what bushrangers were?

Ned Kelly does it for us.
It's making a genre movie out of this period like they did with Westerns in America. All the films that have been made about bushrangers have been factual stories about actual bushrangers, Ned Kelly, Mad Dog Morgan, all that lot. This is fictional. It's been two years of nightmarish dealings with finances but it's finally happening and now it's in its third week of filming so it's gonna happen which is great news for me.

You wrote the script.
I wrote the script and I'm doing the music. It stars Ray Winstone, Emily Watson, Guy Pearce, John Hurt and Danny Huston.
I went to Winton where they built a little town for the filming. In Queensland.

There's nothing out there. I went to this tiny town where they were rehearsing and it was fantastic – to have written something and to watch these actors do it, really great.

And you wrote it in the office between songs?
Yeah. Johnny Hillcoat is a dear friend of mine and has done a lot of videos for us. He's also made two feature films, the first one *The Ghost of the Civil Dead* – I acted in and some other of my band members did the music to. The second film, *To Have and to Hold*, we did the music to. So we have a long history. He came to me and said would I write bushranger movie.

Your first shot at a film script?
Yeah.

Does it relate to your songwriting thematically?
No, no. It's sad, it's violent. *[grins]* In that respect . . . Hopefully everyone's not just dribbling Nick Caveisms out of their mouths throughout.

Does it connect at all with your father's interest in that area? Where I gather he was something of a specialist?
I grew up in Wangaratta which is next to Glenrowan and they call that 'Kelly Country' so you grew up with these stories and, yeah, my father would hold exhibitions of Ned Kelly memorabilia when he worked in adult education in Wangaratta. He had an exhibition of his armour and so on, and wrote an introduction to a book about him called 'Ned Kelly: Man and Myth'. So I'd taken in a certain amount of knowledge. But this is completely fictional and it's not dealing with the usual aspects of the thing – the Irish situation; bushrangers generally were Irish set upon by the British and they had enough and went off into the bush and drank a lot and committed low-level crime. It's not dealing with that. It's dealing with very different sorts of things.

Does it at all relate to the Southern Gothic literary influence on your work?
Probably not. No.

Has Southern Gothic gone from your writing? The last song I could see where it seemed to be an underlying force, perhaps, was 'Dead Man in My Bed'. Is it something that's faded from your work now?
I just was reading a lot of it back whenever that was. I haven't read much for years and years now. But there are always those grand themes that go on – Southern literature seems to deal with grand themes – a hyper, extreme style of writing. That's why I responded to it and certainly I relate to that in the way I write today. To get into one of my records, you have to enter my world, the world of that record. You don't drag one of my records into your world. If you understand the difference; I don't know if I do. But it's an alien, romantic, extreme world, which

is of my making. Some people enjoy entering that world, and other people don't feel that's necessary in order to listen to music so they prefer to listen to music which augments their own lives as such. I think that's why, to a degree, my music will always be marginal. End of lecture. *[claps hands]*

Southern Gothic: you never or hardly ever went to that place and what you wrote came out of your own imagination. It seemed to be a real world, but you imagined it all. Did you perversely refuse to go there so that you wouldn't see the real thing?
That was all totally received information – movies, books, blues music. At the time of writing I had no experience of the South at all – one night we played somewhere down there I think, that was all.

Was that a positive choice – I'm not going to research this?
I didn't feel it was necessary. I was creating something that was mythical, not meant to be real. I remember ringing up my mother, who's a librarian, and telling her I was writing this book about the sugarcane industry and asking her if she could find out something about it – this was before the internet, which I don't use anyway. She sent me back this pamphlet, a two-page thing for kids at school, and that was the extent of my research on sugarcane growing which was absolutely fundamental to the story. But I didn't feel it was that necessary. I know the flora and the fauna is all over the place in that book, it's not consistent to the South at all. And then, although it is set in the South of the USA, a lot of it feels to me as though it's in Australia. In some ways I wish I had set it there. I don't know why I didn't.

In so many areas of your life – religion, music, relationships – you seem to have developed out of chaos and confusion into self-respect. Is that how it feels to you?
I feel more confident in the worlds I've created. I certainly feel more content and happier. I'm definitely happier than I was ten years ago and to me this is a good thing even though I feel required to make excuses for it all the time. A lot of that comes from narrowing down the experiences I actually have so that I'm very much involved in my family and my work and some friends. It's very simple and that's intensified things on one level and made things simpler. And in that respect I'm happier.

You've written lots of different things but are you thinking of writing an autobiography?
I had an idea that from my own personal view I'd quite like to write an autobiography, but by going back throughout my life and interviewing the people I can remember – old girlfriends, Penny Charade, who I knew when I was thirteen, what's she like now? I abandoned that idea; too much like hard work and a masturbatory type of affair. So the answer is, Fuck, no! Well, I wouldn't mind

getting right some of these apocryphal tales from the biography that is out there – well, tales that I don't remember and keep cropping up in articles about me.

On the religious side, you said you believed: was that the result of long thinking about it or a Damascene moment – which one of the lyrics on the album suggested?

I can't remember not believing. I certainly can remember periods when I didn't give it a thought, when it wasn't a factor in my life. I've certainly never been an atheist. Never had any conscious disbelief. There was a period when I struggled with the whole thing because being someone who uses words, you need to be able to justify your belief with language. I would have arguments about it and I would always lose because it's not a rational thing, it's an absurd thing. The atheist always wins because you can go back to logic and belief in God is illogical, it's absurd. I gave up arguing about it because there's no debate; it's something that comes from the heart, something I just feel intuitively. At the end of these arguments, I'd go, Well, I dunno, I just feel that way! For me it comes from the place that inspiration comes from, from a magical place, a place of the imagination. And I'm comfortable with that.

Again I was looking back at the lyrics of the new album and I was struck by the lines about your father's words on beauty in 'Nature Boy'. Is that actual or an imaginary father?

The first verse is true. It comes from me being at my grandmother's house; the news came on the TV and I saw the attempted assassination of George Wallace. I was shocked; I knew it was the real thing. My father said to me, yeah, this stuff goes on and there are other things in the world too, beautiful things. Which was a good thing to say.

Wonderful thing to say. I know you lost him early but great to have memories like that.

Yeah, you hang on to them.

Phil Sutcliffe, Interview transcript for a *Mojo* feature, 21 October 2004

Acropolis Now!

Michael Odell

- *Place: Piano bar, Residence Georgio Hotel, Athens, Greece*
- *Date: Saturday, 4 December 2004*
- *Vibe: A surreal afternoon. In a Bogart-like interlude, a waitress comes over and says someone called Marty Thomas is on the phone. Would Mr Cave take the call? Cave says, 'I don't know anyone by that name. So no.'*

Nick Cave is struggling with the dress code for 200BC. In an Athens restaurant, which aims to recreate the ambience of ancient Greece, he sits at the centre of a thirty-foot table as toga'd servants pour sweet wine into goblets and a spit-roasted carcass is passed overhead. Between the Doric columns are beds, should you require a mid-prandial rest. On the walls gods loll and point or stab animals with spears.

In his brown, chalk-stripe suit Cave looks like a Reservoir Dog who has blundered onto the set of *Alexander*. As the Bad Seeds get trolleyed in historically accurate fashion around him, teetotal Cave smokes a succession of highly anachronistic roll-ups.

He recommends the lamb. He explores the photo opportunities with *Q*'s snapper ('You're not getting a Kylie shot of me in a toga,' he warns), and, for a man so often compared to the devil or a vampire, he seems a genial host.

In fact, on a scale of one to smashing-Kylie's-head-in-with-a-rock (the grisly text of their duet 'Where the Wild Roses Grow'), Cave is in jovial mood and with good reason. His dates in Athens and Thessaloniki mark the end of a sold-out European tour. And today is the last day of filming of his screenplay *The Proposition*, a story about Australian bushrangers starring Guy Pearce, John Hurt and Ray Winstone, being shot on location in the outback.

A quarter-century into his career Cave has evolved from the proto-Goth lunatic attacking his audience at Birthday Party gigs to the multi-tasking artist, as comfortable at his grand piano as he is writing on theological matters for *The Times*. It's as much a surprise to him as everyone else that his recent album, *Abattoir Blues/The Lyre of Orpheus*, has sold 80,000 copies in the UK alone.

In the limo ride back to his hotel he's quite the elder statesman, remembering how the Greeks smashed up a now defunct venue at a Birthday Party gig in 1981. Confronted with a tape recorder, the famous reticence returns. 'Oh God . . .' he moans.

That's not a good start. What do you mean, Oh God?
I just hate . . . Put that. Just start with, Oh God . . .

Okay. You think this album is a masterpiece?
I say that about all my records because people believe it, and it becomes the accepted viewpoint. But yes, I'm very proud of this record and it's been a pleasure to play it. We wrote it as a band rather than me working alone in my office.

Yes, you usually work nine-to-five in a suit. Sounds a bit dull.
What am I going to wear? Bermudas and flip-flops?

How about trainers?
No. I'm going to do something serious. I would feel extremely uncomfortable sitting at a piano in trainers. Trainers?! I couldn't bring myself to demean myself or my material. My muse wouldn't bear it. I've always worn suits as soon as I could afford to have them made. They're only 600 quid but I feel serious. I feel the part.

You've got Leonard Cohen's suitcase in your office. What's in it?
Nothing of Leonard's in there, unfortunately. Just crap. It's my wife's. She got it from a friend who was involved with Leonard. I don't kneel by it or sit in it. He can have it back if he wants.

Tell me about Orpheus's Lyre . . .
Oh, is this where you try and forge a link between my music and us being in Greece?

Yes.
Well everyone knows the myth of Orpheus and his lyre, don't they? You didn't? That's intriguing. You need to sue your school. I'm worried about you. It's a story that is from before the Rolling Stones. Anyway, I grew up with it. I've been aware of it for as long as I can remember. I'm not even sure it was my father who told me about it. Obviously the tale of Orpheus, who makes music so beautiful it can wake the dead, was something that spoke to me but I wanted to change it. So in my song he makes such a godawful racket. He makes a deadly sound.

You're very settled now. Wife. Kids. Steady career. And you love Hove, don't you?
I feel more towards that place than any place I've ever lived in, except maybe Australia. I'm thinking of a particular stretch of the promenade and certain back streets of Hove. I feel happy there and I feel invisible. I've always felt an alien or intruder or gringo or a guest. I'm happy to remain in Hove for the duration.

So your wife will wheel you along the prom in a wheelchair and a tartan blanket when you're seventy?
And she in stilettos and a nurse's outfit, yes.

Do you campaign on parking and dog shit?
No. Not yet. Although I did campaign to have Brighton's West Pier turned into an ape island.

What do you mean?
It was the front page of *The Argus*, the local rag. 'Rock King Has Idea for Pier', or something. We wanted the pier's iron frame to be covered in vines, lay grass on top and throw a few monkeys on it so that it was this strange island sticking out to sea the community could watch.

That's a bit more like it. Now you're sounding a bit like the madman of old.
I felt demented when I arrived in London in the '80s. Now, like my parents, I feel the world is crazy, not me. I'm a tourist now, so I like London again. I can go to Buckingham Palace and buy a tea towel.

I don't believe you.
I have. I went to Buckingham Palace and bought a tea towel. I've got it hanging in the kitchen, but we really don't need to go there. I like tea towels. It felt symbolic. *[Bad Seeds percussionist Jim Sclavunos later confirms that Cave collects tea towels. At their Greek shows over the weekend, Lyre of Orpheus tea towels are available for five euros.]*

Are you a royalist?
I'm a tourist. But I'd rather have the Queen on my tea towel than Tony Blair.

Why?
[suddenly bored and grumpy] Oh, I don't know.

'Breathless', from the new album, is an unironic love song. It's unusual, perhaps, because no women end up in tears or in casualty?
I'll exclude my wife from this. I've always found that women I've written about have been flattered even when I haven't been nice.

Was [former lover] PJ Harvey okay with the songs about her on ['97 album] The Boatman's Call?
I don't know. It was all over by the time it came out. We haven't talked about it.

Didn't you start going to church to get over Polly?
What?! No I fucking didn't. Where'd you get that from? Come on. That's just not

true. I wasn't that wounded, to be honest with you. I wrote a great song, 'Far from Me' [on *The Boatman's Call*], about her, which was a fucking cracker. That song was by far the high point of our relationship. It lives on.

What about Tori Amos? You said the 'twinkling cunt' line in 'Green Eyes' [also on The Boatman's Call] was about her sewing sequins into her pubic hair. I bet she wasn't flattered by that.
That's simply not true. It keeps getting repeated in the press, but it's not true.

It's here in this music magazine from 1997. The journalist asks, 'You have first-hand experience of this?' and you say, 'Yes.'
I lied. I start to lie when things get really tedious. Anyway, I met Tori in the lobby of a hotel once afterwards. She seemed a lovely girl. She didn't send any letters of complaint. I think even if it were true it's kind of flattering. I mean, how sweet. What a sweet thing to do . . . to sit there and sew sequins into your pubic hair.

You've managed to maintain a very balanced view of being a junkie, haven't you?
I was a junkie for twenty years. I'm not going to deny all that. That would be silly. I don't trust the whole reborn thing, whether it's religious or cleaning up. You're still absolutely the same person. It would be like denying my entire youth. Perhaps if it was a deeply hideous time I would, but it wasn't. People take drugs to feel good and that seems a legitimate reason to do it for me.

Won't that be a tough rationale to defend as a parent?
I'd have a lot more difficulty if my son came home in a Burberry cap carrying a six-pack under one arm and a football under the other. If he started binge-drinking like a huge proportion of the English male population does, I would be worried.

That's class snobbery. What if he wore a Burberry suit while he got pissed?
No, it's Burberry that's the problem. And junkies don't punch the shit out of each other every night. They don't trawl the streets looking for heads to kick in. They just sit there and quietly dribble into their lap. They're passive and harmless. There is a difference.

Who impresses you musically right now?
In relation to what's going on in music today, I consider myself head and fucking shoulders above, musically, lyrically and as a live band. I mean that in all humility.

But you claim not to listen to pop music, so how do you know?
Well, maybe I'm wrong. Maybe everyone's really great. But the fact that the Red Hot Chili Peppers are one of the biggest bands in the world makes me want to

hang my head and weep. I'm forever near a stereo saying to the band, 'What the fuck is this GARBAGE?' and the answer is always the Red Hot Chili Peppers.

Really? There are a lot worse.
Really? Well that's my point exactly.

Hearing Johnny Cash when you were nine drew you to music. You ended up recording with him.
I worked with him in the studio. We weren't friends, but he was a great man. It was very sad when he died, obviously, but in some ways it gave me hope. He sang right up until he died. And he died not long after his wife died, which is a beautiful thing, too.

You've said you are forever trying to escape the myths around you . . .
Do you know it's a breach of gentlemanly code to repeat back a man's quotes to him?

You didn't ask me to sign any code. Go on, be your own PR for a day.
I wouldn't do that job. But I suppose if anything rankles it's that I sit down and do interviews and the article will always say I look like a fucking vampire in the first sentence. I realize I am implicated in that. I've written some pretty dark, death-obsessed music, but there is more to me than that.

Stop dyeing your hair, perhaps? Be Nicholas again?
I don't think so. It's been black since I was a teenager. I dyed it when my first girlfriend, with whom I was besotted, left me. Just vanished. I'm brown naturally.

And you're quite warm and friendly, too, aren't you? I saw you stroke a cat yesterday. Do you regret cultivating an image as a dark lord?
I don't cultivate any image. Granted, I see the macabre in life but I'm just as capable of stroking a cat as the next man.

The next night in Thessaloniki Cave entertains 3,000 Greeks, but his struggle to avoid vampire stereotyping hits a snag. A bat flies into the venue and dive-bombs the stage and audience. Nevertheless, his high-kicking, Gothic Rat-Packer routine hits the mark. Backstage he takes receipt of an end-of-tour cake and gives flowers to the choir. But he's not quite done. Unlike many pop stars Cave does not really curate his image, but he does care about words. Our earlier discussion of 'chavs' in Burberry needs tweaking. Cave approaches with a carefully prepared statement.

'I've been thinking about your suggestion that my dislike of English men in Burberry drinking lager amounts to class snobbery,' he begins. 'But you are English. That's why you deal in class. I'm Australian, a land where a cunt is a cunt.'

Michael Odell, _Q_, March 2005

Old Nick

Simon Hattenstone

Nick Cave is sitting behind his desk, long of limb and droopy of 'tache. He's wearing a suit, of course. Super-smart. And yet there's something distinctly spivvy about him. I feel as if I'm being interviewed for a job by a second-hand car salesman in a John Waters film. But instead of cars, Cave is flogging film scripts, novels, lectures and, of course, music.

Cave is one of rock's greats. While many of his fans expected the once heroin-addled Gothic punk to be long dead by now, he's actually creating more than ever. He gets up early, goes to work in his office (a flat connected to his house in Hove), does an honest day's work, returns home in the evening to his wife and kids, and starts out again the next day. He doesn't take drugs, he doesn't drink, he doesn't even smoke. In one way, he says, life is no longer worth living; in others, he says, it has never been better.

It's thirty years since Cave first made himself heard with the Birthday Party. He was tall and gangly, black-haired, with spectre-white skin, beautiful despite his spoilt-boy's snub nose – and inexplicably angry. Unlike their British counterparts, the Birthday Party – all of them Australian – weren't railing against the monarchy or the establishment. They were simply railing. The music was cacophonous and spit-furious, and occasionally heartbreakingly tender. They were always going to implode, and when they did in the early '80s, Cave went on to form the Bad Seeds, who were to all intents and purposes his backing band. He took more drugs, drank more, moved from Melbourne to London to Berlin to New York to São Paulo, all the time travelling farther down the road to nihilistic obliteration. His lyrics preached Old Testament-style hellfire and damnation, then he discovered the New Testament and wrote love songs, even if they still ended in bloody despair.

Whenever you think you understand Nick Cave, he chucks something different in your face. As he segues into his fifties, his latest album with the Bad Seeds,

The Bad Seeds (left to right: Conway Savage, Warren Ellis, Blixa Bargeld, Thomas Wydler, Mick Harvey, Nick Cave, Jim Sclavunos and Martyn Casey) photographed in Putney, London, April 2001.

Dig!!! Lazarus, Dig!!!, visits familiar New Testament territory, but now Lazarus is in '70s New York, and he's lost and confused and can't make head nor tail of the modern world. In another persona, as Grinderman on a previous album last year, he blasted out songs about being a literate ageing rocker who can no longer get the chicks. The accompanying video shows young people shagging, pigs, goats, rabbits, everybody at it – except Cave. 'I got the no-pussy blues,' he screams in libidinous despair. In between, he and fellow Bad Seed Warren Ellis turned their hand to a classical film score for *The Assassination of Jesse James by the Coward Robert Ford*.

In Cave's office, there are two pianos, a double-neck guitar and enough books to fill a library. His desk is cluttered with the paraphernalia of his work – lyric sheets, pens, the old-fashioned cassettes on which he records new songs. Above his head is a painting of Christ in all his suffering. There are leather sofas and prints on the wall of cats in varying degrees of derangement. He says he would find it impossible to work at home with his wife, the model Susie Bick, and their seven-year-old twin sons. He often complains that musicians are the laziest bastards in the world, writing twelve songs every two years, and they haven't got a clue what real work is like. Much of the time, he sits in the office, doing nothing, waiting for inspiration, ditching ideas. These dead periods are not enjoyable, but they are necessary. Sunday is his day off.

When Cave gets a passion for something, it often becomes an obsession. I ask about those cats. He tells me they are by the Victorian artist Louis Wain, a man who became schizophrenic after his wife died and whose illness is reflected in his increasingly delirious portraits of cats. 'Look, Google it.' 'Google it' is one of Cave's favourite expressions. Ask about his past and he'll often tell you to Google that as well.

There is something terse and scary about Cave – which is not surprising, considering he's spent so long modelling himself as a modern-day Beelzebub – but he can be gentle and seductive, too. He smiles and laughs (even at himself) more often than you might expect. YouTube the Birthday Party and the Boys Next Door (their original incarnation) and you can find the two extremes of early Nick Cave. On 'Shivers', he looks like a punk Bryan Ferry – a gorgeous, suited-and-booted crooner. On the live recording of 'Nick the Stripper', he is screeching self-loathing lyrics, dressed in a nappy.

Cave grew up in rural Victoria, Australia. His father, Colin, taught English and maths at the local school; his mother, Dawn, was its librarian. Cave loved the epic landscape, but hated the attitudes of small-town Australia. It was the early '70s and he was influenced by David Bowie and Lou Reed and Iggy Pop – songwriters, performers, heroes of pop's avant garde. Everything cool seemed continents away in London and New York, and Cave wanted some of it.

By the time he was twelve he was getting into trouble, so his parents packed him off to a boarding school in Melbourne. That's where he met the boys who went on to become the Birthday Party. 'We were interested in art and we weren't particularly interested in sport, so we were considered homosexuals. There's no two ways about it – we were the school poofters.' There's a story that Cave and his friends walked through school one day carrying handbags, and when people shouted abuse at them, they walloped them with the bags, each of which contained a brick. Is that true? He looks weary. 'Oh, you're only interested in the truth rather than a good, entertaining article.'

Does he prefer a lie? 'No, but there are times when the truth is necessary and times when myth-making is necessary. When you're talking about rock'n'roll, myth-making is what it's all about. Who wants to know the fucking truth about Jimi Hendrix? We want to know the myth. We want to know he got on that plane to England with that electric guitar, acne cream and pink hair curlers – that's all he brought.'

Guitarist Mick Harvey met Cave at school and has played in bands with him ever since. 'He always stood out,' he says. 'He flew in the face of authority.' Was Harvey one of the handbag boys? He laughs. 'What stories has he been telling you?'

Harvey didn't take drugs and for a time was teetotal, but the others more than made up for him. One night onstage, with Harvey playing drums, Cave threw a bottle over his shoulder and it hit him on the head. Harvey was livid. 'But then, he was totally out of it.' Did he worry for them? 'No, when you're that age you don't really think about the long-term effects. A couple of people did overdose in the mid-'80s. Then Tracy [the Birthday Party's bassist] developed epilepsy, which I suspected was through a combination of taking drugs and drinking very heavily, and we know how that ended.' Tracy Pew died after an epileptic fit in 1986.

Punk provocateur Lydia Lunch supported the Birthday Party in 1981. She and Cave didn't hit it off. 'We were on two separate planets. I was wild, uninhibited. Even though he's an extrovert onstage, he was very shy.' Lunch calls Cave one of the great poets, and remembers the first time he showed her his work – thousands of handwritten words, so small you needed a magnifying glass to read them. 'He was so hyper-conscious and so sensitive, which is beautiful to me, but it's a painful road to take.' Was he depressive? 'He was a heroin addict – of course he was fucking depressive.'

When Cave was nineteen, his father was killed in a car crash. Colin Cave was a serious man who believed culture was the answer to society's ills: beauty would save the world. His philosophy seemed to inspire and enrage Cave – he himself looked for beauty, but what he found was corrupted and destructive. At the time of his death, his father and he had drifted apart. Where was he when he found out his father had died?

'I really don't want to go into all that.'

Why not? 'It upsets me. Google it, just Google it.'

When I get home I do Google it, and discover that Cave had been at a police station, being charged with burglary. His mother, as usual, was at the station bailing him out. Shortly afterwards, having failed the second year of his art course at college, Cave and the Birthday Party left Australia for England.

A few weeks after our first meeting, I meet Cave and most of the Bad Seeds in London where they are recording a trailer for the new album, *Dig!!! Lazarus, Dig!!!*. They are re-enacting a seance in a darkened room. Cave is wearing a turban – he looks strange even by his standards. He is improvising his lines and keeps bursting out laughing. I tell him he's corpsing. He's never heard the expression, but he likes it. I'm staring at his hair. Surely, it can't be that black now . . . yet the sideburns and 'tache are a perfect match.

His twin boys, Earl and Arthur, are there – Arthur plays drums, Earl is on guitar. I ask Earl who's a better guitarist, him or his dad. 'Me,' he answers instantly. The boys are excited. They are about to head off for the premiere of *Doctor Who* with Kylie Minogue. Cave had his one reasonably big hit with Minogue in 1995 – 'Where the Wild Roses Grow'. It gave him commercial viability and her a new creative credibility. The song is about a man who can possess his beloved only by stoving her head in.

Love, possession and violent death are recurrent themes in his work. Perhaps his best-known song is 'The Mercy Seat', about an unrepentant con on death row, which was recorded by Johnny Cash shortly before he died. Cash is one of Cave's heroes – another songwriter wrestling with the notions of redemption and retribution, and the man who showed Cave that popular music could be bleak, with a whiff of evil. He also admires Leonard Cohen and Nina Simone, two singer-songwriters who have plumbed the depths.

He tells me how Cash's producer, Rick Rubin, rang to ask permission to record 'The Mercy Seat'. 'My stomach is dropping out at this point. I said, "I'll think about it, Rick," and I waited half a minute and came back and said, "Nah, I don't have any objections," and he chuckled and said, "I didn't think you would."'

Why did he wait? 'I wanted to play it cool.'

The notion of cool has always been important to Cave. At times, in his white, three-piece suits, he has almost come across as a parody of himself, hovering close to *Saturday Night Fever* territory. Did he work at it? 'No, I was just always cool.' He laughs, but I think he means it. 'Sometimes it crosses paths with what's fashionable, and then I become obsolete again.'

Susie Bick, Cave's wife and a former Vivienne Westwood muse, watches while the video is made. She is beautiful, with black hair and very pale skin, not wholly unlike Cave. When they met, she says, 'We had just broken up from relationships and we were both heartbroken. We were mostly thinking about being heartbroken. It was very intense, but even so it took us about two years to go on a date. We were a bit shy, actually.'

What's Cave like? 'He's just adorable. He's just the warmest person, he's got the biggest heart.'

But isn't he supposed to be the antichrist? 'I know!' She giggles. 'He's so the opposite of what people imagine. And he's the best dad in the world.' It's not what we want to hear about Nick Cave.

Cave and fellow Australian, Warren Ellis, are sitting at a table, eating burgers and whingeing about the way they are portrayed by the media – drugs, booze and bad behaviour. 'Such an old story,' says Ellis, who is Cave's chief collaborator.

He joined the band in 1995, to play a bit of violin on the album *Let Love In*, and stayed. Both were addicted to heroin, but Ellis was trying to stop.

Now they regard themselves as workaholics. 'The day we finish mixing this, it's like, "Right, do the next one,"' Ellis says. 'It's really addictive. The more you make, the more you want to make.'

Even in their junkie days, though, they worked hard. Cave says addiction didn't hamper creativity, except when they were sick or out scoring. He hasn't touched drugs for ten years. 'I'd like to say Susie stopped me. But the truth is that nobody can kick that stuff for you. You have to do it yourself. That I was head over heels in love with the most beautiful woman on the planet didn't hurt, though.'

Look through Cave's work and you see the geography of his influences – Australia in the landscape, Germany in the sound and fury of early Bad Seeds records, America and Britain in his pop heroes. While living in Germany, Cave spent three years in a bedsit – the walls covered with religious and pornographic images – writing his 1989 novel *And the Ass Saw the Angel*. It tells the story of Euchrid Eucrow, a vengeful mute living in a fundamentalist community in America's south. Overwritten maybe, but the book is a beautifully imagined horror story illuminated by stark images ('Mah father loomed over me like a crooked stick'). More disturbingly than Cave's songs, it portrays a world of gratuitous cruelty and a religion founded on retribution.

Eucrow, in his feral world, and Cave have this at least in common – both hear voices in their heads. Sometimes Cave's voices tell him he can do anything and leave him spent and exhausted: in the past, he took heroin to still the voices and himself. Sometimes, especially at the beginning of projects, the voices tell him he's a hopeless loser.

Another day, another suit. It's mid-January, and Cave is carrying a heavy case and heading off to Paris to promote the new album. He is slurping his tea and we are talking children. As well as the twins, he says, he has two sixteen-year-old boys. Blimey, I say, two sets of twins. 'Erm, no. They were very . . . they were quite close to each other.'

Months? 'Well, less, actually.'

'Bloody hell, Nick,' I say as it dawns on me what he's saying.

'It's a wonderful thing, but...'

'Did it not cause domestic strife?'

'It was difficult at the time, but it turned out great in the end.' Jethro was born in Australia, Luke ten days later in Brazil, where Cave was living with his mother, the stylist Viviane Carneiro. 'To my eternal regret I didn't make much contact with Jethro in the early years. I now have a great relationship with him.'

He's not telling me anymore. 'Google it, you fucker. Google it. There are things you read in *Hello!* and you think, "Why the fuck are these people talking about these type of things?" There's this culture of confession and admission, and I find it nauseating.'

For all that, Cave did once make an astonishingly personal record – *The*

Boatman's Call in 1997. It is regarded by many as his most beautiful album. It's about breaking up with Luke's mother, falling in love with the musician PJ Harvey (another woman with dark hair and pale skin who bears more than a passing resemblance to him) – and having his heart broken by her. It's one of the most nakedly romantic, and desolate, records ever made. In 'Far from Me', the penultimate song, he sings, 'Did you ever care for me?/ Were you ever there for me?'

Was he aware at the time . . . ? 'That I was doing the big confessional record? No, no. When I was making half that record I was furious because certain things had happened in my love life that seriously pissed me off. And some of those songs came straight out of that.' Does it embarrass him now? 'I don't regret making it but, yeah, it does a bit, because the songs are of a moment when you felt a certain way. When you don't anymore, you just think, "Fuck – please!"'

He asks if I've seen the video he and Harvey made for the song 'Henry Lee', and raises an eyebrow. 'Fucking hell! That's a one-take video. Nothing is rehearsed at all except we sit on this "love seat". We didn't know each other well, and this thing happens while we're making the video. There's a certain awkwardness, and afterwards it's like, oh . . .' So you were beginning the relationship in this three-minute video? 'Yeah, exactly.'

He says he and Susie were recently trawling the internet and came across the video. 'She said, "I do think it's a wonderful video, but I must say I do find it rather hard to watch."'

His love songs always evoke the inevitability of loss – a feeling fuelled by his father's early death. In 1998 at the Vienna Poetry Festival, Cave gave a lecture on the love song in which he said, 'The actualising of God through the medium of the love song remained my prime motivation as an artist.' Even on *The Boatman's Call*, one of his most secular records, many of the songs are like contemporary psalms. In a *South Bank Show* profile, the filmmaker Wim Wenders said, 'His songs deal with a desire for pure love or this longing for peace in spite of all the turmoil and unrest happening inside him.' Author Will Self put it more earthily, calling them 'songs of spiritual yearning dressed in Ann Summers'.

I ask Cave why his work is so dominated by God – in the early days, a vengeful God at that. He says that's hard to answer – he's never been the type of writer who looks at the world and expresses what he thinks; instead, he writes and in the writing his vision of the world is shaped. 'The brutality of the Old Testament inspired me, the stories and grand gestures. I wrote that stuff up and it influenced the way I saw the world. What I'm trying to say is I didn't walk around in a rage thinking God is a hateful god. I was influenced by looking at the Bible, and it suited me in my life vision at the time to see things in that way.'

Why? 'Well, things were crap at the time . . . in my personal life.' Because of a vengeful God? 'No, I was just crap. It wasn't a gnashing of teeth, Job kind of thing, though I did have a lot of skin complaints, things like that.' He smiles. 'Yeah, I had a lot of pestilence visited upon me by a vengeful God – you know, scabies, crabs, general stuff like that.' Wasn't that because of the sex and drugs?

The Bad Seeds (left to right: Mick Harvey, Martyn Casey, Nick Cave, Thomas Wydler, Warren Ellis and Blixa Bargeld) on the set of 'Fifteen Feet of Pure White Snow', filmed at Bethnal Green Town Hall, 10 April 2001.

'Well, you've got to blame someone, haven't you?'

I ask whether he really does believe in a greater force, or would he just like to be a believer? 'I do believe, but my belief system is so riddled with doubt that it's barely a belief system at all – I see that as a strength rather than a failing.'

Cave says you can roughly divide his work – the '70s and '80s is Old Testament, the '90s and onwards is New Testament. 'After a while I started to feel a little kinder and warmer to the world, and at the same time started to read the New Testament.'

He has a way of smiling when he feels things are wrong or have been misinterpreted. A little-boy smile. 'Look,' he says, almost apologetically, 'when I look back, from twenty onwards, I was actually having a pretty good time, I have to say. I don't look back to "What a miserable fucking time". In general I'm a pretty up, buoyant, optimistic kind of person.'

Do people think you're a moper? 'I hope they don't, but I suspect they do.'

Maybe that's because there are so many songs about . . . He completes the sentence for me: 'Death and shit.'

So is Nick Cave a character? 'I don't think so. It's not that I don't feel those things – I feel those things very strongly.' He has his lows, when everything feels unbearable and insurmountable, but they are less frequent than they once were. Perhaps, like Leonard Cohen and Samuel Beckett, once he's put his existential angst to paper, he can get on with the important business of living life. 'At the end, we're kind of observers – creative people, I mean. I feel like an observer, and I'm pretty much able to step out of things and see how things are playing out.'

I'm staring at Cave's jet-black hair, wondering. Does he think he's getting too old to rock at fifty? 'Yeah, I do think that sometimes. I mean, the whole fame thing is incredibly undignified, anyway. You're allowing yourself to be exposed. A lot of it you can get away with because you're young, but you should know better by the time you reach fifty. But, for me, I get such huge benefits for my own psyche, creating, working, that it doesn't at the moment seem an option to do anything about that.'

Actually, he says, there is so much rubbish talked about age – as if, when you hit certain landmarks, you start to think and act differently. He's getting quite worked up as he talks and it becomes apparent that age itself is the new authority figure to rebel against. 'There's a certain wisdom we are supposed to get, and I'm not really convinced that happens. I mean, you're wiser to a degree. But there's a certain archetype – a tried and tested road for artists in their autumn years: more meditative, less concerned with temporal things and more concerned with spiritual things, all that sort of stuff – I was looking forward to that, but it hasn't really arrived.' In fact, Cave says, if anything, he's gone the opposite way. He's been doing the deathly stuff for decades and now he's more concerned with the physical world. 'There are things that preoccupy me now that feel weirdly adolescent.' What like? 'Like sex.' He knows it's supposed to be taboo, a little unsavoury, for a man of his age to write or sing about sex but, sorry, that is what he's interested in, so that's what you'll be getting.

And I'm still looking at Cave's hair. Is that really his natural colour? He bursts out laughing. 'I've been dyeing my hair since I was sixteen.'

What colour would it be? 'I hate to think.'

What about the 'tache and sideboards? 'You have a special little brush and stuff. Look, I'm a high-maintenance kind of guy.'

Will he ever stop dyeing his hair? God no, he says.

'No, I'll dye it till I die.'

Simon Hattenstone, *The Guardian*, 23 February 2008

Nick Cave: Raw and Uncut 2

Phil Sutcliffe

A suite at Manchester's Malmaison Hotel. As tall skinny people do, Nick folds himself awkwardly into the sofa. Striped silver-grey socks, pinstripe suit; narrow trousers emphasizing narrow legs within. Two expressions: the downward turn of his moustache frames a grave-to-stern view of life and experience thereof; but his face has a way of springing from shades of worry to a truly sweet smile and maybe laugh, full of humour and the sheer enjoyability of things. One imagines he looks like that a lot when he's with his wife and kids.

So how do you like touring these days?
I'm really enjoying it I have to say. I haven't always enjoyed it as much.

What's the difference?
The shows we're doing at the moment, the songs are working really well in a live way. The concerts are . . . a joy to do. We can all sit in the same room together and get on with each other – and that's extraordinary after all these years. *[laughs]* We were remarking on it last night – we've sat at the same table and told the same fucking jokes for thirty years and people still laugh at them. After a while a lot of bands do separate I think, they do the show and then they go off and do their own things, but we do the show and we remain together and we eat together – all that sort of stuff.

I think this has something to do with none of us living in the same city, we don't see each other socially, we come together to do tours and make records. We don't rehearse much. *[Two days for this tour, it turns out.]*

Don't you?
No. *[laughing]* We haven't for years actually.

What's that about – you're not careless people as far as I can tell?
We understood that . . . rehearsals only work to a certain point and that is to know when the chorus comes – and even that's not necessary – and how many

choruses, and possibly how the song ends. But apart from that none of the true workings of a song can be found out in a rehearsal I don't think. You find out live. All your great plans, your great objectives from rehearsal, you quickly find they don't work live. Like, 'I'm gonna sit back on this song,' that kind of stuff. To me, going on live you're thrown into this vortex, this maelstrom which for me at least, not being particularly musical, I have no control over. Everything just gets thrown up in the air so rehearsals are largely a waste of time.

The vortex and the maelstrom: is that what's happening onstage or between you and the audience?
Yeah, it's to do with playing songs in front of an audience. I don't know if this is true for everybody in the band but my whole body chemistry, the way I am, changes onstage. I'm a different person in the rehearsal room to the way I am live so the songs become different things.

Is that adrenalin, in lay terms?
Yeah I guess. If you sit in a room on your own and tell a joke, you think it's really good. But you go in front of a hundred people and it falls flat . . . that's not so good, edit that. The thing changes.

But maybe writing lyrics on your own in a room is like telling the joke on your own? Maybe it is a good comparison?
It's my belief that songs become different live, not just in the way they're played but what they actually mean. You can sit down and think you understand a song that you've written, you think you have a handle on what it's about – hey, you wrote it! – but onstage it changes. It goes on its own journey, *[pulls face]* whatever, and you sing the song and you're thinking, 'Eh? Oh, all right, okay, *that's* what it's about.'

Can you put that into words in regard to a particular song?
Something like 'The Mercy Seat' constantly changes its meaning for me. It becomes something extremely personal that has nothing to do with making a song about a guy who goes to the electric chair . . . or whatever the song's about, God knows. It was a long time ago it was written. It can become excruciatingly personal . . . a lot of songs do that. Because when you write songs you can't help but write them in a guarded way, you tend to disguise . . . Lyric writing is about obscuring the truth in some way. Writing songs that have a kernel of truth in them but writing in a way that you're not really revealing all that much.

About yourself?
About yourself, yes.

So you want to write in a way that reveals some wider truth while concealing . . .
Exactly.

Not, 'What happened to me this morning is why I'm writing this song.'
You don't want songs like that. No one wants songs like that. Well, some people like to hear songs like that but I don't want to write songs like that. I have written songs like that. You can get an album like that. But you don't want to keep writing that sort of stuff. I don't think it's healthy.

But some people go for songs which I suppose we'd call confessional . . .
Yeah.

Why don't you like those things?
For me it's a dead end, for two reasons. First, I don't naturally . . . maybe I'm an Australian. My mother was a stoic. She doesn't reveal her emotions; that's the way the Australian is supposed to be. There's something about making heroic your own little pains that sticks in my craw. Heroicising your own personal tragedies, if that's a word . . . I don't feel comfortable with that.

But also if you become that kind of singer, something's gotta be happening in your life that's of interest for you to document, and if it's not you've got nothing to write about. So for me it's much more interesting if it's happening in your imagination. You can lead a completely banal existence and go in and write extraordinary things. That Kafka thing of being a clerk and what's going on in his head is something completely different.

And you've brought up Philip Larkin in that connection.
Yeah, a great hero of mine. The Bukowski model I don't subscribe to. I haven't read him for a while, but he's a lush and it's all about that, the situations he's supposedly got himself into and all that.

So when you were . . . well, I doubt if you'd describe yourself as a lush . . .
Not really.

Well, drinking a lot and so on, you were still not writing about it; you were moving it away from you?
That's kind of what I mean. Most of the time what I'm writing about is what I want and what I need. Not what I have. These days. And back then really. So the more beautiful, spiritual songs came out of the exact opposite circumstances in my life. When I was at my most depleted and unhappy. And I suppose these days when my life is relatively stable there's a kind of yearning in my songs for something else . . . that comes out.

They're very open about it.
That's the way it always has been for me.

To go back to 'The Mercy Seat' and live, any examples of where life wasn't tranquil and you were writing 'spiritual' songs?

'Into My Arms'. It was written in rehab, the first couple of days in rehab when you haven't slept, you're withdrawing from drugs, you're sick, you're under the worst possible circumstances a human being could be put under . . . Well hang on, no, edit that . . .

It's not a concentration camp.
It ain't a concentration camp. But it's not pleasant. The first few days are not pleasant. Please take that 'worst possible circumstances' out, that's not right. But it's not pleasant circumstances and something like that came out of it.

I don't have that experience . . .
You should try it!

Yeah, Nick Cave told me to! But oddly enough I grew up with my father being a morphine addict for medical reasons and going through the withdrawal symptoms if he slept too long, all that which you know about . . .
Absolutely.

All I mean is it's bloody hard for me to be able to imagine someone writing a song in that condition.
You try and make the best of a bad situation, don't you? *[laughs gently]*

Is that your mum speaking?
Exactly. We will persevere. Um. Yeah. So anyway, in a live situation these songs get their opportunity to speak back to me.

And in a song like 'The Mercy Seat' you're suddenly hit by, what, memories of something in your past life? What happens there?
[pause] I think you kind of . . . I'm not exactly sure how to answer that. The songs get written from a . . . a higher part of you in some way. Than the average person that we are. That I am, at least. Those songs come from a more developed place. In time, maybe, you catch up to that. They seem to speak to you . . . it can happen years later, you're singing it and you go, 'Oh, right.' It suddenly makes more sense to you. To me that seems to happen quite a lot. I wish I could think of a better example, but it just happens, there are moments all the time onstage . . . and also the world can change too and suddenly your songs become relevant.

Any example?
You sing 'Tupelo' and Katrina's just happened. You're going round America and . . . that can be nice. I don't mean Katrina happening was nice! *[laughs]* But suddenly things can happen . . . fun and games.

These things are happening just to you, or do you think the audience

shares any of these experiences in some way?
Well, I assume the audience have their own interpretations of things. I certainly do of other people's songs. In fact, it's often very disillusioning when you find out the lyrics to something – oh, is that what they're saying? How disappointing!

I always wished Jimi Hendrix had sung, ''Scuse me while I kiss this guy.'
Yeah. *[laughs]*

So we've veered off into the writing but . . .
Oh, the other thing live is I'm really enjoying playing the guitar a bit. That's an absolute joy. A pleasure. Mostly because it pulls me right back into the band. I can't move away from the mike when I have to play guitar and sing – my natural tendency is to get the mike and go over the foldback wedges and onto the lip of the stage and leave the band behind. When I'm playing guitar I become a band member and that feels really good. I can get out there and then the guitar pulls me back into the band, like you're part of the nuts and bolts of the music, and that's really exciting.

Unfortunately I'm not really a guitarist in the sense that I can play anything but it's a much nicer job. Warren [Ellis]'s job is much more fun than my job. Being the frontman takes it out of you. *[laughs]*

The responsibility you mean?
You're cut adrift a bit. There's a natural separation from the frontman to the band in all ways. There's something that happens onstage between musicians that I found out with Grinderman, playing guitar with them. It's very much about eye contact, playing onstage; the song is developing in its own way and it's really about a very concentrated and intimate contact between the members, a male intimacy that most people don't share, or that men share in the workplace. But the frontman isn't privy to that. It's all happening at the back.

Because you're the flash bastard and they're the workers?
That's right. *[laughs sweet and light]*

And I suppose the intimacy in the band is seen as a muso thing – sometimes scorned, sometimes appreciated?
Yeah, I've never been part of the muso thing through being out the front. I can go back there and point and gesture *[he does in an extravagant fashion like a histrionic conductor, both arms jabbing]* and everyone's like, *[rolls eyes to the ceiling]* 'Sure, right. He's pretending he knows what's going on!' But when I play guitar there's a great warmth; you whack your wah-wah on and you play a little thing and Warren'll look at you and kind of smile – it's a good feeling.

Peer approval?
Mm, peer approval . . .

Have you always been the leader of whatever band you were in?
[gasp of laugh] Not initially. I remember the bass player, this guy Brett Purcell, when we were fifteen. Mick [Harvey] could play the guitar and Brett was the bass player – and Brett said to me, 'You're the one who has no musical ability, so you're the singer.' I'm like, okay. It's one of those things that thirty-five years later you still hear in your ear sometimes – okay, that's me. But let's not get into the voices in my head . . . And then I don't know if I was the leader in the Birthday Party. We were all in it together.

The rock'n'roll gang. So it was with the Bad Seeds you definitely stepped out there.
It became Nick Cave and the . . . I don't know why that happened actually. I'm happy it did. *[chortles]* Actually, it was meant to be.

And what did it mean to you?
I then had a *name*, a public name, that my other work could go under. I think it made other work more possible for me, whatever it was, scripts or novel writing – it's by *Nick Cave* and people know that name and maybe they wouldn't have.

So it was really a brand name career development move.
Yeah, I didn't really think of it in that way. But yeah. It's turned out that way.

Being Nick Cave and . . . must have changed the relationship with the band then I guess.
Oh, I brought songs to the band and they played 'em.

You were the boss effectively.
Yeah.

And artistically?
It changed through these fourteen records – different people rose and fell in terms of their influence over the music. I've always needed someone in the band to interpret what I do or take the songs on to the next level. Possibly less and less so . . . there was a time back in the Birthday Party when I didn't play anything so I was writing the songs and singing the riffs to Mick – like 'Dead Joe' goes, *[grunts it out with sudden alarming ferocity]* 'oh oh oh oh oh oh oh' and Mick would go 'Dang dang dang dang dang dang dang'. I'd go, 'Yeah, like that.' That's how some of those songs were written.

Then I was able to get a bit of piano going and write the songs, basic stuff, and that developed over the years. But I figure I've always needed someone in the band to work fairly directly with in regard to the music.

Did you learn piano specifically to write songs?
No, I'd done some lessons early on; I could play a chord.

So initially in the Bad Seeds, Mick was the right-hand person?
Yeah.

How did it move around from there? You said it was different people at different times.
The last records I've been more involved with Warren [Ellis]. I started doing solo shows and Mick wasn't involved with them, it was just Warren, Jim [Sclavunos] and Marty [Martyn P. Casey]. Then we became Grinderman because these solo shows became more and more outlandish and less and less about me just sitting at the piano, which is how they started off. They started as Nick Cave at the piano doing stately kind of concerts with a quiet little backing band and eventually these solo gigs were becoming so histrionic and loud – they were face-peeling events and people were sitting in baroque theatres and asking for their money back because it was too loud. We were doing a tour of Germany when we decided we couldn't do what we were doing as solo shows within that framework. It just wasn't working. In these seated venues, people were expecting an intimate evening with Nick Cave, and they were sitting there getting their faces ripped off. Too loud, too this, too that. The last German gig with that set-up, a lot of people complained and we thought let's turn it into a band. We'd been thinking of it anyway, but it was very much that the solo thing couldn't contain the music.

You must have thought this chamber Nick Cave was a good idea to start with.
It was. It was really beautiful, actually. Stripped down. People loved it. But things change and develop. You don't have that much control.

So you were still letting it happen, not getting set in your ways as an old geezer?
If you're going to be in it for the long haul, there seems to be two ways of doing it. One is you make the same record over and over again like the Fall and try and keep a certain quality so people say it's another Fall record and they love you and they want it. Or you attempt to change the records constantly and keep people guessing and surprised, keep it alive in that way. We do it the second way.

That is always the fundamental question for me when I sit down to write the record: what it's going to be about. Is it going to be a significant shift from the last one? The writing process is initially to write out the last record. You start playing, you start writing and it's, 'Mmm, not bad.' And then you think, 'Oh, but it's just like that song off the last record.' You have to get that out of you until you land on something different.

Lyrically you mean?
No, musically and lyrically. It keeps it alive. I think we really feel that it's important these days. We feel what we're doing is important. And we've not always felt that way.

You speak collectively there.
I think I can. There's a sense that what we do is some way important and it's our responsibility to keep the thing alive and . . . relevant. No, relevant is the wrong word. Alive is it. It's very easy for us . . . *Dig!!! Lazarus, Dig!!!* has been successful and it's not necessary for us to do another *Dig!!! Lazarus, Dig!!!*. I could go and write another one tomorrow; the blueprint's there. It's much more difficult to go and write something different, but it's much more important to do that and keep the whole thing alive even though you might disappoint people and lose a certain amount of your audience. You don't know. Another *DLD* would probably be commercially successful and everyone would be happy. But keeping the process alive is more important to us than the success of the next record. There you go.

Are you already writing the next one?
Yeah, the next record is the new Grinderman record and that's what me and Warren sit around and talk about. In an oblique kind of way. What is the next Grinderman record going to be about? The great thing about Grinderman is it's a project where we can do anything we like. The Bad Seeds isn't, I don't feel.

Grinderman seems to be something where we can go out and experiment, and if it fails it doesn't really matter. We're allowed to go out and fuck things up. Embarrass ourselves.

Have you?
We haven't yet. We'll try to embarrass ourselves in the future.

Is Grinderman cheap to run too?
Well, it is in the wonderful position where if we fuck up and nobody likes it and nobody buys it, we'll just go and make another Bad Seeds record.

What I mean about the money is nobody's investing heavily in you?
Well nobody's investing in us as heavily as we'd like! Actually. I was not altogether happy with the way Grinderman was . . . I don't think in a way the record company knew what to do with Grinderman – and that was partly our fault because we didn't . . . First of all I spoke to Daniel Miller about it, and the American label, and I said I wanted to do a jazz spoken-word album. They're like, *[sarcastically]* 'Great! Can't wait!' But Grinderman turned into something else, something we thought was kind of significant and had huge potential. I'm not sure if they really ran with it.

The next Grinderman record at the moment is a conversation between you and Warren. Can you share the nature of that conversation?
It's gone through various . . . and then we see how long we remain excited about the concept of the record – there was the hour-long instrumental, no vocals; we were very drawn to that for a while but I think it's forgotten now.

Everyone breathes a sigh of relief . . . The great thing about Grinderman is we went somewhere with that record – and I don't think we fully realised where we could go – but we went somewhere and brought back this information that we were free to be able to discover with that record and go back to the Bad Seeds and make *Dig!!! Lazarus, Dig!!!*. That's how it felt.

What were the conceptual conversations you had before Dig!!! Lazarus, Dig!!!?
What we wanted *DLD* to do was . . . I think the *Lyre of Orpheus* record hinted at what *DLD* was going to do. I see a lot of stuff in there that was developed. But the main thing with *DLD* was we cut the amount of people playing at any given time down – we tried to at least – and that was coming out of Grinderman – Hey, this works, eight of us, or however many is in the Bad Seeds, we don't all have to play at once; maybe we can do a song with just three or four people. It seems more pared down.

Do you talk about lyrics with them too or is that just you?
There are some broad strokes given. I'll ask Warren, what do you want this record to be about? He did say with the first one [*Grinderman*], 'No God and no love.' That was the brief. I respond quite well to those briefs; it gives me immediately something to work with. But what I want to do with Grinderman is get very much away from the personalised lyric, to write a much more generic, less flashy kind of lyric. That's what I'd like to do. So you're not listening to the lyrics very much.

That must go against the grain.
It's difficult for me to do. It's a whole different way. It's difficult to sit in the office and write, Whoa, baby I love you, and . . .

That's where you want to be?
It's hard. These are the lyrics. *[mimes handing them over]*

A couple of things then about the band down the years. Was Blixa Bargeld one of your creative oppos?
No. He always came into the studio and brought his own thing in. You never knew what it was going to be. In fact he largely overdubbed. He did an enormous amount of preparation. We would finish the record and ask, 'Has anyone got anything to add to these songs?' And Blixa would go, 'Yes. I do.' And he'd go in and start, and to me it was always spectacular and unexpected. So he wasn't really someone I sat around and talked with about the albums.

He was more after the event?
He was always curious to know, when he came in, what this record was about, 'Uh . . . what do you want?' I'm talking about a couple of sentences here. And

Blixa was always the person in the Bad Seeds who would come up to you after and go, 'I think we have made a good record here.' Kind of embrace you and give you a kiss, you know. It always felt, oh, that's good. *[laughs]*

Is it basically that the creative partners have been Mick and Warren, with no one else in between?
Yes.

Why do you think the Bad Seeds have attracted such loyalty from the members? People have stayed for years and years on the whole.
What else is anyone going to do? Why wouldn't they?

It's an attractive proposition artistically, creatively?
In some ways I think it is. It's not something that totally dictates the terms of an individual member's life. They can have a whole separate career if they want. Mick does all sorts, film work, this and that. Being in the Bad Seeds, they may seem omnipotent, but it doesn't take that much time. You come in and make a record and then you fuck off again. Or you do a tour – we've spent a lot of time together this year because we've done a lot of touring. But we don't do barbecues together, we don't do holidays in the Bahamas together, whatever other bands do. It's not that we don't get on; it's just everyone lives in different places and they have a lot to do. Marty has to go back to Perth and play in his wedding and Bar Mitzvahs band – seriously.

What about money? That's always crucial in the life of a band. Did you get yourselves sorted from the outset in terms of how it divvies up?
It changes over the years. It started off in a more . . . even-handed way. But as the responsibilities grew . . . *[laughs]* I dunno, the splits are generous – it's not a wage thing, it's splits. I think everyone's pretty happy but you'd have to ask them.

I will. You've asserted yourself, obviously, though, as you imply you've got more.
Yeah, I get more. But I'm the one person in the Bad Seeds who can't just go home. To me it's a constant job so I get paid more for that.

And it's something you've paid attention to. Have you ever fired anyone?
Erm . . . *[long pause]* I'm not sure I want to go there. People might feel . . . I remember we did fire the drummer out of the Boys Next Door.

Was that the bloke who said you had no musical talent?
No, not that guy – that was the bassist. No, we just punched him up. No, the drummer. We fired one of my best friends . . . Mick fired him actually; Mick did the firing back then. A guy called John Cocivera who was the guitarist, very good guitarist, but his hero was David Gilmour and we'd kind of changed and

he didn't . . . so we had to fire him. I was always rather sad about that. He was a lovely guy, John Cocivera.

The thing about being important: what did you mean by that – that the band now has a feeling that it's important?
Important might be the wrong word. I can't really speak for the band but I feel there's a body of work that is significant. It's gone up and down, and in the 200 songs or whatever there are some catastrophic failures of songwriting, unbelievable indulgences.

Such as?
Just look around. *[laughs]* But also some very precise and beautiful songs. Basically the body of work is significant and I've become conscious of that. I didn't used to be conscious of that ten years ago. Maybe it wasn't then. But now I don't wanna degrade this body of work by going out with a bunch of inferior records. Which is normally the way.

That's the responsibility side of what you were saying.
Yeah. And if I feel that it's getting that way we'll either do something radical and change the course of where we're going. Or stop. It's not the only thing I can do. There are other things I can earn a crust with. But at the moment I'm still proud of the records we're making. Proud is a funny word for me to use because I actually have no particular interest in the records we made in that I never play them, I never engage with them other than in the live situation. I don't even remember what's on them. But I have a sort of vague overriding feeling that something happened, just the sheer volume of it is kind of good. *[laughs]*

That sense of value, does it include an idea of what it is and what it does artistically?
[very firm] Yeah.

Describe away please.
It has a beneficial effect on people. I've always been told that it did. Everyone gets their fan letters and people coming up and saying . . . You go, yeah, yeah, yeah, but I feel it does have a lasting resonance in certain people's lives. That aspect I value more now.

Do you know what that might be, that beneficial effect?
No. Not really. Whatever those songs are that I listen to that have that reliable effect to change things; I walk into the room feeling one way and I know I'm going to walk out feeling better. I think my songs have the capacity to do that.

Has the notion of catharsis got anything to do with it?
I know what catharsis means on one level. But I'm not sure if listening to music

is cathartic for me. I always loved music as a kid and a teenager but I was always told very clearly by my father – he was an English literature teacher – that it was hardly an art form, that it was bottom of the fucking heap.

And, um, for some time I felt I was involved in an inferior art form, that I'd failed art school so I wasn't good enough to be a painter and I'd ended up doing, you know, this other kind of work which is rock'n'roll. It took a few records before I realised that what I was doing was working with an art form which is hugely important. In fact it may well be that it's at the very peak of this pyramid – if there is such a thing. That rock'n'roll music has the capacity to do things to people that other art forms don't. It certainly does it to me.

What does it do to you?
It can change my entire body chemistry. In a lasting and significant way, it can make me go from feeling exhausted, depleted, unhappy, depressed into feeling fuckin' buoyant and brilliant and joyful in a matter of seconds. And I can't get that from reading a book or looking at a painting or even Shakespeare. I can't get from Shakespeare what I can get from the Ramones.

What is that 'what'?
You never know what it is.

Must be something to do with those people in the Brill Building writing two-and-a half-minute songs and having to get it all in there.
I have a huge amount of respect for those people, to be able to do that. That whole thing, sitting in an office and writing songs, I always thought was a great thing and a really honourable thing. Which is quite different to the musician or writer who is walking around the world waiting for something to happen in his life, for when the Muse comes down, all that stuff. I'm a nuts and bolts kind of guy when it comes to that. Those people slaving away in that Brill Building! *[laughs in wonderment]*

And that nuts and bolts approach applied to you before you took to your office?
It's difficult to tell what my approach was early on. I certainly had a dedication to it early on. I didn't have a particular love for it because I didn't think what I was doing was particularly worth it. I think it took a few records before we got anywhere doing anything halfway good.

Do you remember writing your first song?
Yeah, I do remember it. I wrote this song which was very much based on this Australian singer Stevie Wright's 'Evie (Parts 1, 2 and 3)', an epic love song in three parts. I had a girlfriend I fancied in school called Julie so I wrote 'Julie Parts 1, 2 and 3'. *[laughs]* This epic . . . I couldn't sing it to you.

That's all right.

But it was heavily derivative! I was only thirteen.

Was it a eureka moment despite all that?
No. I don't have that feeling even now with songwriting. Songwriting is always just the hardest thing to do – out of the things I'm involved in.

What other music or other arts were inspiring you then?
In my childhood fantasies I wanted to be a rock singer. I would come home from school, race upstairs and put on David Bowie records, lock the door and jump around and sing. Especially *David Live* where you get the audience applause at the end of the songs. I did a lot of that on my own – you know, the kid with the tennis racket. But I didn't really equate that with actually having to get down and write something and do what was necessary. In fact, I never felt I had any natural talent for it, so it was very much a fantasy. But I did certainly feel very strongly that thing of putting the record on, how I changed and became this godlike person to myself, the schmuck that I really was.

That comes up so much in your interviews: the godlike and the schmuck. Not that it's unique to you; we all have it in us . . .
Exactly.

What is that fantasy of approbation, being admired?
What I didn't think was, Hey, I want to do this; I want to become someone. At the time was I was very involved in art; I was painting a lot. Or something to do with literature; I was quite good at lit at school. I thought that was a more noble occupation and I felt I could do it.

What lit you up in art and lit?
I guess the first person in music when I felt I could do this, was Alex Harvey. And nobody in Australia had heard of Alex. I had a friend who was much older than me and he turned me on to the Alex Harvey Band. We waited for his records to come out. They were hugely important to us and the band I was with; we were basically an Alex Harvey covers band. It was easier to sing an Alex Harvey song than a David Bowie song, slightly less challenging vocally. I think there was that kind of mayhem about his character, and theatricality. And his lyrics are something else. I started with *Next*, then I bought *Framed*, and on from there.

What about visual artists?
I was into a lot of religious art at the time – Piero della Francesca and Grünewald. Also I was always heavily under the spell of Brett Whiteley, this extraordinary Australian painter from Sydney – I think a lot of us were. He had the most beautiful line, fluid; stylistically he had his own thing, and he had this morbid streak which I liked as a kid – he did a series of paintings of the Christie murders, though they were by no means his best. Anyway he was a huge influence.

And literature – was the Deep South coming in by then?
Not at that stage, no.

And the Bible.
No, that was in my twenties. What I was listening to mostly in my teens was English progressive rock music. In Australia at that time it suddenly opened up and bands started coming over and all playing this one terrible venue in Melbourne called the Festival Hall. All the major English progressive rock bands came there: Pink Floyd, Procol Harum, Moody Blues, Jethro Tull. And I went to them all. That had a huge impact.

It did?
Yeah. I loved that stuff. *[titters]* My brother was into it and a guitarist we kicked out, John Cocivera. His sister's boyfriend, Barry, worked in a record shop and he was a serious English prog-music nut. He educated us in it, us young kids; he was tyrannical and if you veered off and started liking anything else he was . . . It wasn't worth it. This T. Rex record came out and me and John Cocivera were playing it and he walked in, and that was it, the relationship was over. I remember him standing there going, *[heavy sarcasm]* 'Get it on, bang a gong' – and walking out. That was the rift. And then I started deciding my own musical taste. That said, I know all the English prog rock really well and I listened to it as a child does, with that intensity which I haven't listened to most music with since, sit there and play the record over and over again. So actually I know King Crimson's music really well. And Jethro Tull's. Even lesser bands than that. It's extraordinary to listen to that music now because some of it was really good. Some of it was not of course. But I get in the car *[laughs]* and I play '21st Century Schizoid Man' full blast, especially the live version on the *Earthbound* album – the guitar is so heavy it's unbelievable!

It was strong stuff. But punk didn't like it I'm sure.
Well, there was that throwing the baby out with the bathwater with punk. It needed to happen.

Did Elvis's death hit you at all?
I don't think it did that much. I remember where I was and I remember Lydon's quote about finally the fat-gutted Presley will stop casting his shadow. Something like that. That started to divide me from a blind following of punk. Quotes like that. That wasn't good. *[laughs]* I came to Elvis late because I wasn't around when he was doing his stuff.

He became a character in your songs.
Yeah. I got into it, the later stuff.

Thinking of the cultural milieu you came out of, I read in a biography

written by an Australian of a scene at the Crystal Ballroom in St Kilda where students gathered to discuss Dostoyevsky and Rimbaud. Was that you?

Not me. I wonder what book that was?

He had a wonderful name, Robert Brokenmouth.

Oh yeah, that man's just a fuckin' idiot. That biography is pretty much the Birthday Party as seen through the eyes of the drummer who was the only one he could interview – the drummer who Mick had sacked. Oh, he might have interviewed Mick as well. So, a travesty. If that guy thinks we were sitting around discussing Dostoyevsky and Rimbaud he wasn't there. It didn't happen. We had other things on our minds. But the Crystal Ballroom certainly was a place where a lot of Melbourne bands played, and it became a central place for us. They served food to keep the place open – curried chicken wings. We lived on them for years and years. A little known fact!

You brought your mother up earlier, talking about the stoic side of your character. What is her place in how you turned out?

I always felt really close to her and that I was always very like my mother, that I got a lot more from my mother than possibly my father. We're extremely close. I don't see her so much because she still lives in Australia. But I always live with her when I go to Australia. She was hugely supportive of me *under any circumstances [forcefully]*. I'm talking about circumstances that would blow any mother's mind in terms of what was happening to her child. I was always right. *[laughs]* She supported me. She was a mother to me. Always on my side. Despite how glaringly obvious it was at certain times that perhaps she shouldn't have been.

Which certain times?

I'd get in trouble with the police, let's say, and she'd have to bail me out . . .

Drunk-driving type stuff?

Yeah, the usual. And she would be driving me back muttering, 'Bloody police!' She's amazing. I remember she was obviously worried about my future, not that she showed that. I remember her coming to London and I lived in a squat in Maida Vale – one of the first places we lived in, a really nasty place. All the windows had been smashed out and it was the middle of winter, the toilets had been smashed, no hot water, mattress in the corner. My mother stayed in a hotel and I was loath to show her my current abode. But we did drive past because she wanted me to show it to her and, God knows what was going on in there at that moment, but I pointed to the place next door rather than the actual squat I think. But then I remember being with her when she opened up a copy of *Time Out* and there was an ad on the back page for us doing a gig, or maybe a little review, and the expression on her face was like, 'Oh, there really is a band and they're playing somewhere.' It was then I realised she was really concerned.

It's a big moment in any lad's life.
She was very supportive. But unfazed by things that happened in my career and stuff. She's cool!

You had a comfortable middle-class life over in Australia and then you come here and, for money reasons, have to live in shit. What were you looking for?
It was twofold for me – on one level, the manager at the time, so-called, managed to get us tickets out of Australia to England and that's what every Australian dreamed of. All we had goin' was the band at that stage and you knew you were never going to get anywhere in Australia; you knew that as a fundamental truth. We'd had the same maximum 200 people coming to our gigs for years. There was the scene, and it was never going to get anywhere.

There was the ceiling and you could see it right above your heads?
Yeah, everyone could and we were one of the successful bands. The unsuccessful ones were still playing at parties – and creating extraordinary music, actually, because no one was going to get anywhere so why not do what you wanted to do. The manager lasted a week during which we managed to sign a contract with him that said he gets all the money and distributes it – Keith Glass. But he never did distribute it to us. That contract stayed in place for most of the Birthday Party. We kept saying to 4AD, you know you send the money to this guy – he never gives us any. They just said, 'It's the contract.'

We were in such a state of chaos, living hand to mouth, that no one could get it together to do anything about it. What do you do about something like that? Well, a friend of mine who was a speed dealer and spent a lot of time in prison – and is now dead *[laughs]* – he was in an Australian band that got fucked over in a similar way, he said to me, 'You've got to do something about this guy.' I said, 'I don't know what to do.' [He said] 'Oh, I'll bring a friend over.'

This guy comes around who's kind of terrifying so I say, 'I don't want this to get out of hand, you know.' He says, 'No, no, just a simple conversation – we don't touch the kids. That comes later.' I'm like, 'Look, man, I don't . . .'

You headed him off?
Yeah. That was back in Australia. And that was Keith. I think Mick did manage to sort something out with him, but that was after many years. We lived in pretty dire circumstances.

How did you take to that?
I didn't mind it, actually, in the sense that we were all together and we were in London and we could scrape up enough money to get pissed every night – that's if you drank a couple of bottles of cider really fast. That sort of thing. *[laughs]* Some of the work was hideous – the temp work and construction work and factory work and washing dishes. We could have done without that. But . . . otherwise we didn't have any money.

Nothing educational about the experience?

I dunno. There was something we found difficult about going to a factory in the dark and coming out in the evening and it was dark again. That was strange. I still can't get it around my head that sometimes I pick my kids up from school in the dark . . . Anyway, mustn't grumble. As my mother would say.

Well, that's very English too.

Her mother was English.

So there you were living in shit and . . .

But what was more disappointing to me was not the living circumstances; it was what Britain had on offer artistically was fuckin' disgraceful. We'd been duped! Some of us had got the *NME* in Australia and would read the back pages and see who'd been on each night and it seemed like this wonder-world. I remember Rowland Howard saying, 'Imagine! We could go and see this band. Or this band. Or this band tonight.' With the wonder of a child. And when we got there, this band, that band and that band were all fuckin' crap! They were really bad and really boring and obviously something had happened in England with punk and now something else was happening – things like Echo and the Bunnymen, Teardrop Explodes. The singles sounded really good and the write-ups in *NME* were great, but when we arrived we thought it was fuckin' dreadful. Some kind of abomination.

And that a huge impact on our band, the way we behaved, the way we became as a band live. Me and Rowland sat at a gig with four bands playing, a showcase – I dunno, Teardrop Explodes, Echo and the Bunnymen, Psychedelic Furs and some other band – and we thought, 'We're not going to do this; this is not how we're going to be.' And then our gigs were so few and far between we just went fuckin' mental. We had this thing called a rider, which we'd not experienced before, which was just an enormous amount of alcohol at three in the afternoon! So we were broke and suddenly these concerts became something different because that was what was happening. Some people just responded to that.

Raw aggression?

I think we were . . . raging. Something had happened, we felt a complacency. We became good friends with the Fall and the Pop Group and pretty much that was it. We knew them, we got on and we partied.

Looking at those early songs, what you were writing then; there were wild descriptions of what you were up to, a story about you attacking a woman member of the audience and Mick pulling you off.

He was worse than me actually.

So you were all at it – a whole new relationship with the audience?

Well, it wasn't like the audience were just standing there. After a while we had this guy who used to hang around with us, Bingo, who was an ex-marine and he used to stand on the side of the stage and he'd show us what he'd picked up from people at the front of the stage – iron bars and all sorts of shit. Especially touring around Europe. That particular tour someone billed us as 'the most violent band in Europe' and the people who came along were serious fuckin' nutcases. So there was self-preservation . . . Bingo was a fan who used to follow us around. After a while we said, 'Would you mind standing up here instead of being down there?' He became a fireman.

Between Boys Next Door and Birthday Party, you started writing and . . .
Boys Next Door you can forget about.

I recognise your voice in the Birthday Party lyrics right through to now. Something new was coming through.
Still in Australia, the Pop Group's Y album came through [in 1979] and the EP single 'She Is Beyond Good and Evil'. That had a huge impact on us. Pere Ubu's first and second albums, whatever they were called [*The Modern Dance* and *Dub Housing*], had a big influence, and you can hear that in certain songs. They had a significant impact.

But something was coming up out of you too.
A blues thing was coming in lyrically. Uh, literature.

The song 'Zoo-Music Girl', for example?
That's more a literary thing, coming out of Dada literature, the Alfred Jarry plays, the Ubu plays – the spirit of it, the abstractedness and heavy imagery. It wasn't coming from other people's music, it was founded in what I was reading at the time.

It sounds as though it was releasing your voice.
Isn't that always the way, though? Seventeen or eighteen and certain things happened to me that totally influenced me. Certain people. They were painters, people at art school. The people at art school had a huge impact on me because they were really about fuckin' everything up. There was a lesbian girl, hardcore and terrifying. She'd do these beautiful paintings and then she'd get some black paint and paint a big cock with big fuckin' hairy balls over the top of it and hand that in. They were really exciting paintings and this stuff was informing a certain kind of attitude towards things, a kind of art that went against what was traditionally considered to be the normal notion of what is good. A lot of Dada. I'm young here! That was having an impact.

Then there's the violence as well – you're going to murder her and in the next line, 'Oh please let me die beneath her fists.' Both ways!
I always had an instinctive talent for that sort of stuff. I don't know where it came from. But I never thought a love song worked unless it had some kind of darker edge.

And that's where you were starting to bring it out.
At that age there was a certain voice that worked through a lot of blues music, some of those murder ballads. At that age I found it shocking but at the same time very exciting. I don't feel that now but then I felt it was genuinely shocking, and in some ways that's what we were looking for. There are songs there that became outrageously so . . . And also our lives were chaotic. We were pissed off and our shows were violent. There was a need for that sort of thing.

Another thing I noticed was there are a lot of stinks: 'King Ink kicks off his stinkboot and puts the stink on us.' There's a powerful olfactory sense of how life is.
'King Ink' was written in that squat and it *did* stink. We were living in Walterton Road, which only had black people there. For us Australians, who went pretty much straight to live there, first it was shocking to see so many black people because in Australia we'd had the White Australia policy – which wasn't something we'd even thought about, it's just the way it was. But also they were hugely aggressive to us; they tried to get us out, they smashed all the windows, they spat at us on the street.

Racism?
Total. And we were, 'Fuck, man. What is this place?' I was hugely naive about everything in England. Cosseted little middle-class boy from Melbourne thrown into the real world. We had gang people smashing on our front door! We locked the door. There was a violence going on towards us and the songs reflected that. I didn't understand anything about that. I probably still don't. That was an English thing that had nothing to do with us. We did not understand, being Australian, except in the most basic terms what was going on in England – even what the Sex Pistols were about, the politics of punk, it meant nothing to us. We came from a private school. All that meant nothing.

And racism?
It was so much a part of the fabric of Australia we didn't even realise it.

You mean about the Aborigines or . . .
The Aboriginals and the fact that there were no black people in Australia.

And then it came at you the other way round, which must have been baffling.
It took us a while to work it out. We didn't have English friends. No one saying, 'Hey, maybe you ought to shift over to this street instead.' We didn't get on with the other English musicians. We were also junkies. I was a junkie. In Australia, because it's near Asia, heroin is pretty much the drug of choice. Go to a party and pretty much that's what everyone is into. Certainly in my period it was like that. Suddenly you came to England and you just didn't go to a party and shoot up.

Which you did in Australia! *[laughs]* No big deal! In England it was like you were down there on the bottom with the paedophiles. So we were marginalised in a lot of ways and we got pissed off. The Birthday Party comes out of that.

But I don't think we ever got comfortable with the English thing. They couldn't handle it. Tracy Pew, the bass player, he said, 'I'm not ever going back there, I'm going to live in Australia.' He went back to university and died a couple of years later. There was something so intolerable to the way Australians were. At that time I went to Berlin. We did a tour, and the atmosphere after the show was all these people saying, 'Oh, we love what you're doing,' and, 'Come here with me; I'm a filmmaker, come and be in this film.' Suddenly we were welcome and no one gave a fuck what our habits were; it was this creative artistic scene that was really exciting. I just stayed in Berlin. I thought, Fuck, why not? Filmmakers and painters all living and working together – very exciting. I don't think I've said that before about England, but it was different for us on so many levels that it was traumatic.

It was a crash course in being a foreigner.
Yeah. I remember Germaine Greer saying, 'An Australian never feels more alone than when he's in England.' It's something within us that feels different, something we don't understand about the place. I think that's why Australians here hunker down together and form Aussie ghettos.

Maybe you'd have been better off in an Aussie ghetto . . .
We never got on with those sort of Aussies either. That's what we'd fled. *[laughs]*

Monday, 8 December 2008: Nick Cave's basement office on the Brighton seafront
The office area is quite spacious with the only furniture an enormous old wooden table bearing a computer, a few papers and books including dictionaries, plus a chair on either side.

Nick waves me to the job interviewee side, as he remarks, because he's familiar with the work side.

All around on the walls and even leant against the walls among piles of stuff awaiting allocation are paintings and Polly Borland photographs. To the left are floor-to-ceiling shelves which run on into a substantial alcove which also features his grand piano, its keyboard on the desk side, and a microphone on a stand but no recorder of any sort. Among the newer books lying around are encyclopaedias and general history books.

He offers tea – and half his sandwich, which is some kind of sausage so I decline, but with the second cup he brings out a slice of iced cake and kindly splits it with me.

He says he's sent text messages during interviews before now but promises he won't. He also turns the computer screen away from his line of sight.

There's something impressive about being in amongst all these books.

There's a lot there. A lot of them are from a friend of mine, Mick Geyer, a radio DJ in Australia, who was a cool figure on the Australian music scene although he didn't do anything himself musically. But he was one of these people who dedicated himself to finding weird and wonderful music. He brought it back to us, who didn't have the time to do that sort of thing. He made what were called the Geyer Tapes. You seem them all over the world. You walk into someone's flat and see a cassette with his distinctive handwriting on it – 'Ah, you've got a Geyer Tape.' Just the most remarkable, obscure sort of music. And he died about four years ago, and a lot of that's his library which he gave to me.

In 2004 I asked you whether there was anyone you talked to when you were in the midst of writing and you said you talked to him.
He's the only one. I've never been able to replace him, sadly; there's no one else I feel comfortable enough with or trusting enough with or has no agenda one way or the other or that actually has a clue anyway! I have lots of friends but this guy could say, 'Hey, you've got something there, something's happening.' He could say those good things or bad things at the right time.

Has no longer having him to consult made you more independent?
Definitely. I've always been kind of superstitious and I've thought if something like that goes, the whole thing sort of suddenly becomes precarious. But actually I'm learning more and more and year by year that all the superstitions, the rituals you do to provide luck in the creative field, it's all useless. You just have to go in and work. If you go in and work, things get done, I find. And if you don't, things don't get done. *[laughs]* There are things I know, because they've slid around the borders of my creative process at times, that I know are hugely detrimental to the flow, certain voices you hear inside yourself about your own capabilities or lack of them. I know those voices very well, and I can see how people can get paralysed and do get paralysed by those voices. I managed to work out a way to deal with them which is that it doesn't really matter. What you're doing doesn't really matter. If you can convince yourself that it's not important then you have the freedom to do something that is important.

So there's a bit of self-kidology, bluffing going on?
Yeah.

You have to fake it.
Yep, you've got to fake it.

I know there used to be a period when occasionally you'd get some bad reviews – in among all the good ones – and back then in the '80s you got very involved in talking and thinking about the press . . .
Yeah, but the voices I'm talking about go way back before that. We don't need to put faces to them, but the things you hear as a child, things you hear at school.

I still remember very clearly certain things that were said to me that didn't feel like they had any importance at the time, it wasn't like I was crushed to death, but they never go away.

Any examples?
Basically, right back from the first, being told, 'You are not the musical one.'

Oh yes.
'You are not the musical one.' It's only like fifteen albums later or something I'm saying, 'Hang on, maybe that guy wasn't right.'

One of the band members was saying that the suit thing seemed to happen on joining the Bad Seeds as if it was some kind of osmotic force . . .
You mean we asked them to join the Bad Seeds because they wore suits? We saw some guy on the street and said, 'Do you wanna be in the Bad Seeds? Oh and can you play anything?' In fact the band don't all wear suits; they just look like they do. I always wear a suit, Warren always wears a suit. Jim, he does. I always wanted to wear a suit as far back as I can remember, before anything; I used to look at the blues guys in their suits and think they looked really cool. It was only when I could afford to buy the fuckin' things, though.

No Oxfam cast-offs for you.
Well, yeah, early on I did that but I'm a kind of funny shape. Thomas our drummer could walk into any second-hand shop and come out with eight classic suits because he just has the right build. But I never could, so I had to wait until I could make enough money to get a tailor to make them for me. And now I've been going to the same tailor – who's sadly disappeared off the planet this year – Peter Arkus in Berwick Street, since about 1982. I think he met an American woman and went to live with her in Boston. Shocking, how dare he?

I don't feel I wear a suit in a dandyish way. I wear it as a worker. Someone who prepares themselves for the job, you know. It's always been like that. A certain amount of preparation needs to be done to get yourself ready to come down here and do it. It's what I do. There's no debate that goes on in my head.

Has being a bandleader developed you as a person, as an artist?
As a person? I think the whole thing of being in a band retards you in other aspects of life. I have on occasions met people in bands who can do shit like change light bulbs and keep marriages together, stuff like that, but in general being really in a band tends to have a devastating effect on every other aspect of your life outside of getting onstage.

Very early on, if the band's at all successful, you don't develop basic coping skills, shall we say. You're living this wonderful adolescent fantasy that can go on and on and on. But the rest of the world moves on, people grow up and develop and become adults . . . have views and shop and catch an aeroplane without having a manager put them on it. People in bands notoriously don't develop at the same rate and when they finish with the band there's this huge shock.

You know, Eric Clapton spoke about how he went on a holiday without his manager for the first time in years and he stood in the airport and he just didn't know what to do; although he'd flown on planes thousands and thousands of times he just didn't know how to catch a plane. It's a lifestyle choice.

Here you are in two bands at once . . .
Well, the good thing about being in a band, about being a bit famous, is when you ring someone up, people ring you back straight away. Certain frustrations about day to day life that people have to deal with don't apply when you're a bit famous.

I've never seen anywhere an explanation for why you chose the name the Bad Seeds for the band – genuine question, mundane as it seems.
We'd put out a record as the Birthday Party which was called the Bad Seeds and in the middle of standing around with Blixa and Mick, I think, talking about what we were going to call this band . . . I said I wanted the Bad Seeds, and Blixa said it was a problem that we'd had a BP record of the same name out but to me it was kind of Biblical and cool at the same time. I dunno, who can remember these things? Although I was accosted one day by Sky Saxon of the Seeds and he goes, 'You fuckin' bastard, stealing my band's name!' *[whimpers]* 'I'm sorry . . . can I have some acid?'

I hope he obliged.
Oh yes.

A generalisation that's often said about you is that your music, meaning your lyrics, divides into an Old Testament period and a New Testament period. Is there anything in that, do you think?
That sounds a bit . . .

Tosh?
It is tosh, yes. What happened in Berlin was I started to write a novel and the novel had an Old Testament feel about it so . . . it was about a religious community. I was forced, initially for research purposes more than anything else, to start reading the Old Testament and get a feeling for that kind of thing. It drew me in. It also took me back to my childhood, and I found I knew a lot of what was going on in the Bible, that I'd absorbed a lot of it from when I used to be a choirboy. So I read it. And considered it and used parts of it in the novel and based characters around Biblical characters and used it as the bedrock for the novel.

So that was going on in the background to several albums, writing and reading the Old Testament?
Several years.

You were beavering away in that cubbyhole in Berlin, on a typewriter too.
Absolutely. Several typewriters that I borrowed off Berlin friends. Manual ones. Tippex and more Tippex and more. Because I was in quite a state then. I could have written the book a lot quicker. It may have come through in the writing but I was taking a lot of amphetamines, so sometimes when I hadn't slept for a long time . . . I could be working on a fucking paragraph for three days, so the page ended up about this thick *[holds thumb and forefinger an inch apart]* with Tippexes on Tippexes on Tippexes. The book reads like that. On the other hand there was a lot of time wasted. This is the way things were back then.

Basically I'd go there, stay in that room for a few days and nights awake. Then at the end when things were getting too unhinged I'd go to this club called the Risiko, this bar, where everyone went every night – everyone on the Berlin scene went to this club. Or one or two others. But this was the main one at that time, and we'd sit there and drink ourselves into unconsciousness and get back to bed and sleep and wake up again and off I'd go. Beavering away. The Berlin scene, at least for the first couple of years I was there, was amphetamine-fuelled – same for everybody else who was there.

Mick was saying that it was the best place in the world for amphetamines because the East Germans were shipping it over into West Berlin in order to undermine Western Civilisation.
That may be the case. I think there was a lot of sense in that idea. People deteriorated very rapidly in that place. Some people hung in there but a lot of other characters didn't. All sorts of stuff was going on. But this amphetamine was so strong that you could stay up for seven days and seven nights. I'm not talking about with little lie-downs, I'm talking about being completely without sleep. I remember literally crawling up on my hands and knees – I lived on the fourth floor – crawling up these stairs and then crawling into my bed because I'd been up for a week and then someone going, 'You want some speed?' Okay, yeah, and *[mimes jolt]* suddenly you're back up and ready to go again. It was extraordinary stuff but it had terrible psychological effects on people at that time. Some didn't last very long at all, I mean seriously didn't last. It was radical stuff. And fed that whole movement.

It didn't get you?
It got me psychologically but it didn't. I guess I applied it in some way to work. If I hadn't had that it would have been different. You'd go to clubs and see people sitting weeping on their stools for no reason and curled up in corners of rooms. Just through exhaustion, total exhaustion. I didn't worry about the fulcrum of the Berlin movement, Einstürzende Neubauten, who were genuinely radical and innovative. To see them in action was a total privilege. To walk around Berlin and visit this artist in his studio and then drop in on Neubauten was to me an absolute privilege – that place at that time.

What was going on in Neubauten's studio that so fascinated you?
I remember going in there one day and they're all craning forward and nodding listening to something and I couldn't work out what it was, this sound. I went into the studio and there's this enormous pile of offal and a dog they'd miked up was rooting around in it! Another time I was in there and all you could hear was this, boom, boom-boom beat, and Blixa, who was rake-thin at this stage, he barely even existed, he's miked up and Lofty, who was a big guy, has got him by the neck and he's bashing him in the chest getting this incredible reverberating sound. When you listen to their records it's full of this stuff, but it's seriously beautiful music at the same time. So there was genuinely radical stuff going on in Berlin at the time. I felt very much in awe. I felt like we were welcomed into a community that existed way before I was involved in it. And Neubauten and Blixa were the centre of it. I always felt privileged to be involved with them and to have Blixa join the Bad Seeds.

Is it true that you were the king of bar poker?
We did play a lot of bar poker.

And you were very good at it and made money at it?
I don't think anyone's very good at poker. It's a game of luck, isn't it? Me and Blixa did play poker a lot. There was a room out the back at the Risiko where you could sit and play poker. Quite a lot of money got passed around. The stakes were relatively high considering that we didn't have any money.

The great thing about the Risiko was we got free drinks. Blixa was the barman. That really helped. And there was a wonderful place run by a barman called Alex, a wonderful character, a big guy and an extraordinary character. I'm not quite sure what happened to Alex, but he had his own appetites and the profits of the Risiko pretty much went into looking after Alex, so much so that all the records got sold and toward the end he managed to find in a doorway this box of German *Schlager* LPs which someone had thrown away, and so that was the music we listened to for a considerable time because he'd sold everything else.

What's Schlager?
Old German beer-hall music and general shit. It was a great place.

One song from that era I wanted to raise with you because it's still in the set and covers a lot of ground – 'Tupelo': why does that song endure for you?
Because it's so simple; it's free to go wherever it wants to go, it can morph at will to become part of the set. It's very different to what it was four years ago. I play guitar in it. It's a completely different song. So that's why it endures. It's malleable.

You mentioned how it became a topical reference because of Hurricane

Katrina. But back then it seems your imagination was using the Bible and making Elvis a Jesus figure and . . .

It's got the whole fuckin' kitchen sink thrown into it. The thing about my songs is they've all got the kitchen sink thrown into them!

There's the odd moment of restraint.

Nah, restraint never was my forte. At that time I was also reading a lot of Southern Gothic literature which had a huge impact on me – William Faulkner and Flannery O'Connor in particular. That had a big influence on my style of writing. I've always had a real love for the heavy prose writers – Nabokov, Faulkner, Herman Melville. Even the modern crime writers, for example, James Lee Burke or James Ellroy. Or Bret Easton Ellis. The big, heavy-duty prose stylists. They have a love of language. Language is way more than just a way of putting across an idea. In a way the language itself is possibly more important than the idea. Or there are only a certain number of ideas, but they can be said in a variety of different ways; it's how you say them that's more important than what you're saying. I've always had a love for those sort of writers, from as far back as I can remember.

In fiction, most often I come away from a book that I love and it's about the words that have been used, not what it's taught me. I don't believe that fiction can teach you much, in the end. Language itself can have a hugely beneficial effect on you in the same way music can. Music can change the way you are, the way you move around in the world and do an enormous amount of good for a person. For me language is about the same thing on a level that's not necessarily intellectual; it's about the music and the rhythm of the words that operate on some other level.

That's what grabs me.

And that's what you try to do?

Well, it's what interests me in the new novel [*The Death of Bunny Munro*, published in 2009]. I know *The Angel* clearly has a lot of problems, and this new book is not like that. It's much more spare. But it's still about language and the incredible effect language can have over a person. Someone says, 'What was that about?' Oh, I guess it was about this, this and this . . . or I don't know but I loved it. I often feel that way.

I like all those authors except I can't face Bret Easton Ellis.

That's the effect he has on a lot of people – it affects the way he's rated as a writer too. If you slow down and start reading him sentence by sentence, he's fuckin' unbelievable, that guy. His writing is bursting with ideas.

Sometimes I get halfway through books that are supposed to be great and people love them and I think, Why am I reading this? Because to me the language they are using is only there to tell me what's going on. I guess I'm not that into it. I'm absolutely dreading doing interviews for this novel because it's really about the way it's written and there's just nothing to say about that.

You were in the studio in Berlin recording 'The Weeping Song' the night the Wall came down . . .
Yeah.

Is it true you couldn't even break off finishing the track to see the Wall come down?
Yeah, that did happen. I remember Blixa coming in while I was doing my vocal, *[hollers at the top of his voice]* 'The Wall has come down! The Wall has come down!' And I'm like, *[shouts]* 'Get the fuck out of here! I'm doing a vocal!' *[laughs]*

I guess it's about you getting locked into your work above everything.
When I come into this room until I leave, that's it. Anything could happen out there but it has to wait until I've finished. It used to just bleed over everything, though. I can actually close the door on it now.

I presume family could intrude if there's some crisis?
Have to be a fuckin' big one! *[laughs]* The kids have got TB? Suddenly? Fatal illnesses only.

Back then you were portrayed as not interested in the affairs of the world at all. Is that fair?
Yeah, at that period in Berlin – but hey, the papers were in fuckin' German and so was the TV! *[laughs]* So it didn't hold that much interest to be honest. I didn't speak German.

You don't speak other languages . . .
It's not like I don't. A lot of us didn't speak German because everyone spoke English to us – they all got the chance to use the English they'd learnt at school. I didn't learn German at school, I learnt Latin.

Just you and the Pope then.
Yeah, me and him. Mick did German at school so he was able to speak it in Berlin. It took Blixa quite a while but pretty much everyone was happy to speak English. Rather than blithering away, it was easier to speak in English. But I didn't read a paper, that's true. That was just the way it was. I do now.

Did you leave Berlin because of meeting Viviane in Brazil?
No.

What was it about then?
I think I slightly wore out my welcome; that's my theory. People started to, uh, make suggestions: maybe it's time you went and got somewhere else to live? I was staying at Dresdener Strasse a long time with Christoph Dreher, who played

in Tom Wydler's group Die Haut. And at some point it got a little heavy round there with drugs and strange people being around, up in his office there where I was living – I was camped out there for a couple of years actually. In the end he said, 'Maybe it's time to go.'

I thought, Fuck it, I'm going back to London. That other sinkhole. I went and shared a house in Clapham for a while. Lovely! *[laughs]* It was a little grim. Though I guess you can make anything out of anything. It wasn't the best period. I was suddenly going back to a place where I didn't know anybody. I knew a couple of Australian people. It was back to that hunker-down-in-London feeling.

And then you had you had your Brazil interlude.
I was in Clapham for about a year I think. Or eight months. I'd been sitting in this dark room in Clapham for eight months and then we went to Brazil to do this tour, walked out of the airport at Rio and the sun was out, beautiful girls on their mopeds, fuckin' palm trees – the whole thing was really alive and I didn't go back. *[laughs]*

And you had a love at first sight thing?
Yeah. I got snapped up.

You are a catch.
Don't write that 'snapped up', please! Yeah, met Viv there – that was in São Paulo; we played Rio first then we went up there. São Paulo was a fuckin' trip, an incredible city, like nothing I'd ever seen before. Stayed there for a few years.

One thing Conway [Savage] said to me, having joined for The Good Son tour, just when you were getting involved in Brazil: joining the Bad Seeds helped him to stop 'speaking out of the side of his mouth'.
[laughs] I don't know what the fuck he's talking about but it's a lovely quote.

Well I asked him what he was talking about and he said it was an Australian thing, it was about not being direct, not saying what he thought . . .
Right. And Conway thinks he says what he thinks these days.

And the Bad Seeds taught him how.
In my view Conway is the most obscure person on the face of this planet. He continues to be. Brought him out of himself? Well, maybe. God knows what he was like before that then. Because decades can go past before Conway speaks. Then a quiet line will come out. A withering line. *[laughs]* But Conway certainly has changed very much onstage, from the introverted piano thing he used to do on his own country music, to an extraordinary piano player who's immensely watchable onstage at the same time.

There's a story from 1988 where Tony Cohen got sacked as soundman. You were both taking heroin, and agreed between you that you both had to stop. And shortly after that you went to Broadway Lodge for your first shot at rehab . . .

That had nothing to do with Tony Cohen. Did he say that?

No, he didn't say he made you go into rehab, just that you had that conversation before you did go in.

But junkies have that conversation every night. Every night they say, 'We've got to stop this, man,' and then the next morning they start again. I was a junkie when I came to London in the early '80s; it wasn't a new thing. It always suited me in the sense that I'm an unbelievably, to a fault, a creature of habit. And that's what heroin is. It makes life very simple and your choices very simple. You wake up and you're sick and you get your drugs and you're well and then you go to bed and you wake up and you're sick and . . . It simplifies everything, it habitualises everything and for some people that's exactly what they want in their lives. It certainly was exactly what I wanted in my life. Other drugs don't do that. Heroin does that. Other drugs cause enormous amounts of chaos. Alcohol for example. If you're a chronic drinker, an alcoholic, your life is in chaos. Every night you do something and the next morning you wake up and wonder what the fuck . . . Heroin's not like that; you just vegetate. *[laughs]* It makes you the same every day. The same person every day. Which is fine. There's a lot of merit to that.

But eventually it stops doing that; it's a physical thing, it stops having the capacity to do that. The idea of things being not like that is impossible to face. So it's terrifying to stop. It's actually not that hard; it's a lot harder to build a brick wall than it is to stop heroin. But it was always what to do once you stopped. That became very quickly my problem. So we just continued. You know, the stopping's easy. It's just that you start again.

You stopped at Broadway Lodge.

I stopped for seven months.

Was that all?

Well, for me it was unbelievable. An unbelievable feat. But for that seven months I pretty much didn't leave my house. I watched maybe five videos a day and ate every evening an Indian takeaway and that was pretty much it. I just couldn't cope.

You didn't work?

I did very little. I had an electric piano there and I wrote the odd song. I wasn't drinking either. And then I went to Brazil, and I remember very clearly walking out into the sunlight and just thinking, Fuck this for a joke! In Brazil you couldn't get heroin, it was cocaine and alcohol.

I wanted to ask about how it went from there to . . .

That first fuckin' rehab was just a nightmare. I don't want to talk about that but it was old school. The idea back then was to destroy the person that you were and rebuild a better person. Now they've reviewed that line of thinking. But you went in and you were systematically taken apart. It was a real bad scene. *[laughs]* When I came out of there I felt really broken, in some way. A broken that I didn't feel before I went in. I'm really happy with the way things have turned out in general and I'm not one to look back in a negative way; I look back on my life and I'm really happy with it, but there is no happiness around that period. It wasn't a good eight months. But then I went to Brazil and everything changed, it was like I'd walked into the light.

And the light included going with your habitual personality, all that.
Yeah. For a couple of years it was wonderful there.

I'm guessing you started writing again there.
Yeah, I did. Nowadays the rate at which I can produce these days makes all of the time back then look as though I was just fuckin' around. Writing was like I'd produce one every couple of weeks and now there's something going on at fifty that wasn't at thirty or forty. I don't know how long that will last, but at the moment if I wanna do something I can just do it. I don't feel impeded.

So you got off drugs, then you got back on . . .
I've never been one to disparage drug-taking. I've always maintained if I could have carried on I would've. But I lost the capacity to function so it became fairly black and white. I had a little help, to be honest, because I met my current wife. I'm really pleased I made that decision on so many different levels. But that's not to say of that twenty years we're talking about I wasn't having . . . There were great periods of my life – Berlin, Brazil – and drugs were very much tied up in it.

You said in an interview immediately after that first terrible rehab in an interview with Nick Kent that you'd been afraid that you might emerge 'emotionally and spiritually bankrupt'. You told Nick Kent that you weren't after all, but now you've just told me that you really were, that it was horrible.
That quote to me sounds like some shit I'd been told to say in that place. Bullshit. Look, you go into one of those places for seven weeks and I don't care who you are, you stay in there and they fuck with you, they fuck with you. Like I say it's really different now, a whole different kettle of fish; the whole way people deal with addiction is completely different. But back then I don't think anyone knew what the fuck they were doing. So that quote is a brainwashed kind of remark.

But I know Nick Kent got me like day two out of rehab and . . . that's Nick Kent. I guess he was lookin' at me as a kind of experiment to see what actually happens, how this guy went in and how he was when he came out. And I assume I wasn't a particularly great advertisement for sobriety at that point. Certainly in Nick Kent's eyes. I was a stone heavier.

Bleedin' heck.
Yeah, put on a few pounds and I was . . . rattled! Clearly rattled.

The next thing that happens from the outsider's point of view is that, after going back on drink and drugs in Brazil, you become a father – twice as you've said since, one son in Brazil and another in Australia born at almost the same time. How did knowing you were going to be a father and becoming one hit you?
It's a little cut and dried to say I was back on the drugs because in Brazil I was just drinking a lot. But having said that, they were very chaotic years in Brazil – precisely because of that. Because I was fuckin' pissed out of my head! *[laughs]* Who knows why you make certain decisions, but the thing is with my kids is, they're all hasty decisions and the best decisions I ever made in my life. You know, 'I'm pregnant – shall we have the baby?' 'Yeah, what the fuck?'

I didn't have much to do with Jethro initially, the boy who was born in Australia, to my eternal regret. But he was over there and I wasn't. I was every bit the run-of-the-mill proud father despite everything. Very much a hands-on father to Luke. Not to Jethro, but to Luke.

Was that something you knew about yourself in advance, that you would be a good father?
I always had a love of kids. I got on with kids, little kids particularly. Better than adults actually.

So it was just right and proper in its own way.
I'll never be one to plan in advance or have any overriding ambitions. It may seem like that, but it's not that way at all. So the idea of having the kid was, in a way, done with a certain amount of levity, you know, Let's give it a shot. Mmm.

Do you think it showed through into your music at all?
I think it might have done a little bit with some of those early songs, some of them were about that . . .

What are you thinking of in particular?
'Papa Won't Leave You Henry'. That was composed more or less completely in my head without writing it down while standing over Luke's crib. I used to sing that song to him and develop it and make it up. I was always singing stuff to him. And – it ended up being an outtake off *The Boatman's Call* – a song I wrote for Luke called 'Sheep May Safely Graze'. Stole that title. It was rather sentimental: don't worry, everything's going to be all right little guy. Blixa took me aside and said, 'Listen, how about you just sing that one to your boy when he grows up and spare the world?' *[laughs]* At that point he put a cap on that shit. I thought, Okay.

Good to have friends, eh?

Absolutely.

To pursue the heroin story, you've said you wrote 'Into My Arms' from
The Boatman's Call in rehab – was that the next big try at getting off it?
I went to six rehabs. *[laughs]*

You did say you were a creature of habit.
It wasn't by choice. The first one was because I'd been busted three times in a
short space of time in London and it was decided by the lawyer that if I went and
did a stint in rehab that would be to my favour. That was the first one, Broadway.
Then one of them, the next one I'm not sure, I was dropped unconscious at the
front door of the place by my manager and just woke up to find myself there –
that wasn't too good.

In the UK?
In the UK somewhere. He'd had enough and he dropped me off there. I decided
for some reason to stick that one out. Some I didn't stick out. One in Jersey I did
for four weeks maybe, and then one in Bury St Edmunds. But none of those were
my decision, I have to say; they were all, 'If you don't do this, this'll happen to you.'

From friends.
Across the board.

People who cared?
You could say that. People who cared, yeah, and people whose interest lay in
having me sober. Whatever.

Because you are a cash cow?
Um. Oh, I don't want to get into that. It's celebrity. You attract all sorts of fuckin'
wackos who think it's in your interest to let them help you in life and you're
often vulnerable to that sort of stuff. At times. Anyway . . .

Six times and you finally did it with your wife's support; you want to
say anymore about that?
Yeah. I just was decided. I did go into another place. It gave me enough time to
get away from it. Physically and to deal with the withdrawals, all that. But for me
I felt I'd made the decision and that was that. I'm fuckin' stopping. It felt like a
different decision and it felt like a decision that was my own.

Is that the key?
That's what it felt like to me.

That's why it stuck.
Weeeell. It was really easy. I wanted to know what all the fuckin' fuss was about.

Suddenly I just wanted to. Despite all the fuckin' chaos that had been going on, I just didn't want to. It didn't matter what anyone did to me. I didn't want to. At some level I didn't want to . . . I stopped. From that point, maybe ten years ago, it's never felt a difficult thing to do. It's never felt to me like it's been that difficult.

And then you completed the set by giving up smoking recently.
Mmm, more or less. *[laughs]* There's other things. Smoking I didn't find that hard, I gave it up from one day to the next.

To go back to the effect on your work, it seems that you kept on working with the exception of that period after your first rehab . . .
That one still gives me the fuckin' heebie-jeebies when I think about it.

It feels like coming through the '90s produces a new you, whether it's mainly about getting off the drugs, your habits, and moving forward into this recent accelerating period of creativity.
I don't sit and think about what's going on at all. All I know is I can look back at a given year and say, Fuck, I did that, that and that – quite a lot. But what actually happened, now that I do look back on the ten years, it did take me three or four years, which I was totally unaware of at the time, to get my act together, although I didn't realise it at the time because I was very happy. It hasn't been ten years of unbridled creativity.

I think something happened very much before we went into do *Lyre of Orpheus*. Going into the studio with Warren and Jim and Marty and writing together – suddenly for me as a songwriter it sent *woomf*! The possibilities. As a songwriter I was like, Why didn't I think of that before, that you don't just sit at the piano on your own, in your own fuckin' head? There's been this sudden opening up which has been amazing ever since.

In Manchester you traced that back to the quieter period, the solo tours and so on.
It was an introspective period. I was sort of lookin' for something. There was *No More Shall We Part*; I worked out certain things for that record, especially playing and singing at the same time. I sat down and played piano and sang at the same time, and I think it vastly improved my capacity as a singer.

When you were writing or recording, was that?
Recording. And then *Nocturama*. Even though people don't seem to go for it very much, it's really searching for something, that record. It might be one of the best records we ever made; there's a huge searching going on all over the shop and . . . not really finding it. *[laughs]* Though the song 'Babe, I'm on Fire' hinted at something. But not long after that I went in and started jamming like you do in your first band in a garage. We just clicked. We'd been playing together for fuckin' years and suddenly it clicked.

And also out of that came a relationship with Warren. Warren is very similar to me in terms of his production rate; it can be huge. And he's one of the most consistently enthusiastic musicians. Enthusiastic doesn't do him justice; he's obsessed with music and the creation of music – an enormous amount of energy. For me and him to work together, a lot can get done. I can allocate things and it's like a little factory, with him in Paris and me here.

You said about how on The Boatman's Call *you went into confessional mode but didn't want to continue that way. Did it bring your writing into a sphere of realism in the way you were expressing yourself?*
Well I've always wanted to pull back from the theatricality of my writing – it's always been one of my ambitions in life to do something simple and concise but it's often beyond me. It's very difficult for me to do. But there was a period where some of those songs were simple. I guess to do something that's simple and concise takes a lot of confidence – although it may seem it should be the other way round. For me to write and write and write is possibly a bit like the person who talks and never shuts up – they don't do it because they are confident, they do it out of a terrible lack of confidence.

That's suddenly sounding like a response to the voices saying you're shit.
Possibly.

So you blurt.
With the new novel I've just written I'm really pleased. The first chapter which I've now gone back and rewritten, it was like everything was in there – it was an incredibly dense piece of writing. Now I've been able to calm it all down, weed it out and it fits really nicely. To me, the very simple stuff like 'Into My Arms', 'Lime Tree Arbour', they're the audacious songs as far as I'm concerned because I was able to write something simple and stand back, rather than the Tourette's thing which overtakes me sometimes.

The song 'Hallelujah' on No More Shall We Part *is an example of a gentleness that really works.*
Yeah, I always liked that song. There's a humour and playfulness too.

And you'd never have written earlier about the bloke wandering out in his pyjamas and resisting temptation and going back home to his cocoa. Nick Cave wrote that!
Yeah, I guess not. But for me at least playfulness with language has always been there, although it wasn't broadly comic – though more comic writing did come in after a while. There's a playfulness to me in 'The Mercy Seat' although it feels kind of heavy. I'm having fun with the language. But I guess more a comic element was coming in. Life got funnier, that's the thing.

How did that happen?
In the last ten years, life just seems really funny a lot of the time. As opposed to funny in the sense that you've just got to laugh about it. *[laughs]* And maybe there's times it wasn't. I started to see life in a more comic way. I think that's bled into the writing.

Saying life is funny, is that about what kids give you?
No, I can look at it in a different way, maybe I can be more inclusive. Or I can be included a bit more. But I'm not particularly sure about that.

Well there's an element of farce in 'Hallelujah' – the guy's in his pyjamas out on the street.
He's off his medication. There was certainly a period of time when it became interesting to me to make rock'n'roll music about doing the dishes, shall we say – about married life, or family life. I was reading people like Larkin, this humdrum view of the world which felt interesting for a while to apply that to rock music, to talk about certain things which weren't generally characteristic.

When I interviewed you four years ago, Lyre of Orpheus ***time, you said you were going to 'have a bash' at writing about the middle period of love; you said rock was usually all about the first flush or the sorry end . . .***
I did do that. For a bit. Then I thought, Fuck it, that's enough of that!

Would I be correct in identifying 'Jesus of the Moon' as one of those?
No! I wouldn't have thought that at all.

I've misunderstood it then.
Oh, it's not that easy – 'Jesus of the Moon' to me is just a straight kind of love song. But what's different is that rather than being a sad end, the male character is saying, *[slaps hands together]* 'Well, these things end!' Anyway . . . Girls are walking down the street saying hello and who can blame a man for . . . It's got that, 'Sorry! Bye!' air about it. But done in a tender way.

I was throwing out a lot of those marriage songs around *Dig!!! Lazarus, Dig!!!* and not pursuing them because I didn't want to write a record of that sort of stuff – I wanted to write a record with a lot of visceral energy. The last thing I wanted was a ballads record, but I'm drawn to writing ballads because I write on the piano. I was writing a lot of those kind of ballads and I like 'Jesus of the Moon' a lot so it hung in there.

I thought it ended happily.
Between the man and the woman? Well, I don't want to disappoint you. One must stay and one must depart, I think it says.

I had it in the balance.

Well, he may go and make a fool of himself with the ladies and then come crawling back.

In 'We Call Upon the Author to Explain', for the first time in your songs you acknowledge 'socio-economic divisions' . . .
That verse is taken straight out of some current philosophical work on the state of the world. Can't remember what it was. It's one of those books talking about the great problems we're gonna get into. That verse deliberately sits outside of the context of the rest of the song in style with ridiculous words like 'socio-economic divisions'. It is in a way a remote thing for me. I do read the newspapers, and I do have some kind of a handle on that sort of stuff, but I'm still not very interested in writing about it. I don't feel for one thing that I have the authority to write about it – if I have opinions about anything they're usually just shit that I've culled from newspapers anyway. I don't feel I have the real information about any of that sort of stuff. I've always found it difficult to have those conversations that I see people having all the time, where they sit around going, *[slaps the table]* 'Fuckin' so and so did this and why don't they do that!'

I like 'Mass extinction, darling, hypocrisy/ These things are not good for me' ['Abattoir Blues']. Social satire has been creeping into the periphery and then rejected in recent albums. One where you did go for it was 'God Is in the House' [No More Shall We Part, 2001]. It seems a one-off though you still play it live.
I guess it is. It's a bit more complicated than it may appear. On the one hand it's talking satirically about small-town thinking, but then my own voice is in there quite a lot in terms of things that I privately have problems with myself. But it gets a laugh. *[laughs]* It's irony hits irony.

And it is an organised satire.
I actually don't like songs like that. I don't like . . . who's that guy? Great songwriter?

Randy Newman?
Exactly. I mean he's obviously a great lyric writer, but they don't touch me, those songs – I know they affect other people hugely. Or some of those Roger Waters lyrics.

Randy does other stuff, you know, 'Old Man on the Farm'.
Yeah. There's the opening song to *Toy Story*.

Randy covers the waterfront.
I know, but it's that wry, ironic, one-eye-open look at the world, I just don't . . .

***In 'Love Bomb' you refer to* Gardeners' Question Time *and* Woman's

Hour: *does this reveal your displacement activity when you're writing.*
No, actually that comes out of my script I wrote which became the novel; and that comes out of the central character who is a sexual predator – though that's kind of a grand term for what this guy is, because he's not very good at anything. But one of the things he does is listen to *Woman's Hour* to get tips on chat-up lines and the way women think. In the script he puts *Woman's Hour* on and cruises – it's a comic device.

Gardeners' Question Time well, who can resist? I'm no gardener, but I do drive a lot and listen to the radio and . . . halfway through it you think, what the fuck? Why am I listening to this?

In the late '90s you started writing songs where the backdrop suggests the apocalypse, Armageddon, has happened. Is that right?
It's more talking about the apocalypse that's happening incrementally. It always felt like an interesting backdrop for what I'm writing about. Having said that, I've just done the music for John Hillcoat's film of *The Road*, the Cormac McCarthy book; the backdrop is that the apocalypse has happened and it's a father looking after his son, who was born after the apocalypse. They're walkin' along and the landscape's gone, everything's fallen down, everything's covered in ash, you don't even know what's happened, there's no food and people are eating each other – it's as grim as you can get. But at the heart of it it's a father looking after his son and it's really beautiful, really heartfelt. The thing that's most affecting about the movie to me is that the apocalypse has happened but there's something horribly, um . . . what's the word?

Familiar?
Yeah, familiar to me about this, and the film is beautiful because of that. While we were doing that, being sent rushes and stuff, Warren and I were with the Bad Seeds driving around America, parts of San Francisco and so on, and it looked *exactly* the same. Huge areas where people were pushing along their shopping trolleys and the shops were boarded up and closed down, very few people around. It seems to me sometimes that it's something that happens gradually . . .

Anyway, I liked the apocalyptic backdrop for a human story; that's what I'm trying to get at. I don't think my songs are really about the apocalypse at all, but there is that backdrop. More often than not it's metaphoric. Something like 'Moonland' is about a guy, a metaphor.

He comes out of a meat safe and then he gets into stalking a woman, right?
Well, he's following . . . I took the guts of the story out.

To create an enigma?
I'm trying to work out this new way of writing songs and it works quite well at times. We were talking before about trying to do something that was simple. It's

like an affliction I have that I can't let go of an idea and I end up coming in with fuckin' ten pages of lyrics for a song and everyone's kind of rolling their eyes as I put them up on the piano *[spreads arms to full wingspan]* and say, 'Okay, are you ready?' *[smiling]* And now, very much what happens in the recording studio, because we don't rehearse songs and we don't practice them before we record them, sometimes I've told them, 'This is how the verse goes and this is the chorus,' and they just watch and I'll nod the chorus in. We go bang! and play the song and the question then is, 'How long was it?' Not, 'How *good* was it?' How *long* was it? And the guy'll go, 'Seven and a half minutes!' All right, then very fast I can go, take that, that, that and that out *[deleting gestures with pen]* and then, 'Let's play it again,' and *[intercom voice]* 'Five minutes!' Okay, more out. And the more this tale became condensed the more powerful and haunting. I mean, the guy's looking for the woman that he loves – she's obviously left him for someone else, he's not her favourite lover, something like that – and he's going through this internal apocalypse! And now onstage that song is fantastic; it's turned into a real funk classic!

The meat locker bit – to totally demystify it – I vaguely remember Kurt Vonnegut Jr being in the Blitz and spending the time in a meat locker and when he went outside everything was gone.

That would be in Dresden, Slaughterhouse-Five.
That's right! Exactly.

And that part is autobiographical.
He mentioned it in an interview I think.

Well it's a belting first line, the mystery, why is this guy in a meat locker?
I think the new stuff off *DLD* . . . I wrote 'Today's Lesson', the second song, with a very weird sexuality about it – the Sandman, the Inseminator, all that. I was really, really, really pleased with it. I thought, Fuck! It was touching on stuff that felt quite new for me. It was to a degree mysterious about what was going on – and my songs are usually so literal in that they tell a story and you can pretty much tell what's going on. But this felt like suddenly I was free to digress or not to tell the whole story – 'Moonland' came out of that and various other songs.

You don't want to meet the Sandman, do you? Who's the most rotten character you've ever created?
Mr Sandman's a candidate; he's a date-rape type.

Actually I thought the Grinderman character had that side to him as well.
Grinderman has a kind of double; a song called 'Electric Alice' and Grinderman have the same imagery going on and 'Electric Alice' is out in the silver rain,

something like that, and the next song is 'I'm the Grinderman in the silver rain' – it's, you know, victim and . . .

He's a rapist.
No, no, no.

Rape is his favourite form of sex; that's how it strikes me. It's savage, it's rough; that aggressive predator comes through in a lot of the songs.
It's sexy, man! *[laughs]* The girls love it! Actually Grinderman are the rock'n'roll equivalent of chick lit in my opinion. The girls really like it!

The band goes down well with women?
Yeah. You put it like that. It sounds real bad but . . . They appreciate it, that it's muscular music and . . . lyrically it's not a barrage of heavy-metal lyrics but it hasn't been muted. There are lots of things you can't say these days. Dammit! That you could say thirty years ago. And, shit, the stuff you could say sixty years ago! I mean those old blues guys, outrageous.

A lot of metaphors again.
Only so they could get those songs on the radio. 'One-eyed cat peepin' in the seafood store' – 'Shake, Rattle and Roll'.

Just a few more questions about your music. Age and mortality starts to come into your view, although I know you're still a young man.
It changes. What it does is it changes people's perception of what you write about – I could be writing about the same stuff I was when I was young, although I'm not. Because it's a fifty-year-old man singing it, it takes on something different, it actually becomes something uncomfortable and we're enjoying that aspect of it. You know what I mean?

You mean singing about sex when you're a middle-aged man?
Yeah. There's certain labels you get when you start doing that sort of thing – 'dirty old man'! Which I've been called many times by different people – 'You're just a fuckin' dirty old man.' I find quite rich territory about that – fuck' em!

In a sense that sounds like it's friends calling you a dirty old man.
Well, I've got people who are in the middle of being friends and enemies, if you know what I mean. There is something that's slightly discomfiting about the whole thing which we're all enjoying at the moment. It's all about context, isn't it?

Despite the high body count over the years, I don't hear mortality as a theme in your songs in the way I do with Bob Dylan or Leonard Cohen these days.
I'm not as old! *[laughs]*

True.

They've gotta get in their mortality songs 'cause if they don't do 'em now, they're never gonna fuckin' do 'em.

Good thing they noticed that. They're sharp fellows.

There's always that to fall back on. There's a few things people fall back on when they've basically run out of steam – I'm not suggesting either of those two people have run out of steam 'cause I love 'em both, but politics is another one. We see that happen all the time. They make wonderful music for a while and then they cast their eyes around the world and start doing these songs about . . .

The ecology.

Yeah, and oooh dear . . . I guess that's the thing about those sort of songs that are political – I object to being told what to think by a fuckin' rock star. Of all the people in the world to tell me what to think, a rock star is the last person I want my information coming from.

Really?

Because they're the last people that have any realistic encounter with the world. They're not real people; we're not real people.

Of course you bloody are!

I don't think we are. The more successful you get, the less real and the more cartoonlike you become. These people don't know what it is to be a real person, so why should they be giving out the information?

But last time we talked you said you'd finally come to accept that rock music is the best art form of the lot and you'd embraced that and were glad about it, and you illustrated it from Van Morrison, Veedon Fleece, as the fount, the avatar for you. So when you say this is the greatest thing in the world and then argue it's made by detached idiots – what do you mean?

What I mean is that a detached idiot can do the most extraordinary, beautiful things, but I don't want my politics coming from them, or to be told what to think by them, or have my information come from them about how to live. Because I don't think these people have any fuckin' idea how to live. That's why they're in a band.

I love artists that understand the nature of what they are as rock stars, and these are the ones that are cartoon characters. I mean, you can literally draw these people in a couple of strokes of a pen. You know what, Michael Jackson is like or David Bowie – you don't expect these people to be real, functioning, nor do you want them to be. And the ones that try to come across like they are really annoy me. *[titters]* I'm not gonna mention names because I always get into trouble.

Nick Cave on the set of the video for 'Fifteen Feet of Pure White Snow' at Bethnal Green Town Hall, East London, 10 April 2001.

Mortality then, you say you get to that when you've run out of steam, but . . .
I wrote my death songs early!

But not about your death.
I have written one actually; it's called 'Lay Me Low' [*Let Love In*, 1994] – it discusses what the world's going to be like after I die. A comic song. In fact it mentions – it goes, 'Lay me low, I'm going to get a thirteen-page feature in *Mojo*.' At least that was certainly what I was singing live – it rhymes! 'Cause it's fuckin' not easy getting on the cover of *Mojo*. The amount of bowing and fuckin' scrapin' it takes!

You might make it to be eighty-five . . .
Probably.

And still singing. Do you foresee those things, or do you not think that far ahead?
No, I don't.

Well, there's all those white rockers heading up there now and I think they reckon to carry on just like the old blues guys.
I think that is what they look at. There's no reason why not; there's just been this terrible miscalculation that it's a limited time you have as a rock'n'roller. There's certainly complacency and we fuckin' can't have that, *[slaps table]* not on this ship!

I'm just foreseeing the Nick Cave comeback album aged eighty-five featuring loads of guest stars and almost certainly including Keith Richards.
Absolutely. Where's this, in heaven?

No, here; he'll outlive the lot of us.
Still climbin' up coconut trees.

I was just thinking about the John Lee Hooker comeback album, although it was nice he got the money and all.
I actually liked that one with Santana, 'The Healer', that song.

Okay, let me turn to the filmmaking bit. Soundtracks seems a topic on its own aside from the Bad Seeds and Grinderman.
It is very much like that. We have almost a company where people ring up and ask us to do music. At the moment is we get paid by the studios, Hollywood or whatever, and we hand in a score and they take it away and cut it to the scenes. A lot of filmmakers want to be able to do that, not have you write three seconds for this shot and seven seconds for that one.

Is this just a way to make some possibly better money than you do from records and touring?
You don't make better money.

You don't?
It's not bad, not that great. It can get great. But it's exciting to work with Warren one-to-one on something that's not lyrically orientated and is just a pure musical thing. In many ways I feel I can sit back and we work pretty well together. Warren is a multi-instrumentalist, he can play most things that need to be played, and for me it's a delight because it doesn't feel like it's my gig. First of all we're doing music for a film so that whole problem of original creation disappears completely; you've got a movie in front of you, so all you have to do is record something that suits that particular scene. You don't have to sit there thinking, 'What's the next fuckin' song gonna be about?'

You've seen the whole movie before you write?
Sometimes, sometimes not.

As soundtrack composers, based on The Assassination of Jesse James *and* The Proposition, *do you have a 'sound'?*
We have, yeah. I think we're gonna move away from that with the next; I've written a new film script, a Hollywood film, for John Hillcoat who made *The Proposition* and *The Road*. The music for that has to be real fast, more than piano and fiddle. It's a film set in the Depression in Virginia. It's from a book called *The Wettest County in the World* [by Matt Bondurant]. I've written the screenplay for it. It's about the illegal alcohol industry in Franklin, Virginia, in 1929–30. It rocks!

Gangsters, violence?
Not city gangsters, it's in the hills. Such a beautiful book; it was easy to write, came off the page.

Easier than writing the earlier ones?
Because the book was already there.

And The Proposition . . . *up to here*
You mean how it came about? John Hillcoat was trying to get an Australian Western together since I first knew him which was back in punk days, '79 or something, and at some point, five years ago, he got another script and it wasn't right; it was an American story dumped arbitrarily in Australia and it didn't work. I said that and he said, 'Well you fuckin' write one then!'

I said initially I'd just do the story and then get someone else to do the dialogue. It was really enjoyable because he was filming the Bad Seeds record *No More Shall We Part*, behind-the-scenes shit for one of those extras they put on CDs, whatever they're called – complete waste of time – and so I'm going, How about his happens? 'That sounds good.' And what about if this comes next?

We're mixing our album and discussing the movie at the same time as he's filming us. We came out of that with a story. I thought I'd write it down in treatment form, but I just started on page one writing the dialogue and it was pretty easy. I didn't think I could write the dialogue, but it was quite fun.

Your early scriptwriting adventures . . .
John Hillcoat's first movie, called *Ghosts of the Civil Dead*, which had a prison setting. He was straight out of film school and he was getting different people to write bits of it. In the end it was a complete mess but a pretty hardcore prison film. Then there was another one he did which didn't work so well. But *The Proposition* worked out real good. Full of surprises. Real watchable. Rocks along. For our first real film together it worked really well.

Back in '79, was he a musician or did you just meet him on the arts scene in Melbourne?
He was a filmmaker then too. Just around the music and drugs scene.

And a mate since then.
He lives up the road here. Although he's been in Hollywood for a while. His wife's Polly Borland, who did some of these pictures [in the room].

And some of your album sleeves.
Yeah. We're very good friends. We've got another one going up – whether it gets made remains to be seen.

Got a name for it?
No.

You weren't involved in the script for The Road?
No. I passed on it, actually. I probably shouldn't have. Although Joe Penhall did a great job. I got offered another Cormac McCarthy book too. They're really difficult to make into films unless you're prepared to really change them. *The Road* is different and the Coen Brothers one, but before that, they're so linear – these random acts that happen, no dramatic arc.

But they work.
They work as novels but I don't think they'd work as big Hollywood films. That requires redemptiveness and all that sort of stuff. Unless you're gonna really change the book, so I turned those down.

What's the title of your new novel?
The Death of Bunny Munro.

Have you been writing this alongside a whole row of recent albums?
No, I wrote this on the European tour, on the bus actually. No hang on, on the American tour too, on the bus. I wrote it in hotel rooms as well. I had a laptop; never had one of those. This was amazing. I'd always had to wait to get back to my office before I could really sit and do anything but now . . .

Did that surprise you or had you been hatching it for some time?
Well, it was already a film script, I gotta say that. I knew what I had to write.

But the film's not going to be made?
John was going to make it. It's an English film and it's just fuckin' really hard to get the money to make a small English film. There's a certain amount they'll give you and it's a real gamble to give you more and we wanted more because we wanted to make a certain type of film that felt more than a grubby little English

film. It just proved difficult . . . so when John got the offer to do *The Road*, I wrote it into a novel. And now the novel has expanded the idea hugely. Just your average book though, about 240 pages.

Acting is something you can't do – true?
Is that a quote?

No, it's me asking a rude question. I'm out the door soon so it doesn't matter much.
Yeah, I dunno if I can't do it or not. I've never been interested enough to give it a proper shot. But you know when you do something and you've got a knack for it? Or you don't. With acting I never felt I had it.

It comes up in videos of course, the need to play to the cameras.
I don't. Or photos. Stiff as a fuckin' board. I always warn directors, You don't want me to do anything. They say, 'No, come on, it'll be great!' It won't.

Onstage there must be an element of acting. Must just be more natural to you.
Oh, that's something completely different.

Thanks, I think I'm done.
Well, if it's not a complete drugathon that would be good. Don't wanna use up all me stories, you know, because there's me autobiography.

Oh you're doing one? You promised me you wouldn't last time.
No, I'm joking. There's no story. There was. But now I just sit in an office and work. There is no story. What do they do with those writers' biographies? Some of them have a life but most of them don't. I suppose they write about what they wrote about.

Yes, literary biographies. Critical biographies. Still the connection between people's lives and their work is so fundamental I don't tire of asking about it.
That's why Larkin was always so fascinating to me – what he was creating and that mythic life working in the library and then the quotes about, oh, how do you write? 'I always like to do the dishes first.' I found those things very moving, far more moving than what we talked about, the Bukowski syndrome of having to live every woeful tale.

Whereas in a sense, you did.
I've done a bit of both, but my Bukowski behaviour wasn't to fuel some . . . I didn't do it and then write about it.

Yes, mostly it wasn't confessional.

What I'm most proud about in the whole thing is that it moves around, it doesn't stand still. The only periods when I get a bit uneasy is when I feel the records didn't move on much, they didn't change. My heroes of that sort of thing were Dylan and . . . that he could keep coming back and do something that made you think, 'Do I like Bob Dylan?' All over again. And sometimes you said yes and sometimes you said no.

Yes, not every album, but sometimes one after the other do it – John Wesley Hardin, Nashville Skyline, New Morning. Then the religious thing . . .
That's when I got into Bob Dylan.

I just re-read our 2004 interview and you talked to me about that back then. Slow Train Coming and 'Gotta Serve Somebody'.
I never heard him before that except for *Nashville Skyline* which my brother had and I loved that record. It's not like bog-standard Christian. It's nasty, one of the scariest records I ever heard.

Yeah, you're a sinner and I'm gonna rip the arse off you, you bastard.
And by the way, praise the Lord!

Phil Sutcliffe, Interview transcript for a *Mojo* feature, 25 November 2008

Contributor Information

Michel Faber has written five novels, including *Under the Skin, The Fire Gospel* and *The Crimson Petal and the White*, and three short story collections, including *The Fahrenheit Twins*. His less illustrious achievements, in the years before literary renown, include shoplifting Nick Cave and the Bad Seeds' rare flexidisc 'Scum' from a Melbourne record shop.

Barney Hoskyns co-founded the online music-journalism library *Rock's Backpages* (www. rocksbackpages.com). He is the author of, among other books, *Across the Great Divide: The Band and America, Waiting for the Sun: Strange Days, Weird Scenes and the Sound of Los Angeles, Hotel California: Singer-Songwriters and Cocaine Cowboys in the LA Canyons* and the acclaimed Tom Waits biography *Lowside of the Road*.

Antonella Gambotto-Burke is the author of four (soon five) books and a writer and critic for numerous newspapers and magazines, including *The Mail on Sunday, The Weekend Australian, The South China Morning Post*, and *Vogue*. To her great amusement, she awoke one morning in 2005 and found herself married to a Grinderman fan. Find her at: www.antonellagambottoburke.com.

Mat Snow, who edited this anthology, is the award-winning former editor of the music magazine *Mojo* and football periodical *FourFourTwo*. Born, bred and based in London, he continues to write about these subjects and a few more besides. He has dined out on the story of 'Scum' for many years.

Simon Reynolds is a pop culture critic and author. His books include *Energy Flash: A Journey Through Rave Music and Dance Culture* and *Rip It Up and Start Again: Postpunk 1978–84*. His seventh book, *Retromania: Pop Culture's Addiction to Its Own Past*, will be published in 2011. Born in London, he currently lives in Los Angeles.

Jack Barron first wrote about music while doing a doctorate at Oxford University on the difference between 'stoned' and 'normal' conversation. His writing and photographs have been published in *The Guardian* and numerous magazines. Clean and sober since 1994, he has made documentaries and children's programmes for UK network TV and worked as a substance abuse counsellor.

Since the 1970s, rock journalist **Nick Kent** has been a fabled insider, controversial chronicler and legendary participant in London's music scene, in at the births of the Sex Pistols, the Clash and the Damned. *The Dark Stuff* collects some of his best work, while 2010's *Apathy for the Devil* recalls his life and career.

Music journalist and DJ **Kris Needs** edited *Zigzag* in 1977–82 and has also written for *NME, Sounds, Creem* and *Flexipop*. The author of books about Primal Scream, Keith Richards, the Clash and the New York Dolls as well as his memoirs, Kris contributes to *Mojo, Record Collector* and *Shindig!*, raving about Grinderman at every opportunity.

Andy Gill is Chief Rock Critic of *The Independent*, and has written for such magazines as *The Word, Mojo, Q* and *NME*. He is the author of two books about Bob Dylan, *My Back Pages: Classic Bob Dylan 1962–1969* and *A Simple Twist of Fate: Bob Dylan and the Making of Blood on the Tracks*.

James McNair is a Glasgow-born, London-based journalist who has written for numerous publications including *Mojo, The Independent, Q, The Daily Telegraph* and *The Evening Standard*. He shares Nick Cave's admiration for the late, great Alex Harvey, and his favourite Cave song is 'Are You the One That I've Been Waiting For?'.

Unwisely but willingly, **Jennifer Nine** (a.k.a. Karen Shook) frittered away over two decades in the music circus: record labels (major to minor), the highway lure of tour managing, the folly of artist management, radio, hackery. In 1994 she traded Montreal and Toronto for London, where the streets were once paved with music papers.

Ginny Dougary is an award-winning journalist whose interview profiles with the rich, powerful and influential have made front-page news. A founding member of Women in Journalism and author of *The Executive Tart and Other Myths*, she has also contributed to anthologies including *OK, You Mugs* (about movie actors) and *Amazonians* (new travel writing by women).

Jessamy Calkin is features editor of *The Telegraph Magazine*, after previous stretches on *GQ* and *Tatler*. She sensibly retired early from her noisy, slightly messy career as road manager with the Bad Seeds on their first tour of America, and several outings with Einstürzende Neubauten.

Robert Sandall was a music journalist and broadcaster whose wry and elegant style never obscured his passion, knowledge and insight. *The Sunday Times* his principal canvas, he also wrote for *Q*, *Mojo*, *The Word*, *Rolling Stone* and *GQ*, and co-presented BBC Radio 3's eclectic and experimental *Mixing It*. He died in 2010.

Sydney-born and raised writer, broadcaster and public relations consultant **Debbie Kruger** (www.debbiekruger.com) spent over four years researching and writing the pioneering *Songwriters Speak* (2005), in which forty-five of Australia and New Zealand's greatest songwriters of the last half-century, among them Nick Cave, discuss in depth their art and craft.

Author of acclaimed books on Queen, the Police and AC/DC, London-based journalist **Phil Sutcliffe** writes about music for numerous publications including *Mojo*, *Q* and *The Los Angeles Times* and has interviewed such greats as Paul McCartney, Paul Simon, Bruce Springsteen, Pink Floyd, Kate Bush, the Police, Radiohead, Nirvana and, of course, Nick Cave.

Michael Odell grew up in a Croydon house full of military brass band music (his English father) and salsa (his Bolivian mother). He has been writing about music and family life for twenty-five years, with his work appearing in *The Guardian*, *The Times*, *The Observer*, *The Voice*, *Q* and *Elle*.

Simon Hattenstone is an interviewer and features writer for *The Guardian*. His books include *Out Of It*, a childhood memoir of illness, purple rage and Pink Floyd, and *The Best of Times*, about the later lives of England's 1966 World Cup winners. He has just completed his first novel, *A Man of Diminished Stature*.

In 1980 photographer **Bleddyn Butcher** left Australia for London, where he met fellow self-exiles the Birthday Party, who remain the single most astounding phenomenon he has ever witnessed, onstage or off. He has documented them and Nick Cave's successor projects ever since for numerous publications, and for five years he edited the Nick Cave fanzine *The Witness*. As a writer, he presently awaits publication of his first book, *Save What You Can – Part One: The Day of the Triffids*.